John Webster Grant was born in Truro, Nova Scotia. A graduate of Dalhousie University, Dr. Grant was ordained in the United Church in 1943, and served as a Chaplain in the Royal Canadian Navy. He was a Rhodes Scholar to Keble College, Oxford, where he secured his D. Phil. in 1948. He was twice granted the degree of D.D. *(honoris causa)*—in 1961 by Union College, Vancouver, and the following year by Pine Hill Divinity Hall, Halifax. Dr. Grant began his teaching career in 1949 with the appointment to the Woodward Chair of Church History at Union College. During 1957 and 1958, he was Visiting Professor at the United Theological College of South India and Ceylon. He was appointed Editor-in-Chief of The Ryerson Press in 1959, leaving the position in 1963 to become Professor of Church History at Emmanuel College, University of Toronto.

In addition to being General Editor of this series, Dr. Grant was the Editor of **The Churches and the Canadian Experience** and the **New Look Paperbacks,** an informative series for young adults. He is the author of numerous books, including **Free Churchmanship in England, God's People in India, The Ship Under the Cross, George Pidgeon: A Biography, God Speaks...We Answer,** and **The Canadian Experience of Church Union.**

# The Church in the Canadian Era

JOHN WEBSTER GRANT

# The Church in the Canadian Era
*The First Century of Confederation*

Volume Three of *A History of the Christian Church In Canada*. General Editor: John Webster Grant

McGRAW-HILL RYERSON LIMITED

Toronto   Montreal   New York   London
Sydney   Johannesburg   Mexico   Panama   Düsseldorf
Singapore   Rio de Janeiro   Kuala Lumpur   New Delhi

# THE CHURCH IN THE CANADIAN ERA

Volume Three of A HISTORY OF THE CHRISTIAN CHURCH IN CANADA

ISBN 0-07-092997-1

Library of Congress Catalog Card Number 70-37320

1 2 3 4 5 6 7 8 9 10   THB-72 0 9 8 7 6 5 4 3 2

Printed and bound in Canada

To Gwen

# Foreword by the General Editor

The publication of these volumes is a direct result of the initiative and persistent prodding of the late Dr. Lorne Pierce. Dr. Pierce had determined many years in advance that The Ryerson Press, of which he was Editor-in-Chief, could most fittingly contribute to Canada's centenary celebrations by sponsoring a definitive study of the place of the Christian Church in her history. His hope, now brought to fruition, was that a team of church historians should collaborate on a three-volume work. Dr. Pierce foresaw not only the need but the difficulty of such an undertaking. There were a number of specialized studies, and a few denominational histories, but source material was scattered and the necessary community of scholars was lacking. Instead of admitting defeat he set out, typically, to create the conditions under which an inclusive history could be written. He stimulated the collection and organization of archival material, especially within his own communion, The United Church of Canada. He played a leading part in the formation in 1959 of the interdenominational Canadian Society of Church History, within whose membership he hoped to find his authors. He published a number of studies upon which a larger work could be based, notably Dr. Walsh's *The Christian Church in Canada* (Ryerson, 1956).

The team of writers took shape during early meetings of the Canadian Society of Church History, and the story most naturally lent itself to division into periods of French, British and Canadian dominance. Assignments were soon made: the French Era to Professor H. H. Walsh, the British Era to Professor John S. Moir, and the Canadian Era to myself.

The work now being offered is the most comprehensive account of the history of the church in Canada that has yet been written. In the main it is based on past studies, but these have been extensively supplemented by original research. We hope that readers will find it both useful and enjoyable, and that students will find in it suggestions for areas of future research.

Each author has been left free to interpret the evidence in his own way, and it is only to be expected that some differences in viewpoint will be evident. Nevertheless, the project has been a team effort. There has been constant mutual consultation and criticism, and all the writers have accepted two general assumptions about the nature of their task.

One of these assumptions, embodied in the reference of the title to "the Christian Church" rather than to churches, is that this history should be ecumenical in both range and sympathy. Such a commitment does not imply an ironing out or even a playing down of the controversial elements in the story. It does involve a recognition that the history of each communion is part of the history of all communions. This assumption is not easy to maintain in dealing with periods when Canadians tended to regard their various denominations as, in effect, so many separate religions, but without it the story loses any vital link with the common source and common destiny that are integral to the existence of the Christian Church.

The other assumption is that the Canadian locale should be taken seriously. Once again writers are bound to no particular estimate of the significance of the existence of Canada as a nation but only to an awareness of the setting within which the church has lived and worked. This assumption is no easier than the other, for much of Canadian church history has seemed to consist of little more than the importation of European and American forms and folkways. Inevitably, however, the Canadian environment has affected the churches and in turn been affected by them, with results that have sometimes received inadequate recognition from both religious and secular historians. The writers of these volumes concern themselves not only with the institutional development and the devotional life of the church, but also with its public witness and especially with its relation to the development of the Canadian character.

The time at which the present project comes to fruition is in many ways fortunate. On the one hand, the recent spectacular broadening of dialogue among members of various branches of the Christian Church is beginning to make an ecumenical perspective more natural for all of us. On the other, the growing interest in church history evident in many university departments is initiating a dialogue with secular historians that promises to be equally rewarding. This work will amply justify itself if it leads to a quickening of interest that will result in the filling of some of the many gaps in our knowledge and understanding that still remain.

Each writer will undoubtedly wish to acknowledge some particular debts. I am grateful to Dr. Moir for his constant willingness to give and receive criticism graciously, to The Ryerson Press for conceiving the project, and to McGraw-Hill of Canada for adopting it. I should especially like to record my indebtedness to the late Dr. Walsh for the constant inspiration of his enthusiasm and the stimulus of his creative mind, as well as my deep regret that he did not live to see the completion of our work. It has been our collective wish that this series may be a worthy memorial to Dr. Lorne Pierce, scholar, churchman, and Canadian.

JOHN WEBSTER GRANT

# Preface

Every historical investigation has its own bias, and many readers will probably be more aware of some of my preconceptions than I am. At least one criterion of selection has been consciously adopted, however, that of relating the history of the church to the development of Canada as a nation. In seeking to do justice to this theme I have undoubtedly done less than justice to some equally important aspects of the story. Confederation brought no sudden interruption of colonial patterns of church life, and my emphasis on national issues has inevitably led to some neglect of the regional peculiarities that figure so prominently in Dr. Moir's preceding volume. Moreover, as some readers of the manuscript have correctly pointed out, attention to public activities and changing outlooks has led to some overshadowing of the week-by-week preaching of the word and administration of the sacraments, the inner life of prayer, and the countless acts of charity that undergird the church's ministry to the world. I am especially aware of many individual Christians—here Brother André comes immediately to mind—whose lives deserve an attention that cannot be given in a work of this nature. Within the allotted space, however, it has seemed important that this particular book should deal with the subjects it does.

In addition to those already mentioned in the Foreword, I should like to thank the Rev. C. Glenn Lucas, Dr. T. R. Millman, and Dr. Arthur G. Reynolds for reading earlier drafts of the manuscript and making many helpful comments. I should also like to thank those, too numerous to mention by name, who have allowed me to read unpublished manuscripts or examine private papers, or who have otherwise contributed insights and items of information. I owe a particular debt to students in graduate courses who have discussed the manuscript with me and chosen essay topics with a view to furthering the project. One of their most helpful contributions was a search of religious periodicals during the 1860s that greatly advanced my understanding of the role of the Protestant churches in confederation. Those who have made suggestions will be aware both that I have profited from them, and that the judgments I have made on the basis of them are my own.

JOHN WEBSTER GRANT

# The Church in the Canadian Era

xi

# ONE

# The Church In British North America, 1867

The churches were more conspicuous than the church in the British North America of 1867. One heard comparatively little about Christians as such, a great deal about Roman Catholics and Anglicans, about Canada Presbyterians and the Auld Kirk, about Wesleyan and Episcopal Methodists, about free-will and predestinarian Baptists. Over the years there had been some improvement in the mutual relations of these denominations. Polemical titles like Thomas McCulloch's *Popery Again Condemned*[1] and Benjamin Nankeville's *Christian Baptism Scripturally Considered*[2] had become less common, and closely related communions were beginning to send fraternal delegates to one another's assemblies. Denominational positions were still matters of deep conviction, however, and accessions of members from other churches were greeted with unembarrassed delight. Membership in a particular denomination ranked high as a badge of personal identity. To know a man's religious affiliation was to have an important clue to the politics he professed, the school system he supported, the moral taboos he observed, and even the newspapers he read. Religion also played a major role in determining lines of cleavage within colonial communities. The framers of the British North America Act found it necessary to devote more space to the rights of religious than of ethnic minorities.

The fragmentation of church life by denominations was compounded by their distribution over a number of colonies that had been peopled at different times and from different sources, had developed along different lines, and despite improvements in communication remained at the time of confederation comparatively isolated from each other. The churches themselves were strongly marked by regional diversities in ethnic background, external affiliation, and local experience, so that even members of the same denomination could vary greatly from province to province in social status, political outlook, and theological conviction. It was not easy, for example, to confuse Maritime Baptists with their colleagues in Canada

West. A Baptist from the Annapolis Valley was a New Englander whose ancestors had wandered north but who had never lost contact with co-religionists back home.[3] A Baptist from the Ottawa valley, by contrast, was a displaced Scot who was fed the Bible "with porridge—and—with regularity."[4] The Methodists of Canada West were more North American in outlook than those of the lower provinces, while in some Presbyterian circles the attitudes were reversed. As for the Catholics, it is probable that traces remained even in 1867 of differences between French Canadians and Cape Breton Highlanders that had shocked the sensibilities of Bishop Plessis of Quebec half a century earlier. In the course of a pastoral visitation in 1812 he had noted not only the ramshackle condition of the chapel at Port Hood but "the multitude of dogs within it and the babbling and bawling of forty or more children in their mothers' arms."[5] With a common history still largely to be made, the church of 1867 can most readily be introduced by describing its situation in the various regions of British North America: the Atlantic provinces, Canada East and West, and the North-West.

## SURVEY OF THE CHURCH BY REGION: *The Atlantic Provinces*

The Atlantic provinces had already reached a fairly mature stage of social experience. They owed their wealth mainly to an export trade that had been stimulated by the Napoleonic wars, by protective tariffs that had continued after Napoleon's defeat, and perhaps in slight measure by a reciprocity agreement with the United States that was in effect from 1854 to 1865. These influences had ceased to operate in 1867, and the provinces were reluctantly seeing political and economic leadership pass to the more advantageously located Canadas. The Atlantic region exhibited in microcosm most of the cultural diversities of British North America, variations being readily observable as one moved from one county to the next. Ethnic and religious patterns were determined less by provincial boundaries than by the set of coastlines; seafarers are notoriously sensitive to even slight variations in compass pointing.

In Newfoundland, where for centuries the colonial office had deliberately neglected the local population in the hope of discouraging competition to British fishermen, the churches accepted almost total responsibility for social organization. They ran all the schools, and political struggles were little more than an extension of their rivalries. The elections of 1861, for example, "were attended with much tumult and riot, religious animosities making the bitterest element in the struggle."[6] Fortunately for the economy of the island, and indeed for its peace, the three major denominations were for the most part geographically segregated. Irish Catholics occupied much of the Avalon peninsula and were a majority in St. John's, from which they had for some years been able to control the colonial assembly. Anglicans predominated on the south coast and in Bonavista and Trinity Bays, where their loyalty to the church had been fostered in early times by the Society for the Propagation of the Gospel and later also by the Newfoundland School Society and its successor, the Colonial and Continental Church Society. The stronghold of Methodism was Conception Bay, from which a series of stirring revivals carried the message to the distant outposts of the north coast. Farther away again, on the inhospitable coast of northern Labrador, Moravian missionaries had been at work among the Eskimos since 1771.[7]

Sections of the Maritime provinces that fronted on the Gulf of St. Lawrence or Cabot Strait looked mainly to Europe, but also had fairly close sea links with the Canadas. They suffered from a measure of cultural isolation, however, and were forced back on their own resources more than most other Maritimers. The great majority were Roman Catholics or Presbyterians, both fervently attached to traditional forms of piety and little given to change. The Catholics were mainly Irish in the Miramichi valley of New Brunswick, Acadian along the rest of the New Brunswick coast and in isolated pockets elsewhere, and Scots from the western isles in Antigonish and in most of Cape Breton Island. The Presbyterians were overwhelmingly Highland Scots, although those in the Truro area had come from Ulster by way of New Hampshire. They were divided in allegiance between the Church of Scotland and the considerably larger Presbyterian Church of the Lower Provinces, which had come into being in 1860 through a union of various Scottish groups that had seceded from the national church. Prince Edward Island, unlike the rest of the area, was a patchwork of religious groups. Even there, however, Catholics and Presbyterians predominated.

Western New Brunswick and western Nova Scotia, which the Bay of Fundy served to unite rather than to divide, came within the ambit of the United States and were constantly subject to its influence. In every town or village of any consequence one would have seen at least two chaste New England meeting houses, each with separate doors for men and women. The larger would be Baptist, the smaller Wesleyan Methodist, and a third chapel of similar style would indicate that there had been a split in the Baptist congregation. Most Baptist churches were Regular, holding to Calvinist theology and closed communion. The upper St. John Valley and two counties of western Nova Scotia belonged, however, to the Free Baptists (Free Christian Baptists in New Brunswick), who believed in free will, preached the possibility of Christian perfection, and were commonly regarded by their rivals as Methodists in disguise. The Fundy basin was the Bible belt of the Maritimes, and religious excitement was consistently at a higher pitch than elsewhere. In the towns and some of the Loyalist villages, however, the Church of England offered a decorous alternative to revivalism. Despite occasional losses to "sectaries" it was more than holding its own.

The Halifax area had a cultural and religious pattern of its own. The social life of the city was dominated by an English official, commercial and military class. The bulk of the population, both in the city and in the fishing coves, was of German or Irish background. The English and the Germans were mainly Anglican, although in Lunenburg county many of the Germans stubbornly maintained the Lutheranism of their ancestors. The Irish were Roman Catholics. Within the same area lived more than half of the black population of British North America, descendants of the freed slaves of Loyalist masters or runaways from the United States. Almost all of them were Baptists, thanks mainly to the pioneer preaching of David George,[8] the lifelong interest of John Burton,[9] and the long shepherding of Richard Preston.[10] George and Preston were Negroes, Burton an Englishman whose sympathy had been aroused by the plight of the black community.

### Canada East

The French Canadians of Canada East were in 1867 overwhelmingly rural, peasants closely tied to the soil and living largely by a barter economy. Their farms were laid out in long strips, originally along the all-important St. Lawrence and later in *rangs* or rows parallel to it, so that settlement was continuous and community life close-knit. Robert Rumilly has described them as "a rural, hospitable and sociable people, respecting their priests, raising many children, never omitting their prayers, emptying a glass when so minded, swearing a little more than they ought to, smoking great quantities of tobacco, and warmly clad to brave the rough winters."[11]

In a French-Canadian community the Catholic Church was an all-pervasive presence. The parish priest was the *habitant's* natural adviser in economic as well as in spiritual matters. The parish church was the centre both of his religious and of his social life, and after mass he would wait outside the church door to chat with his friends, learn of forthcoming activities, or listen to a political speech. The parish school, usually run by a religious order, provided education for his children. The local doctor or lawyer, although perhaps a trifle sceptical about some points of Catholic doctrine, was aware that he owed his professional standing to a classical college that was maintained by the church. The community itself was a creation of the church, for a *rang* has no natural centre and the parish church perforce became the nucleus around which a town or village would grow up.

The attitude of the *habitant* to his parish priest was neither the idyllic trust portrayed in old-style French-Canadian novels nor the timorous subservience sometimes imagined by English-speaking Protestants. Parishioners criticized their priests and disputed fine points of doctrine with them.[12] Lawsuits over the location of parish churches were common. Political loyalties were strong, and the prestige of the *curé* might be rivalled by that of a local politician or professional man. Even criticism, however, was of an institution that was universally known and accepted. The local parish clergy belonged to families similar in background to those to whom they ministered, and parishioners had relatives serving as priests elsewhere, so that for most people the church was in effect part of the family. To most French Canadians it seemed closer and more important than the government, for such intimate matters as the keeping of records of births, marriages, and deaths were in its hands. Most important of all, the church provided the structure of belief and conduct within which the society functioned. Disaffection within the social and ecclesiastical system was common, but serious revolt against the church was almost unthinkable.

Although most rural areas of Canada East were solidly French in language and Catholic in religion, there were important exceptions. Protestants were still a majority in six counties in the Eastern Townships, an overwhelming majority in several. This region, which had originally been settled by New England Yankees, was religiously one of the most volatile in Canada. The major denominations all had strongholds, and most of the province's three thousand Second Adventists and two thousand Universalists lived there.[13] Other areas of considerable Protestant strength were the Gaspé Peninsula and the Ottawa Valley, and in the latter region Irish Catholics were also numerous.

The two major cities of Quebec and Montreal differed both from the countryside and from each other. Quebec was not only the archepiscopal see but Canada's second city, larger as yet than Toronto. The authority of the church was seldom challenged there, with the result that a certain amount of independent thought could be regarded with equanimity by the authorities. Montreal, Canada's metropolis and the centre of its commercial life, was by contrast the church's greatest problem. An earlier tradition of daring heterodoxy survived there, and lapsed Catholics were fairly numerous. The most ardent defenders of the faith also lived in Montreal. They were constantly on guard against heterodoxy among professors at Laval University in Quebec, and theological conviction mingled with civic pride to inhibit easy relations between the ecclesiastical leaders of the two cities.

Protestants, a large group in Montreal and relatively more numerous in Quebec City than today, dominated commercial life and were active in politics. In the cities they favoured the more traditional denominations, notably the Churches of England and Scotland. Montreal was also the centre of vigorous attempts, chiefly under Baptist and Presbyterian auspices, to convert French Canadians to Protestantism. The results were statistically not impressive, but sufficiently worrisome to call forth repeated warnings against Protestant propaganda in episcopal *mandements*. There were a fair number of Irish Catholics in Montreal and Quebec, which had been ports of entry during the famine years of the 1840s. In 1867 they were exercised over, but generally unsympathetic to, Fenian attempts to gain Canadian support.[14]

*Canada West*

Canada West, now Ontario, was still largely agricultural but hospitable to commercial enterprise. In population it had forged ahead of Canada East, although its rural areas had practically reached their peak a generation before confederation. During the last few decades the province had passed from frontier austerity to relative affluence, and citizens became more aware of its possibilities as they travelled along improved roads and even railways. The resulting optimism gave rise to an outspoken Canadian nationalism that was taken up by such church leaders as the Anglican John Strachan, the Presbyterian George Brown, and the Baptist R. A. Fyfe. Religiously the most notable feature of Canada West was its aggressive Protestantism, which formed a natural counterweight to the Catholicism of Canada East. Another conspicuous point of difference was the denominational pluralism of the upper province, which by the 1850s had compelled the state to adopt a position of ecclesiastical neutrality.

One could not travel far in the rural areas without becoming aware of the almost ubiquitous presence of the Methodists, although the Bay of Quinte region was their Ontario heartland and its social patterns reflected as nowhere else their long-continued occupation. Their preachers, most of whom were self-educated natives of the province, conducted informal services of worship, proclaimed the necessity of personal conversion to Christ, and through local class leaders enforced a strict spiritual and moral discipline among their flocks. Displays of intense emotion, which had once been a regular feature of their meetings, were now usually reserved for such special occasions as camp meetings or protracted meetings. Institutionally, the Methodists were divided into several segments. The Wesleyans, who claimed the allegiance of sixty percent of the total, were affiliated with the original Methodist Conference in England. They had the tightest organization and generally the highest social standing. The Methodist Episcopals, who claimed to continue an earlier tradition imported from the United States by pioneer preachers, boasted of their freedom from overseas control and offered stiff competition in the longer-settled eastern counties. Other Methodist groups were relatively small. The Wesleyan Methodist New Connexion, Primitive Methodists, and Bible Christians, all of whom had British connections, were liberal in church government and conservative in piety. The British Methodist Episcopals, who despite their name had no British connections, were descendants of slaves and free Negroes who had found a refuge in Canada.

The members of several other important denominations were more heavily concentrated in particular areas or among particular ethnic groups. Presbyterians predominated in most Scottish settlements. In the eastern part of the province, they inclined to the Church of Scotland; in newer settlements further west, to the Canada Presbyterian Church. The Auld Kirk was more formal in worship and more attached to old-country ways, but more relaxed in doctrinal and social stance. The Canada Presbyterians were orthodox, self-reliant, and devoted to good causes. Anglicans were widely, although thinly, distributed. In Protestant Irish settlements in the back counties, where they were especially strong, they belonged almost exclusively to the evangelical wing of the church. Although they adhered strictly to the Book of Common Prayer, their services were plain, and a cross on the altar would have been a source of scandal. Baptists, who were heavily concentrated in several counties north of Lake Erie, were known as people who took their religion seriously. Some congregations traced their origins to American-style revival, others to English or more often Scottish immigration. The great majority belonged to the Regular Baptist Union, which professed a Calvinistic theology and maintained the practice of closed communion. The only major rural concentrations of Roman Catholics were in Glengarry county in the extreme east, where they were Scottish, and in Essex in the extreme west, where they were French. Elsewhere they were almost entirely Irish.

Other religious groups were chiefly of local importance. Waterloo county, where settlers from Pennsylvania and Europe still used German both in worship and in daily intercourse, had its own unique denominational pattern. The Lutherans, who were numerous both there and in the Morrisburg area, had been handicapped in early years by a shortage of pastors and by the poor quality of some ministers who had come from Germany. With the foundation in 1861 of the Evangelical Lutheran Canada Synod, however, they looked forward to better times.[15] The Evangelical Association, which owed its existence to American revivalism, had close affinities with Methodism.[16] Various groups of Mennonites carried on the plain ways of their ancestors, not only in Waterloo but in Welland and York counties.[17] Other rural concentrations were of Congregationalists in Brant and Wellington counties,[18] Quakers in York and Prince Edward,[19] and people calling themselves simply "Christians" in the area immediately east of Toronto.

Religious tastes in the cities and larger towns were more sophisticated, reflecting the attraction of transatlantic traditions. Anglicans were relatively much more numerous than in the country, and some of them were more hospitable to the embellishment of worship with music and dramatic form. Most urban Presbyterians belonged to the Kirk and had a very respectable place in society. The Methodists had always had difficulty in establishing themselves in the larger towns. The Wesleyans, who were most successful in doing so, filled urban pulpits when they could with college graduates and at least made sure that their occupants would not offend with rustic mannerisms. Roman Catholics, by contrast, were overwhelmingly concentrated in the cities and towns. Almost all Irish and recent refugees from famine, they had been able to accumulate few occupational skills and still stood on the bottom rung of the social ladder.

In almost all sections of eastern Canada the native Indians were by 1867 at least nominally Christian, and some of them already looked back on a long Christian tradition. The Micmacs and Malecites of the Maritime provinces were practically all Roman Catholics, although the dedicated Baptist missionary Silas T. Rand was constantly itinerating among them and pleading their cause with all who would listen. A similar situation prevailed in Lower Canada apart from a few Protestant enclaves among the Mohawks of Caughnawaga and Oka and the Abenakis of Pierreville. In Upper Canada, by contrast, almost every denomination had its Indian following. On the northern fringes of the province, where missionary work was still in its pioneering phase, some bands would only be reached in the early years of the twentieth century.

## The North-West

The present western Canada, known in 1867 as "the North-West," was still largely Indian country. A few white men had made their homes along the Red River for more than half a century, and Ontario settlers were beginning to take up farmland on the Portage plains nearby. In British Columbia, which had been opened suddenly by the Fraser gold rush in 1858, a motley population filled temporary mining camps and gave Victoria the reputation of being something other than "a little bit of olde England." In earlier times Hudson's Bay traders from the Orkneys had vied with French Canadians who were almost as far from home, and both had left behind a mixed race that was completely of the country. Apart from such intrusions, the land belonged to its original inhabitants, and the pressure of population had not yet altered their nomadic pattern of life.

A modern road or railway map of western Canada gives few clues to the geography of the region when it was still Rupert's Land. In the days of the fur trade the travelled roads were the rivers, the only dependable transports, the convoys of the Company. The main approach to the northwest was by the Saskatchewan River to Edmonton and the Rocky Mountains or northward over Portage la Loche to the Mackenzie system. The far north was thus relatively accessible, while entry to the open prairies was more difficult and from the fur trader's point of view unprofitable. It was therefore possible to establish permanent Christian missions in the Yukon almost as soon as in southern Saskatchewan.

The work of the church in western Canada was equally different from that of a later era. It was essentially not a home but a foreign mission, and its aims and methods can most readily be understood by analogy with similar enterprises that were being undertaken during the same period in many other parts of the world. Its overriding purpose was the conversion of "heathen" to Christ, and most of those who offered themselves for the work were zealots whose sense of urgency prepared them to face any hardships if souls might be won. Like overseas missionaries, too, those of the North-West assumed a virtual identity between European and Christian values and therefore regarded "civilizing" the native peoples as an integral part of the process of christianizing them.

Three agencies were responsible for practically all Christian work that had as yet been undertaken among the Indians of the North-West. The Church Missionary Society, which was Anglican, had a chain of missions that reached from the Red River along the waterways to Fort Yukon, which W. W. Kirkby reached in 1862.[20] They also had several posts around James Bay, and in 1862 William Duncan had begun an extraordinary experiment in regimented Indian community life at Metlakatla on the British Columbian coast. The Oblate order, which was Catholic and French, competed vigorously with the CMS all along the route, with special attention to the Edmonton area.[21] The Canadian Methodists had missions in what is now northern Manitoba, and in 1863 George McDougall had begun what would be an epic career among the Indians of the Alberta foothills.[22] By 1867 only the buffalo-hunting Indians of the grasslands and the Eskimos of the Arctic remained almost untouched by the Christian mission.

Western missions were foreign not only in motivation and method but in the literal sense of depending on European initiative and support. The CMS was an English organization, and apart from a few "country-born" clergy its missionaries were English. The Oblate enterprise was directed from France, although the order recruited several of its outstanding missionaries in French Canada. Methodist work had been begun by the Methodist Missionary Society of England at the invitation of the Hudson's Bay Company in 1840. From time to time, indeed, there were signs of interest among the churches of British North America. Bishop George Mountain of Quebec toured the area in 1844 in response to a request from Indian converts, although no direct help from Canadian Anglicans followed. In 1854 the Canadian Methodist Conference officially took over the western missions of its denomination.[23] In 1866 James Nisbet opened an Indian mission and school at Prince Albert for the Canada Presbyterian Church.[24] Work among white settlers was undertaken by Canada Presbyterians at the Red River in 1851 and by Canadian Methodists among the miners of British Columbia in 1858. The Anglicans of the Red River were served by the CMS and the Colonial and Continental Church Society, however, and the first Presbyterian missionary in British Columbia was sent from Ireland. By the time of confederation Canadian churches were beginning to realize that the west was within their area of responsibility, but their effective occupation of it was still in the future.

### British North America

Greatly as the British North American colonies varied in background and history, attachment to the church was in 1867 one of the most notable features they had in common. Loyalty and affection were most conspicuous in French Canada, where the church seemed omnicompetent, and in Newfoundland, where there were practically no competing attractions. In other colonies there were usually more choices to be made and therefore greater incentives to independence of judgment, but the possibility of being attached to no church seldom figured among the options to be considered. Even the irreligious usually went to church on Sunday; the religious went more than once, and in most churches for considerably more than an hour at a time. A great many Canadians spent the rest of the sabbath reading religious books or periodicals, and most newspapers coming into the home had devotional columns. This amount of participation, reinforced by the conviction that sermons and religious articles referred to an eternal order whose existence could not be doubted, helped to shape not only formal belief but practical conduct. Most Methodists were in fact abstinent, most Presbyterians scrupulous in observing the Lord's day, most Catholics conscientious in self-examination, most Anglicans faithful in saying their prayers. These outward signs betokened an inner commitment that was usually sincere if not always very deep.

The churches had attained a fair measure of maturity in most colonies. Like society itself, they had left frontier conditions well behind. They had reduced sprawling circuits and missions of earlier days to compact congregations and parishes. They had long since outgrown primitive log chapels, and in more prosperous regions were worshipping in trim brick churches.[25] For several decades some of them had supported arts colleges, and even the more pietistic and rurally based denominations were beginning to desire ministers who had been trained in them. Most churches were moving towards independence of overseas control, and some had already achieved it, although progress towards financial self-support was retarded by the development of more expensive tastes. Having attained a secure place in Canadian life, the churches were looking forward to further advance on the frontiers and to a deeper penetration of national life.

Despite some progress towards sophistication, colonial and provincial attitudes shielded the churches of British North America from the impact of developments that were causing profound disturbance elsewhere. In 1835 David Strauss's *Life of Jesus* had demonstrated the explosive potentialities of biblical criticism. The European revolution of 1848 had brought to prominence a political theorist named Karl Marx who challenged the presuppositions on which every western society, including the Canadian, was based. In 1859 the publication of Charles Darwin's *Origin of Species* opened questions about the nature of man that had long been considered closed. Newspapers made Canadians aware of such dangerous new thoughts, but press and pulpit alike were careful to warn against them. Small coteries discussed the latest ideas from Europe, but the average churchgoing Canadian saw no reason to take them very seriously.

The situation of the church in 1867 was the result of influences that had operated, in some areas, over more than two hundred and fifty years. A Canadian religious tradition was already in process of formation when the first European stepped ashore and inevitably brought with him a heritage of belief and practice that had been in the making since time immemorial. It began to take more definite shape when services of worship were conducted and sermons preached in the new land, and when representatives of various communions sought to persuade colonists to their way of thinking. It was constantly modified by experience in meeting the challenge of the country itself. From time to time it was fertilized by new impulses from without. These four influences—the settlers, the missionaries, the novelty of the environment, and the continued pull of the metropolis—have been decisive factors in determining the shape of Canadian church history.

## THE SETTLERS AND THEIR MISSIONARIES

The early settlers of Canada came, almost without exception, for reasons other than religious. They came to build new empires or to escape lost ones, to make money or to avoid starvation, but not to renounce the corruption of the world or to found religious utopias. It never occurred to them, however, to leave their religion behind. Most of them brought to Canada the beliefs and forms of worship of churches that were recognized by the state or deeply rooted in popular favour—the Catholicism of France or Ireland, the national establishments of England or Scotland, the dominant Congregationalism of New England, the Lutheranism of one of the German states. Many of those who came to Upper Canada, however, brought a religious heritage that had already undergone a mutation or two on the American frontier.

Immigrants were sometimes stubbornly retentive of their previous affiliations, the classic Canadian example being that of Red River settlers who waited forty years for a Presbyterian minister. Old loyalties were sometimes accentuated by the need of self-identification in a new environment, and sometimes dissipated by the material cares and ambitions of the frontier. Much depended on the promptness and efficiency with which pastoral care was provided. Most of Canada's early settlers were not cared for either promptly or efficiently by their natural shepherds. Through lack of concern, lack of imagination, and sometimes lack of jurisdiction beyond the home-land,[26] the old religious establishments failed on the whole to provide accept-able leadership.

The resulting religious vacuum was filled by enthusiasts, usually without the backing of states or state churches, who were willing to undergo limit-less hardships and to adapt their methods to local needs. These volunteers, who ranged from college-trained intellectuals to self-taught handymen, had little in common beyond their willingness. In Quebec, from the beginning of the colony, religious orders rendered services for which the parish clergy of France had neither the inclination nor the aptitude. In eastern Nova Scotia, in the last decades of the eighteenth century, Seceders who had broken away from the Church of Scotland established themselves among Highlanders who had probably never seen a Seceder before. At about the same time, Methodist itinerants crossed the American border into Upper Canada to spread revival among frontiersmen who were largely destitute of religious services. Sometimes a spiritual vacuum attracted a spontaneous inrush of religious feeling. In 1776, when the Congregational ministers of the Maritimes rushed home to New England to be on the right side of a revolution, a young Nova Scotian named Henry Alline had an experience of the Holy Spirit that was soon communicated throughout the area as the "Great Awakening."[27] But for the vigilance of the Seceders a similar phenomenon might have swept the Highland settlements further east under the preaching of the dynamic although unstable Norman McLeod.[28]

The Roman Catholicism of the confederation era was equally a product of revival. French Canada had not been noted for its religious fervour in the early decades of the nineteenth century, when the ministrations of the church were hampered by an acute shortage of priests, by the infiltration of anticlerical ideas, and by the competition of active Protestant evangelists. During the 1830s and 1840s, however, there began a rallying to the church that would last throughout the nineteenth century and even beyond it.[29] The most dramatic turning point was a preaching tour in 1840 by Mgr de Forbin-Janson, bishop of Nancy in France, and in succeeding years other charismatic preachers carried the revival to every corner of the province. The initiative of bishops in founding seminaries and recruiting priests was of at least equal importance, and a new spirit of disciplined devotion that began to emanate from Rome may have been even more decisive. A tightening of moral standards followed, and charities flourished as never before. Among Catholics of Irish and Scottish background, likewise, occasional missions by eloquent priests or teams of preaching friars came to be regular features of parish life.

The varied manifestations of religious renewal had begun to overflow the boundaries of British North America in quite early days. In 1835 Samuel Day of Canada West became a Baptist missionary among the Telugus of India, although under the sponsorship of an American society. During the 1840s Maritime Baptists and Presbyterians began to send missionaries abroad, the latter opening a field of their own in the New Hebrides and soon contributing the Gordon brothers of Prince Edward Island to the roll of Christian martyrs. By 1853 Catholic Sisters of Providence from Montreal were at work in Chile.

The efforts of missionaries and revivalists substantially altered the ecclesiastical configuration of the colonies. Settlers who had belonged to the Scottish Kirk joined the churches of the Seceders who ministered to them. Congregationalists were metamorphosed into "Newlights" and then into Baptists. In French Canada the Catholic Church ceased to be a mere official presence and became a dynamic missionary force. The result was to give many Canadians the impression that their form of Christianity was not merely inherited but actually generated on native soil. It is worth noting, however, that changes of affiliation were usually within limits. Presbyterians moved to other varieties of Presbyterianism. Baptists departed from classic Congregationalism only in their interpretation of one sacrament. Only the Methodists seemed to make converts indiscriminately, and a glance at early class lists suggests that even they found their adherents most readily among the relatively cognate Anglicans and Lutherans.

## ADAPTATION TO CANADIAN CONDITIONS

Although missionaries at first sought only to introduce familiar forms of Christianity into a new setting, they soon discovered the necessity of adapting their approach to the Canadian environment. There was no planned naturalization, no attempt to be Canadian for the sake of being Canadian, but every church discovered that it could succeed in Canada only if it met certain conditions. The most elementary form of adaptation was the stripping away of European adornments that seemed to have little practical utility in a pioneer society. The subtleties of liturgy tended to be reduced among evangelicals to an appeal to the emotions, among French Canadians to an appeal to the senses, and among Anglicans to an appeal to the memory. Many writers have called attention to the scarcity in the Canadian church of intellectual originality and mystical imagination, although learning and piety were always highly valued.

More positively, churches found that in Canada they needed to create for their members a social framework that would have been provided in Europe by other institutions. In England there could be an amicable division of labour between the parish church and the pub across the street. In pioneer Canada secular social activities tended to be disorderly, with the result that the churches involved their members in religious activities to a degree that would have seemed excessive to most Europeans. Small churches also discovered that by pooling their meagre resources they could more effectively serve scattered communities, train an indigenous ministry, and influence public opinion. A desire for church union manifested itself in very early days, and although it sometimes lost ground before divisive forces it proved to be extremely persistent. Unions between Free Church and Seceding groups of Presbyterians in the Maritimes in 1860 and in Canada in 1861 indicated that the drive towards union was gathering momentum at the time of confederation.

In many ways the members of denominations that had never enjoyed state support found Canadian soil most hospitable. In the old world they had been dissenters, tolerated only out of necessity if at all. In Canada they had equal opportunities and had succeeded before confederation in securing equal rights. Their demand for a place in the sun took the form of advocacy of the principle of voluntaryism, according to which churches should be financed by their own members without help from the state. Precedents for voluntaryism abounded both in Britain and in the United States. In England the long-underprivileged dissenting bodies began in 1828 a forty-years' struggle for legal equality with the Church of England, and Canadian Congregationalists and Baptists followed their campaign with sympathetic interest. In 1829 the Seceders of Scotland adopted voluntaryism as a definite principle, and after that time their missionaries promoted it in Canada. The American principle of the separation of church and state was well known, although its republican associations did not commend it to subjects of the British crown. For the most part, however, Canadian voluntarists seem to have been directly motivated by resentment against preferential treatment for denominations that failed to earn it by their missionary zeal. An important result of voluntaryism in practice was to encourage lay participation in church government, for the system depended for its success on financial support by the laity. By 1855 even the clerically oriented Wesleyans were admitting laymen to the financial sessions of their district meetings.[30]

The situation of the Church of England in the colonies was somewhat invidious. British colonial planners had intended an important role for it in their design for transplanting aristocratic institutions to the new world. The transfer of power to unsympathetic colonial legislatures had prevented the church from reaping great rewards for such favour, while fixing in the popular mind an association of Anglicanism with privilege and with the desire for privilege. In England, where the authority of the church was commonly held to derive from its official status, the tendency on the other hand was to regard unestablished segments of Anglicanism as anomalous extensions of the home church. An English bishop remarked of his Scottish and American colleagues, "You do not mean to say that they are Bishops such as we are?"[31] and colonial bishops were no more highly regarded.

Cut off from traditional sources of support, Anglicans perforce became voluntaries like the others and set up representative synods of clergy and laity after the example of the Protestant Episcopal Church in the United States. There remained the problem of determining their proper relation with the mother church in England. Canadian churchmen were unwilling to accept an inferior status, but equally unwilling to sever ties that seemed essential to the maintenance of their identity as Anglicans. This problem was one of the main items on the agenda of the first conference of bishops of the world-wide Anglican communion at Lambeth in 1867, a conference that had long been mooted but was directly inspired by the initiative of the Canadian episcopate.[32] Lambeth set the pattern of a community of autonomous churches held together by periodic consultation, thus anticipating by some years the parallel political development of the British Commonwealth of Nations.

The most conspicuous Canadian circumstance to which the Roman Catholic Church had had to adapt was the English conquest of 1759. This decisive change of fortune, while weakening the institutional fabric of the church and creating a chronic shortage of priests, had the long-term result of making Catholicism an essential ingredient of a renascent French-Canadian culture. It also led to what the nationalist historian Michel Brunet has described as "a tacit agreement between the church, the politicians— both French- and English-speaking—and the economic leaders of St. James and Bay Streets,"[33] by which the church succeeded in retaining its influence on the people in return for its acceptance of political and economic realities. In fact the church was merely pursuing its traditional policy of coming to terms with any government that could claim legitimate authority so long as it was permitted to carry on its own religious and educational program without interference. British rule brought to the Catholic Church a curious mixture of disabilities and privileges. By the time of confederation, it had in Canada East many of the characteristics of a religious establishment, achieving by its permeation of society a status that official favour had never successfully bestowed on the Church of England. Although in other parts of British North America its position was markedly different, the widespread recognition of its separate schools testified to its success in becoming a significant factor in Canadian society.

## FERTILIZATION FROM ABROAD

British North Americans, who in the early years of the nineteenth century had tended to concentrate on local issues, felt with increasing force, during its second quarter, the pull of the metropolitan centres of Europe. Several factors helped to bring about the change. The War of 1812 impressed on Upper Canadians, and for different reasons on the Roman Catholic hierarchy of French Canada, the need for an ideological alternative to American republicanism. Successive waves of immigration that began after the Napoleonic Wars and reached their climax during the Irish famine of the 1840s added a self-consciously British strain to a population that had consisted largely of French Canadians and displaced Americans.[34] Producers of raw materials in all colonies looked more across the Atlantic as they came to depend on the British preferential tariff for export markets. Religious bonds were also strengthened as immigrants followed developments "back home" and as European churches sought in the colonies outlets for their newly awakened missionary zeal. This renewal of contact with Europe coincided with the appearance of important religious movements, all embodying the current romantic spirit, that would have important repercussions in Canada. The most important of these were Roman Catholic ultramontanism, the Oxford Movement in the Church of England, and the anti-Erastian evangelicalism of Scotland.

Ultramontanism means, generally, support for papal power in opposition to national and especially to state control of the church. The implicit reference of the term to an authority "across the mountains" suggests its French origin, and as early as the seventeenth century the French church had an ultramontane wing. As a cohesive movement, however, ultramontanism originated in the early nineteenth century. The Roman Catholic Church, after a period of persecution during the Revolution, was re-established by Napoleon under strict state control as a means of keeping Frenchmen law-abiding and loyal. Fervent Catholics could foresee from such an arrangement only the ultimate degradation of the church. The only recourse beyond the French state being to the pope, those who took their Catholicism seriously eventually became almost unanimously ultramontane.[35]

Fidelity to the pope is compatible with a wide variety of positions, and French ultramontanism was by no means a monolithic movement. Félicité de Lamennais, one of the founders of nineteenth-century ultramontanism, looked to the papacy for spiritual rather than political authority and saw more dangers than advantages in the state connection. When a moderate revolution in 1830 placed the anti-clerical Louis-Philippe on the throne, therefore, Lamennais scandalized conservative Catholics by urging in his journal *L'Avenir* that the church should come to terms with the revolution, abjure its ancient privileges, and gladly accept the opportunities that were inherent in a new freedom. Although he and his journal were soon condemned by a pope who did not share his vision, he left behind him followers such as Lacordaire, Montalembert, and Dupanloup, who continued to maintain a liberal ultramontanism. Others, led by Louis Veuillot, claimed autonomy for the church in spiritual matters but insisted that in such traditionally clerical fields as education the state was bound to enforce the church's will.

Ultramontanism had natural attractions for the French-Canadian hierarchy, who like their counterparts in France had to find ways of dealing with a non-Catholic government. Realism might have suggested that in the Canadian situation the liberal variety was most applicable, but through circumstances and their own conservative proclivities Canadian ultramontanes turned elsewhere. Ignace Bourget, then newly elevated to the see of Montreal, was captivated by the fervour of the ultramontane party during several visits to France and Rome in the early 1840s.[36] By this time Lamennais had been condemned, and it was Veuillot's version that Bourget assimilated. Canadian ultramontanism would be conservative and clerical, pledged to the hegemony of the church over many matters usually defined as secular. As in France, it would seize upon education as the most vital issue in the struggle against infidelity.[37]

Within the Church of England the Oxford Movement is usually considered to have begun in 1833 when John Keble preached a sermon on "national apostasy" at the university church of St. Mary the Virgin. His immediate reference was to the suppression by Parliament of several Anglican bishoprics in Ireland that were almost without communicants, his more fundamental concern with the state's assumption of a right to regulate the internal affairs of the Church of England. The state had actually been exercising such a right since the time of Henry VIII, but the limitation of the franchise to Anglicans had made it possible to argue that King and Parliament were merely acting on behalf of the laity of the church. The right to vote and sit in Parliament was extended to dissenters in 1828, however, and to Roman Catholics in 1829. The result, Keble argued, was to expose the Church of England to the ignominious possibility of alien control. Several Oxford dons, of whom the most notable were J. H. Newman, E. B. Pusey, and Keble himself, determined to resist a menace that was compounded in their view by the appointment of a parliamentary commission to investigate the affairs of the church. They expressed their convictions in a series entitled "Tracts for the Times" and were accordingly often called "tractarians."[38]

Since most Englishmen assumed that the Church of England owed its authority to recognition by the state, complaints that the church was in bondage would have had little effect on them unless it could be shown to have some other claim on their allegiance. The tractarians appealed to the inherent catholicity of the church, guaranteed not by royal or parliamentary patronage but by the gift of Christ through an unbroken succession of bishops from the apostles. Protestants were quick to note the movement's hostility to the Reformation, and their suspicions seemed to be confirmed when Newman adhered to the Roman Catholic Church in 1845. Despite further defections, however, the movement as a whole continued to insist on its loyalty to the Church of England.

In 1841 the inauguration of the Colonial Bishoprics Fund made possible, for the first time, the appointment of a considerable number of Anglican bishops outside England.[39] The high churchman W. E. Gladstone was one of the treasurers of the fund, and Anglo-Catholics were first elevated to the episcopal bench under its sponsorship. By the time of confederation their tenets were becoming well known in British North America through such bishops as John Medley of Fredericton, Edward Feild of Newfoundland, George Hills of British Columbia, and Hibbert Binney of Nova Scotia. These men brought to Canada not only an unfamiliar concept of church order but a new episcopal style. They were austere men, enthusiasts for seemly worship and assiduous pastoral care. They had no interest in the old Anglican dream of a Canadian establishment and distrusted government aid,[40] looking instead to popular support based on councils, or synods, of clergy and laity.

In Scotland too, the encroachment of the modern state on ground claimed by the church provoked resistance. From the early years of the nineteenth century two parties disputed for the leadership of the Church of Scotland. The moderates, many of whom were men of great ability, sought to advance Scottish culture and improve Scottish morals by the methods of common sense. The evangelicals concentrated on conversion and personal piety. The common people complained that the preaching of the moderates was cold and had little good news in it, but the choice of ministers was in the hands of patrons who were men of property and often of cultivated taste.[41] It was only natural that moderates should uphold the rights of patrons and that evangelicals should seek to limit them.

In 1834 the evangelicals under the leadership of the social reformer Thomas Chalmers won control of the general assembly of the Church of Scotland. They proceeded to enact a mild program of reform, allowing congregations to veto the nomination of their ministers and providing for the erection of new parishes in industrial areas. Beginning in 1838, however, the Scottish civil courts rendered a series of judgments invalidating the new legislation, while the church courts continued to assert their prerogatives. The climax came in 1843 when the House of Lords ruled that the Church of Scotland as a creature of the state had no right to independent jurisdiction. At the general assembly that year more than two hundred commissioners entered a solemn protest against the state's usurpation of ecclesiastical power and adjourned to a nearby hall to constitute the Free Church of Scotland.[42] Chalmers had previously defended the principle of church establishments, and the Free Church continued to maintain it. Its contention was that as the true Church of Scotland now set free it had succeeded to the place forfeited by the Kirk that remained in bondage. It was therefore orthodox and retentive of tradition, but also activist, missionary, and full of social concern.

Evangelicals had been the most active supporters of the Glasgow Colonial Society, through which the Kirk had channeled aid to its Canadian congregations since 1825, and most of the ministers whom it had appointed were also evangelicals.[43] Robert Burns, the former secretary of the society, was thus assured a ready hearing when he toured British North America shortly after the disruption in the interests of the Free Church.[44] Ministers and people rushed to dissociate themselves from the "captive" Church of Scotland, and many congregations were divided. In the Canadian setting many Free Churchmen gave up their adherence to the establishment principle and became outright voluntarists,[45] emphasizing the right of congregations to call their own ministers and insisting on lay participation in church government.

Although differing greatly in doctrine, polity, and attitude to the modern world, ultramontanes, tractarians, and Free Churchmen had some important qualities in common. The three movements, in their varying ways, all represented attempts to reassert the inherent authority of the church over against the universal jurisdiction claimed by the modern state.[46] Thomas Arnold recognized their family likeness at the time by lumping together "Popery, High Churchism, and the claims of the Scottish Presbyterians" as enemies of the royal supremacy in which he believed.[47] Each movement, moreover, found its answer to the claims of an Erastian state in a return to traditional elements of its own past, and each released new energies that revitalized the tradition in which it stood.

The impact of European religious ideas intensified strife and division in the small colonies of British North America, where disagreements readily became personal quarrels. It set off bitter controversies within the Roman Catholic and Anglican churches, and virtually ruined the Canadian branches of the Scottish Kirk. It added fuel to local agitation against the official privileges of the Church of England and contributed to their virtual extinction in 1854. On the other hand, fertilization from abroad brought an infusion of pastoral zeal to communions that badly needed it. French religious orders that came to Canada as a result of Bourget's ultramontane contacts stimulated local churchmen to new vigour. The Oxford Movement helped the Church of England to learn self-reliance when its established position was taken away from it. The Free Church became the growing edge of Presbyterianism, transmitting its missionary enthusiasm to others. Most important of all, perhaps, renewed interest in European ideas helped Canadian churches to shake off their lingering provincialism.

## THE TRADITIONAL AND THE CONTEMPORARY

Out of the varied contributions of settlers and missionaries, local circumstances, and European movements, two contrasting attitudes gradually emerged within the churches. One was a desire to maintain undiminished the inheritance of faith and practice that Canadians had brought with them from the older lands of Christendom. The other was a concern to extend and apply this inheritance, adapting it where necessary to contemporary circumstances. The spirit of one was cautious and traditional, that of the other crusading and missionary. Their interaction, which frequently gave rise to misunderstanding and even conflict, also provided much of the thrust of Canadian church history in the century after confederation.

The two tendencies represented natural options for churches in a society that was largely made up of transplanted Europeans. Settlers in a strange land inevitably wished to preserve some links with their past. To them, inherited customs and beliefs were not merely reminders of home, but proofs that they had not left their own identities behind, all the more precious when—as often happened in Canada—the old surroundings had been abandoned with more regret than anticipation. If it was natural for inhabitants of a new country to think occasionally of their old homes, however, it was essential that they should seek to improve their new ones. A desire to take possession of the land, at first tentative, became stronger as the forest receded and signs of effective occupation appeared. In time, a growing conviction that progress had been made gave rise to an assurance that progress would continue to be made, and as thriving congregations grew up in what had been a wilderness the same assurance easily passed over into church life. Tensions in the church between traditionalists and innovators often reflected similar tensions within individuals between inherited loyalties and newly formed attachments.

Even more significant in fixing attitudes was the fact that Canada's churches achieved their major growth during a century when rationalism had been dethroned and both tradition and enthusiasm were back in fashion. Romantics of the nineteenth century looked to the Christian Middle Ages for a cohesion that society seemed to have lost, while historians examined Europe's past with an unaccustomed sympathy. Christians also began to assert their principles with a new confidence, and the church entered what K. S. Latourette has called the "great century" of missionary advance. Both the traditionalism and the activism of the century were reflected in Canada. Queen Victoria and Pope Pius IX inspired, for English- and French-speaking Canadians respectively, a cult of venerable institutions that had never been a part of the experience of the older colonies to the south. Pastors and pamphleteers imbued church members with a vision of Christianity as a dynamic and even irresistable force, engaged in an enterprise of world conquest of which the winning of Canada was an integral and important part.

It was easy, in a situation where ethnic and ecclesiastical affiliations often coincided, for cultural attachments to mask themselves as theological principles. Many Canadians found it natural to assume that God could be worshipped rightly only in transplanted English parish churches, or in trim New England meeting houses, or in imposing Norman basilicas. Progressives were similarly tempted to identify material improvement with divine providence: in 1849 a Presbyterian editor in Nova Scotia had concluded that locomotives and steam navigation were "destined to accelerate the advancement of the Kingdom of God."[48] Even in these confused sentiments, however, Canadians were trying to express some of the fundamental aspects of their Christianity. Those who clung to tattered memories of Christendom were really seeking to conserve the faith itself. Those who rushed to welcome every new technique of evangelism or education did so in obedience to their Lord's commission to make disciples of all nations.

## NOTES TO CHAPTER ONE

1. Edinburgh: 1810.

2. Toronto: Samuel Rose, 1844.

3. ". . . it was this New England background which remained for many years the greatest single influence in shaping Baptist developments and institutions in these provinces." George E. Levy, *The Baptists of the Maritime Provinces, 1753-1946* (Saint John: Barnes and Hopkins Limited, 1946), p. 14.

4. Alumni Association of Toronto Baptist College, *Memorial of Daniel Arthur McGregor, late Principal of Toronto Baptist College* (Toronto: Dudley and Burns, 1891), p. 24.

5. A. A. Johnston, *A History of the Catholic Church in Eastern Nova Scotia* (Antigonish: St. Francis Xavier University Press, 1960), Vol. I, p. 241.

6. Charles Pedley, *The History of Newfoundland* (London: Longman, Green, Longman, Roberts and Green, 1863), p. 435.

7. See Eleanor Mary Fraser, "The Early Moravian Church and Its Mission to the Eskimos on the Labrador Coasts," M.A. thesis, Acadia University, 1964.

8. George's account of his missionary experience in Nova Scotia appears in I. E. Bill, *Fifty Years with the Baptist Ministers and Churches of the Maritime Provinces of Canada* (Saint John: Barnes and Co., 1880), pp. 20-26.

9. *Ibid.*, p. 176.

10. Levy, *op. cit.*, pp. 130-131.

11. "C'était un peuple rural, accueillant et familier, révérant ses prêtres, élevant beaucoup d'enfants, n'omettant jamais ses prières, vidant un verre 'quand s'adonne,' sacrant un peu plus qu'il ne faudrait, fumant de gros tabac et chaudement vêtu pour braver de rudes hivers." Robert Rumilly, *Histoire de la Province de Québec* (Montreal: Editions Bernard Valiquette, etc., 1940-1968), Vol. I, p. 87.

12. Marcel de Grandpré attributes this trait to the training in scholastic philosophy they imbibed through the Catechism of Quebec. "Traditions of the Catholic Church in French Canada," in J. W. Grant, ed., *The Churches and the Canadian Experience* (Toronto: Ryerson, 1963), pp. 5-6.

13. This and similar statements are based on the *Census of Canada, 1870-71* (Ottawa: I. B. Taylor, 1873).

14. H. Senior, "Quebec and the Fenians," *Canadian Historical Review*, Vol. XLVIII, No. 1, (March 1967), pp. 26-44.

15. Carl R. Cronmiller, *A History of the Lutheran Church in Canada* (Evangelical Lutheran Synod of Canada, 1961), Chapters 8, 9.

16. See J. Henry Getz, ed., *A Century in Canada* (Kitchener: G. C. Spaetzel, 1964).

17. See L. J. Burkholder, *A Brief History of the Mennonites in Ontario* (Markham, Ontario: Livingstone Press, 1935).

18. See E. B. Eddy, "The Beginnings of Congregationalism in the Early Canadas," Th.D. thesis, Victoria University, 1957.

19. See A. G. Dorland, *A History of the Society of Friends (Quakers) in Canada* (Toronto: Macmillan, 1927).

20. For Anglican missions among the Indians of western Canada, see T. C. B. Boon, *The Anglican Church from the Bay to the Rockies* (Toronto: Ryerson, 1962).

21. For Roman Catholic missions, see A. G. Morice, *History of the Catholic Church in Western Canada*, 2 vols. (Toronto: Musson, 1910).

22. For Methodist missions, see J. H. Riddell, *Methodism in the Middle West* (Toronto: Ryerson, 1964), Chapters 1-4.

23. *The Minutes of the Annual Conferences of the Wesleyan Methodist Church in Canada from 1846 to 1857, inclusive* (Toronto: Anson Green, 1863), p. 269.

24. George Boyle, "The Foreign Mission Committee of the Presbyterian Church in Canada," *Bulletin*, Committee of Archives of The United Church of Canada, No. 8 (1955), pp. 37-41.

25. John S. Moir refers to the 1830s and 1840s as a period of "tremendous building activity" in Upper Canada. *Profiles of a Province* (Toronto: Ontario Historical Society, 1967), p. 191.

26. For the effects of the state connection in inhibiting the outreach of German churches to colonists abroad, see Martin Niemöller, "The Churches and Migration," in *In a Strange Land*, a Report of a World Conference on Problems of International Migration and the Responsibility of the Churches held at Leysin, Switzerland, June 11-16, 1961 (Geneva: World Council of Churches, n.d.).

27. See Maurice Armstrong, *The Great Awakening in Nova Scotia, 1776-1809* (Hartford: The American Society of Church History, 1948).

28. See Flora McPherson, *Watchman Against the World: The Story of Norman McLeod and His People* (London: Robert Hale Limited, 1962).

29. Accounts of various aspects of Catholic renewal from 1841 to 1855 make up the 1941-1942 issue of *Rapport*, La Société Canadienne d'Histoire de l'Eglise Catholique. But the number of ordinations to the priesthood had already begun its upward climb about 1830. Louis-Edmond Hamelin, "Evolution numérique séculaire du clergé catholique dans de Québec," *Recherches sociographiques*, Vol. II, No. 2 (avril-juin 1961), p. 199.

30. *Minutes of the Annual Conferences . . . from 1846 to 1857*, p. 308.

31. Longley Letters, VIII, p. 39; quoted in Alan W. G. Stephenson, *The First Lambeth Conference, 1867* (London: SPCK, 1967), p. 306.

32. See Stephenson, *op. cit.*, for an assessment of the Canadian role in the calling of the first Lambeth Conference.

33. "The French Canadians' Search for a Fatherland," in Peter Russell, ed., *Nationalism in Canada* (Toronto: McGraw-Hill, 1966), p. 51.

34. See Helen L. Cowan, *British Immigration before Confederation*, Canadian Historical Association, Historical Booklet No. 22, 1968.

35. For a good general account of the movement, see A. Dansette, *A Religious History of Modern France*, tr. J. Dingle, 2 vols. (London: Nelson, 1961).

36. Jacques Monet, sj, "French Canadian Nationalism and the Challenge of Ultramontanism," in Canadian Historical Association, *Historical Papers Presented at the Annual Meeting held at Sherbrooke, June 8-11, 1966*, p. 43.

37. A decree of the Roman congregation *De Propaganda Fidei*, January 11, 1846, pronouncing non-sectarian religious education dangerous to youth, was influential in Canada. Watson Kirkconnell, "Education," in George W. Brown, ed., *Canada* (Toronto: University of Toronto Press, 1950), p. 437.

38. *Tracts for the Times, by Members of the University of Oxford* (London: J. G. and F. Rivington and J. H. Parker, 1831-1841), 6 vols.

39. W. F. France, *The Oversea Episcopate: Centenary History of the Colonial Bishoprics Fund 1841-1941* (Westminster: The Colonial Bishoprics Fund, 1941).

40. Bishop Hills advised parish authorities in 1861 to decline government subsidies that were offered them. F. A. Peake, *The Anglican Church in British Columbia* (Vancouver: Mitchell, 1959), pp. 48, 76.

41. J. H. S. Burleigh, *A Church History of Scotland* (London: Oxford University Press, 1960), pp. 286-308.

42. For the "Claim, Declaration and Protest, anent the Encroachment of the Court of Session; and Protest by Commissioners to General Assembly," see W. Hanna, *Memoir of the Life and Writings of Thomas Chalmers, D.D., LL.D.* (Edinburgh: Thos. Constable and Co., 1849-1852), Vol. IV, pp. 528-551.

43. See A. F. Binnington, "The Glasgow Colonial Society and Its Work in the Development of the Presbyterian Church in British North America, 1825-1840," Th.D. thesis, Victoria University, 1960.

44. R. F. Burns, *Life and Times of the Rev. R. Burns* (Toronto: James Campbell, 1871), Chapter 12.

45. John S. Moir, "The Upper Canadian Roots of Church Disestablishment," *Ontario History*, Vol. LX, No. 4 (December 1968), p. 255.

46. For an illuminating discussion of these movements in terms of their common opposition to Erastianism, see Harold J. Laski, *Studies in the Problem of Sovereignty* (New Haven: Yale University Press, 1917), Chapters 2-5.

47. A. P. Stanley, *The Life and Correspondence of Thos. Arnold, D.D.* (London: Ward, Lock, 1844), Vol. II, p. 187.

48. *Presbyterian Witness*, February 3, 1849.

# TWO

## Measuring the New Nation

Confederation was an offspring of secular statesmanship, born of political and economic necessity, fathered by politicians and railway promoters. Its purpose was not to create a covenant people or to hasten the coming of the kingdom of God but to ensure a continued British presence in North America that would be strong enough to withstand powerful pressures towards continental consolidation. Church assemblies saw no need to comment on the debates that led up to it, regarding it as a project that lay outside their terms of reference. Canadians have always recognized the secular origins of their nation. Unlike many citizens of the United States, they have never been disposed to regard their national constitution as a quasi-religious document. The story of confederation can be told, and indeed sometimes has been told, almost without reference to the church.

From the outset, however, it was recognized that confederation could take place only if the people would accept it, and the opinions of Canadians were moulded in part by the churches to which they belonged. If confederation owed little directly to the churches, therefore, its successful achievement depended considerably on attitudes fostered by the churches. The role of the church was a subtle one, expressed more often in individual actions than in official statements. Of particular importance was the attitude of the religious press, which did not regard itself as bound, like the pulpit or the church assembly, to silence on political matters.

### THE CHURCH'S PART IN CONFEDERATION

Among Protestants, especially in Canada West, a favourable reaction to confederation could almost be assumed. For one thing, they were intensely dissatisfied with the current political arrangements. Under the terms of the act of 1841 that had combined Upper and Lower Canada into a single province, the two sections had equal representation in the legislature. This provision was intended as a safeguard for Upper Canada, which at the time was the less populous province. By 1867, however, immigration had so reversed the proportion that Upper Canadians regarded equal representation as an intolerable injustice. The deadlock that inevitably resulted from such an even balance of forces was the product of religious animosity, and Protestants looked to their growing numbers to give them the upper hand. Representation by population was their obvious recourse, but it soon became evident that in return French Catholics would have to be given a province of their own within a federal system.

Another strong inducement to Canadian Protestants, who seldom distinguished patriotism sharply from religion, was the enhancement of British prestige and power that would result from confederation. John Hillyard Cameron, grand master of the Loyal Orange Order and chancellor of the Anglican diocese of Toronto, welcomed confederation for this reason.[1] Especially attractive, on grounds both of religion and patriotism, was the prospect of attaching to Canada the territories of the Hudson's Bay Company. Upper Canadians had been looking westward since the 1850s, and expansion in this direction was implicit from the beginning in the proposal of confederation. Canadian possession of the northwest would frustrate American designs on the area, give Protestant farm boys a British alternative to emigration to the United States, serve as a counterweight to Catholic Canada East, and provide an outlet for Protestant missionary zeal. George Brown, the leading proponent of voluntaryism in Canada West and a determined opponent of Roman Catholic claims, was both an early advocate of confederation and an enthusiast for western expansion. This combination of attitudes was typical of a large segment of Upper Canadian Protestantism.

Confederation had implications, however, that made some Protestants hesitate. The Montreal *Witness*, which avowed itself non-sectarian but reflected the militant voluntaryism of its publisher, expressed grave fears that Protestants of the projected province of Quebec might not be fairly treated by the large Roman Catholic majority there. Even more worrisome to voluntarists in Canada West was the prospect of seeing the right to separate schools in Ontario entrenched in the constitution. The *Canadian Baptist* was cool to confederation from the beginning, preferring representation by population as more likely to promote the separation of church and state.[2] The *Canadian Independent*, while favourable to confederation, devoted far more space in its columns to problems of religious liberty. Grumbling about the "drawbacks" of the constitution continued even after confederation, and such references were usually to the continuance of separate schools.

Despite such reservations, the tone of editorials in the Protestant church press and of public statements by the few church leaders who referred to the matter was overwhelmingly favourable. The *Home and Foreign Record* hailed confederation for the Canada Presbyterians as "an entrance on a new and higher stage of national existence."[3] The *Christian Guardian* laid before

its readers arguments for and against confederation, but editorials emphasized the missionary opportunities that would exist in an enlarged Canada.[4]
Even in the Maritime provinces, where most people were apprehensive about
the future of the area within a larger political union, some of the most
influential Protestant leaders were strong advocates of confederation. The
editor of the Baptist *Christian Messenger*, while disclaiming any concern for
issues of party politics, made his pro-confederate sympathies clear. The
*Presbyterian Witness*, unofficial organ of the Presbyterian Church of the
Lower Provinces, promoted confederation tirelessly within a largely unsympathetic constituency. George Monro Grant, the minister of St. Matthew's
Kirk in Halifax, publicly avowed himself a Canadian nationalist.

A striking proportion of Protestant churchmen who actively supported
confederation were Presbyterian. The importance of Brown and Grant has
long been recognized, but there were others equally forthright. In Montreal
a group of prominent laymen, mostly Canada Presbyterians but including
some Kirkmen, sought to divert Presbyterians from their preoccupation with
Scottish affairs and to arouse them from narrow provincialism. Most articulate of all was Robert Murray, the young editor of the *Presbyterian Witness*,
whose contribution to the political ideology of Canadian Protestantism has
never been adequately recognized. Murray not only advocated confederation
but formulated a program of Christian nation-building that anticipated in
many respects the social gospel of a later generation.

The positive response of Presbyterians to the idea of confederation had as
its background the Scottish concept of a nation committed to God by a
solemn covenant. Baptists and Congregationalists, reflecting the tradition
of churches gathered out of the mass of society, took up varying positions to
confederation in terms of its probable bearing on specific issues such as
separate schools. Methodists were sympathetic, but regarded political matters
as secondary to the saving of souls. Anglicans were generally content to trust
the judgment of the British government. Belief in divine sovereignty led
Presbyterians further. Brown interpreted confederation as "the duty which
an overruling Providence has placed upon us."[5] To Murray, the new nation
was nothing less than "the goodly heritage, the Canaan we are invited to
occupy."[6]

Less predictable than Protestant support, and therefore even more crucial,
was approval of the terms of confederation by the authorities of the Roman
Catholic Church. There were reasons for concern. French Canadians had
greater voting strength in the province of Canada than they could hope to
retain in a federation, where both representation by population and the
inclusion of the largely English-speaking Maritimes would tell against them.
The Irish had long since learned to distrust British designs, and Fenian agitation was at its height among them in the months just before confederation.
Neither group could be without its suspicions of a project so vigorously

promoted by George Brown, especially when he made no secret of his desire to people the West with Protestant settlers from Ontario. Neither French nor Irish could be immune to a general suspicion on the part of minorities that any change in status favoured by the majority is likely to work to their disadvantage.

There was, indeed, considerable evidence of discontent. The leading English-language Catholic periodical in Montreal, the *True Witness*, cited the condition of Ireland as a horrible example of what was likely to happen to religious minorities under the new scheme. The *Morning Freeman*, its counterpart in New Brunswick, took a similar line. In French Canada there was no evidence of popular enthusiasm for confederation. Widespread distrust was reported among the common people, suspended judgment among the clergy, and hostility among young intellectuals.[7] Among the bishops themselves there were hesitations and reservations, and none of them expressed an official opinion about confederation until it had received the Queen's assent in March 1867.

Long before this time, however, the provincial government had been assured of the sympathetic acquiescence of most of the hierarchy.[8] In the autumn of 1864, the bishops of the ecclesiastical province of Quebec met at Trois-Rivières, and the political situation was prominent on their agenda. Shortly afterwards Elzéar A. Taschereau, then rector of Laval University, journeyed to Rome and returned home with favourable opinions on the proposed constitutional arrangements from two prominent canonists. Late in 1865 the vicar general of the archdiocese of Quebec, C. F. Cazeau, accompanied Bishop Horan of Kingston on a visit to the Maritimes to dispel rumours that the Quebec hierarchy was opposed to confederation. L. F. Lafléche, coadjutor bishop of Trois-Rivières, was a supporter of the project from its early stages. After the royal approval he urged his fellow-bishops to commend confederation officially, and the result was a series of *mandements* that urged the faithful not merely to accept the new order but to oppose those who would undo it. Only Bishop Bourget of Montreal held aloof, and even he refrained from expressing his reservations publicly.[9] Episcopal *mandements* carried great weight, and Lower Canada entered confederation without turmoil if without enthusiasm.

Among the English-speaking bishops, the most active supporter of confederation was Archbishop Thomas Connolly of Halifax, who would later remind Sir Charles Tupper that from the outset he had committed himself to the movement openly and without reservation.[10] The others, apart from Bishop John Sweeny of Saint John, also made their support known. Equally important to the confederate cause was the adherence of leading Irish Catholic laymen of the stature of D'Arcy McGee in Montreal and Edward Whelan in Prince Edward Island. Such men provoked resentments that led to the assassination of the former and the political repudiation of the latter, but they ensured that confederation would not be interpreted as a solely Protestant enterprise.

Official Catholic support for confederation was based less on a sentiment for Canadian nationhood than on a realistic appraisal of the situation. The bishops knew that equal representation of the two Canadas in the provincial legislature could not long be maintained in the face of a growing Protestant majority. They also knew that the available choices were strictly limited. Representation by population in a unitary legislature would expose French-Canadian Catholics to domination by English-speaking Protestants. Annexation to the United States, with its tradition of nonsectarian public schools, would involve even greater dangers to faith. There remained only confederation, which at least promised the creation of a separate province of Quebec and offered the possibility of constitutional guarantees for some cherished rights. Nor could the bishops fail to be influenced by the association of support for representation by population and for annexation with the distrusted Liberals or by the sponsorship of confederation by the friendly Conservatives. Such considerations go far to explain why even Bourget, who seems to have anticipated no good from confederation, could not bring himself to speak against it.

Like Protestants, Roman Catholics were troubled by some of the details of the plan. A reference to divorce in the allocation of powers between federal and provincial authorities gave rise to much heartsearching, for it could be interpreted as an implicit recognition of the solubility of marriage. The divorce clause was, indeed, one of the chief factors in prompting Taschereau's expedition to Rome. Even more crucial was the assurance of public support for Catholic education. In most provinces separate schools received government aid, but merely by the grace of legislators and seldom on terms satisfactory to the church. The bishops wished to have these rights constitutionally entrenched, and the introduction in 1865 of an education bill that seemed to them less generous to the Catholics of Canada West than to the Protestants of Canada East shook their confidence in the promoters of confederation. They were reassured by a provision in the British North America Act that guaranteed the existing privileges of separate schools in Ontario, although at the London Conference of 1867 Connolly was unable to secure the extension of this provision to the informally recognized Catholic schools of the Maritimes. Probably most of the bishops would have agreed with the appraisal of Monseigneur C. F. Baillargeon, then administrator of the archdiocese of Quebec:

> If it be not without fault, if it is not all that we would have desired, we must recall that nothing is perfect in this world, and that in a country like ours, where so many divers interests are at stake, it is

impossible to avoid some mutual concessions, so as to obtain an arrangement that should give satisfaction to all.[11]

It was not only among English-speaking Catholics like Connolly, however, that one heard expressions of genuine enthusiasm for the new nation. Jean Langevin, bishop of Rimouski, saw in the confederation of the colonies "a new way that opens before them a vaster future, that extends prodigiously their horizon hitherto so limited."[12] To Charles Larocque of Saint-Hyacinthe, it was a step that would enable Canadians sooner or later to take their place among the nations of the earth and would thus bear "a fruit without parallel in the annals of our history."[13] Laflèche, who did not share such visions of a wider Canada, grasped confederation with equal eagerness as "a plank of safety" for his people.[14]

## THE CHURCH'S RESPONSE TO CONFEDERATION

Once it had been achieved, confederation posed new challenges to the churches. It increased dramatically the scale on which they had to operate. It led to the opening of new lines of communication among the provinces, available to whoever had the resources and foresight to use them. It created not merely a new political entity but the possibility of a new national identity. From the outset there were churchmen who recognized that confederation implied "high duties and responsibilities,"[15] and indeed over the next few decades the new responsibility of nationhood was one of the arguments invariably urged in favour of projects of extension, union, or moral betterment. Only gradually, however, would Canada take hold of the imaginations of churchmen. George M. Grant's *Ocean to Ocean*, an eyewitness account of the west written after he had accompanied an official exploratory expedition under Sir Sandford Fleming in 1872, awakened confidence in Canada as much by its avoidance of bombastic rhetoric as by its favourable appraisal of the nation's future.[16] When Canadians borrowed American conceptions of manifest destiny, they were inclined to make more of the divine character of British institutions than of the divine election of the Canadian people.

Even when they were not responding consciously to the challenge of confederation, the churches had to deal with the new situation it brought into being. They had to cope with the expanded scale of the nation, represented most dramatically by the acquisition of the northwest. They had to bridge the chasms separating the people of its various regions, now linked by railway and telegraph. They had to come to terms with its emerging self-awareness, still largely devoid of ideological content. The problems of Canadian existence, although seldom at the centre of the church's conscious concern, constituted the framework within which all important decisions were made and all major enterprises undertaken.

## PLANTING THE CHURCH IN THE WEST

Now that eastern Canada had been annexed to Christendom, the most pressing claim on the churches was that of the west. In 1869 the Canadian government arranged for the purchase of Rupert's Land from the Hudson's Bay Company, and on July 15, 1870, this vast territory became part of Canada. In an almost forgotten transaction the British government also handed over the Mackenzie basin, which had never been an integral part of the company domain, and in 1871 the accession of British Columbia on the promise of a transcontinental railway carried the nation at last from sea to sea.

For Canadian possession to be effective, however, the new area had to be not only claimed but won. First of all, it had to be held. As early as the 1840s a group at the Red River, despairing of progress under company rule, had petitioned for annexation to the United States. In 1871, at the prompting of a seminarian named O'Donoghue, the Fenians threatened a foray across the border. It was commonly believed that failure on the part of the Canadian government to maintain order or to develop the territory would eventually lead to American intervention. A second task, therefore, was that of effectively occupying the land. Even if there had not been pressure from without, indeed, Canada's prospects for the future depended on developing her most valuable hinterland. Commercial enterprise would help to build railways and to promote schemes of colonization, but it was the national interest that insisted on them. Beyond occupation there was a third task, that of planting churches and Christian institutions, although only a few churchmen were thoroughly aware of its urgency. The farseeing, at least, knew that the west was the area in which the adequacy of nation and church alike would be tested.

When the transfer of government took place, several denominations were already represented at the Red River, the point of entry to the west. Roman Catholics and Anglicans constituted the largest groups, and their bishops were rivalled in prestige and authority only by the company-appointed governor of the colony of Assiniboia. A. A. Taché, the Roman Catholic bishop, had an experience of the colony unrivalled by any other clergyman. A French Canadian who boasted of being a direct descendant of Louis Joliette and a relative of La Vérendrye, the discoverer of Manitoba, he had been one of the first two Oblates to arrive in the west in 1845. In 1851, at the uncanonical age of twenty-seven, he had become coadjutor bishop of an area designated by the church only as "the North-West," and in 1853 second bishop of St. Boniface. He had gradually built up an establishment on the Red River, imported teaching orders, and persuaded many of the French métis, or half-breeds, who constituted the bulk of his people to settle in compact parishes.

Robert Machray, second Anglican Bishop of Rupert's Land, had taken up his post only in 1865 but had already made his presence felt in the colony. A natural ecclesiastical statesman, he worked patiently to institute a highly centralized program. A combined cathedral and college staff was to serve as the nucleus of a far-flung missionary enterprise in which evangelism and education would complement one another. Full implementation of the plan was still in the future, but the foundation was already laid. The whole operation was firmly anchored in England, where Machray as a fellow of Sidney Sussex College, Cambridge, could count on sympathy and assistance.

Presbyterian and Methodist emissaries were men of widely differing temper. John Black, of the Canada Presbyterian Church, had ministered at Kildonan since 1851 and thus lived continuously in the settlement as long as Taché. Essentially a pastor, he was most at home with his Red River people but had many Canadian parishioners as well. He seldom intervened in public affairs, but he had a canny appreciation of Presbyterian interests and rejoiced by 1870 in the formation of a presbytery of Manitoba. The Wesleyans had long been represented in the Indian work to the north and west but appointed a minister to the Red River only in 1868. They were obviously alert to the importance of the time and place, for the man they selected was the current chairman of the Toronto district. George Young had the necessary pioneer adaptiveness, an abundant supply of self-confidence, and a knack for winning the confidence of others. Unfortunately, however, he had little appreciation of the subtle nuances of an ingrown frontier community. His congregation consisted almost completely of recently arrived Canadian settlers, and he readily accepted their interpretation of events.

Fort Garry, which had hitherto been a sleepy little settlement, was beginning to change in the late 1860s. The railway reached St. Paul, Minnesota, in 1868, and thereafter each year brought greater ease of access to the Red River. At first one travelled by coach from St. Paul, then from St. Cloud, then from Sauk Center. A railway line from the south reached St. Boniface in 1878, Winnipeg in 1879. The CPR was pushed through to the Red River, to Qu'Appelle, at last in 1885 to Port Moody, British Columbia. As the rails advanced, new routes were laid out from various parts of the hinterland, forcing old-timers to keep up with an ever-changing pattern of transport. Letters from residents of the area are filled with expressions of astonishment at the increasing rapidity of communication.[17]

## TROUBLES AT THE RED RIVER

Transition to Canadian rule, which was the key to all other changes in the west, was a badly botched operation. Without waiting for the formal transfer, the Canadian authorities sent surveyors who insulted the local inhabitants and excited fears, probably well grounded, that their land titles would not be respected. The Hudson's Bay Company governor, who was left virtually without information, was in no position to exercise effective authority. The resulting power vacuum was filled in 1869 by Louis Riel, a métis who had once studied for the priesthood and who was related to a number of prominent French-Canadian families. Riel was able to form a provisional government, largely with the support of French métis, by appealing to the legitimate grievances of the inhabitants. Unfortunately he lacked a talent for moderate rule and alienated many of the English-speaking halfbreeds. The most controversial episode of his rule was the "execution" of an Ontario settler, Thomas Scott, on March 4, 1870. What was for some an interlude of self-rule, for others a reign of terror, ended in August 1870 with the arrival of a Canadian expeditionary force under Colonel Wolseley.

During the troubles the local clergy acted in independent but often similar ways. They were all loyal to the crown, all favourable to Canadian rule. Even Taché, who was most unhappy about the manner of the takeover, was proud to be the nephew of a Father of Confederation. Bishops Machray and Taché both offered their services to the Canadian government in facilitating the transfer, although both complained that their advice was largely ignored.[18] The three Protestant ministers sought to calm local feelings, and all were censured by the Canadian adventurer Charles Mair for dissuading the Ontario settlers from taking vigorous countermeasures.[19] Oddly, it was the impetuous Young who acted as an intermediary with Riel for the Canadian settlers, perhaps because he was most clearly their representative. During the critical months, Taché was in Rome attending the First Vatican Council. Machray and Young agreed that his presence would have calmed the situation,[20] although Young may have been unrealistic in supposing that the slightest hint from a Roman prelate would have been obeyed without question by his entire flock.

Upon the restoration of order the various churches sought to build up their establishments to cope with the expected flood of settlers, each giving special attention to the founding of educational institutions. Taché had some special problems of his own. As Protestant settlers arrived from Ontario, the Catholics lost the majority position they had hitherto enjoyed and were increasingly outnumbered. Faced with this threat, Taché sought to attract French-speaking immigrants from Quebec and New England, being able to assure them that pastors and teachers of their own religion and language were readily available. The effort was partially successful, some settlers giving up good positions at home for the sake of what they regarded as a sacred enterprise. Most French Canadians could not be interested in Manitoba, however, and part of the difficulty was that in earlier moneyraising tours Taché had spoken too eloquently of the rigours endured by his missionaries. Meanwhile most of his métis, unaccustomed to farming and uncomfortable in the presence of those who regarded them as inferior, sold their lands cheaply and followed the retreating buffalo westward. The Catholic Church continued to grow in Manitoba, but the struggle for a French-speaking west was quickly lost.

Soon other religious groups entered to stake claims in the newly opened land. The Baptists sent a surveying party in 1869, and Alexander McDonald "the Pioneer" opened a mission at Winnipeg in 1873. A Lutheran congregation was established among Icelanders between the Manitoba lakes in 1876, another among German-speaking settlers in 1879. The Methodist Episcopals, under the vigorous leadership of their new bishop Albert Carman, held their first service in 1875 and reported ten preaching places by 1876.[21] A brief but hectic boom that followed the arrival of the railway in 1879 brought other denominations. The Congregationalists organized a church in Winnipeg that year, the Disciples of Christ one at Pembina on the border in 1881. An important result of these changes was to strengthen contacts with eastern Canada. Most of the Protestant groups looked there for support, while Taché recruited an increasing number of secular priests in Quebec. Only the Anglicans, despite the gift of two melodeons by Canadian women's groups,[22] depended almost entirely on aid from overseas.

Meanwhile the arrival of another group in Manitoba had prefigured a radical change in the religious complexion of western Canada. In 1874 several thousand conservative Mennonites from Russia, worried both by the impact of government policies on their colonies and by the apparent laxity of fellow-Mennonites, left their homes to settle along the Red River. In its eagerness to fill the empty spaces of the west, the government of Alexander Mackenzie arranged a parliamentary loan and made some unusual concessions.[23] Exemption from military service and permission to settle in largely self-governing communities, although helpful in inducing the Mennonites to emigrate, would later expose them to considerable hostility from the public. On the other hand, it was these Mennonites who first demonstrated the practicality of farming the open prairie and thus effectively opened much of western Canada to settlement.

## ANTICIPATING THE WHITE MAN'S COMING

Throughout the 1870s and well into the 1880s the signs of dramatic change were limited to Manitoba. British Columbia awaited the arrival of the railway. The prairie regions in between remained the home of the Indians and the buffalo—the former decimated by smallpox in 1870, the latter practically extinct by 1879. Churches now pressed to occupy areas that had not previously been evangelized. On the plains the two most prominent missionaries were the Methodist George McDougall and the Roman Catholic Albert Lacombe. The two rivals—for such they undoubtedly were—shared a deep affection for the Indians but contrasted sharply in temperament. McDougall was an organizer and planner who gathered the Indians together and sought to prepare them for the coming of the white man's civilization. Lacombe was a romantic who galloped recklessly about the plains holding missions and retreats among the Blackfoot.

In British Columbia, Indian work entered its period of major expansion. The pioneer Anglican missionary William Duncan continued his unconventional but apparently effective program of enforcing Victorian standards upon his new Indian community at Metlakatla. Thomas Crosby revived Duncan's abandoned mission at Port Simpson in 1874 to place the Methodists solidly in the field, and Paul Durieu infused new vigour into Roman Catholic missions as bishop at New Westminster from 1875. In the far northwest, where Anglicans were fairly successful in staving off Roman Catholic competition, the most colourful missionary was Bishop W. C. Bompas, the most effective probably the half-breed archdeacon Robert Macdonald.

Indian work was still conducted essentially as a phase of foreign missions, and indeed was so classified by the Presbyterians until 1878 and by the Methodists until 1883. It still enrolled colourful and sometimes eccentric individuals, apostolic wanderers who were qualified for their task by zeal for souls rather than by understanding of an alien culture. Competition was keen, for precious souls might be lost if the wrong missionaries got there first. Between Protestants and Catholics there was a constant barrage of charges and counter-charges of bribing the Indians with tobacco or of baptizing them after inadequate preparation. Bompas especially drew the ire of the Oblates: "Dressed as a *bourgeois*, a black satchel full of tracts over his shoulder, and a glass of clear water in his hand, you see him going from lodge to lodge, asking everyone whether he wishes to be baptized."[24] The Oblate churches, in turn, were described by McDougall as "toy shops where the poor heathen get their play-things, such as idols, beads, and charms."[25]

The eventual religious affiliation of Indian tribes depended not only on the success of missionaries in making first contact but on the compatibility of their social patterns with the types of Christianity from which they were able to choose. The Oblates were delighted with the response of the tractable Déné of the far northwest. Anglicans had greater success with the Tudukh, whom they found "more lively and affectionate" although "more superstitious" than the Déné.[26] In British Columbia the Roman Catholics were able to plant missions among the interior Salish, who liked their ceremonies and readily accepted their disciplined approach to community life. From the warlike Kwakiutls, Haidas and Tsimshians of the coast they met only rebuffs, but it was among these tribes that the more emotional Methodists were able to establish themselves.

Despite the impromptu approach of some, the missionaries were preparing the way for the Canadian occupation of the west. As the century advanced, their work entered a more settled stage. They encouraged the Indians to form permanent communities where they could attend services more readily, and as a result found themselves charged with various responsibilities to the government. They established residential schools for the education of Indian children. They inculcated European concepts of morality, Protestants and Catholics alike taking a severe view of the use of alcohol and of other customs that appeared to be economically wasteful. As they won the confidence of the people, they were able to make peace among the tribes, so that when the North West Mounted Police came into existence in 1874 they had a comparatively easy task. "It was not the redcoats who had secured the peace," the Ojibway Methodist missionary Henry B. Steinhaur declared, "it was Christianity."[27] The police were needed, however, to curb the activities of whiskey traders from the United States.

Sometimes the role of the missionaries in facilitating the transition was even more direct. George McDougall negotiated two treaties for the government with prairie tribes during the 1870s.[28] He also assuaged Indian fears of a government survey, while Lacombe persuaded the Blackfoot of Alberta to allow the CPR to run through their territory. It was the particular boast of missionaries of all denominations that no Indians connected with their missions took part in the Northwest Rebellion of 1885. The Roman Catholics were reproached for not having the same success with the métis, but they could reply that two of their priests were the only missionaries killed by the rebels.

In retrospect the role of the missionaries poses questions that did not occur to their contemporaries. Many commentators today hold the church responsible for depriving the Indians of their native culture, and the charge cannot be totally dismissed. Most missionaries were convinced that the triumph of the white man's ways was not only inevitable but right, and although in negotiating the transfer of land they sought to protect Indian rights, they showed too little scepticism about the ways of governments. Their attitude to the Indian was sometimes strangely compounded of love and contempt. George Young, an enthusiast for work among the natives, lamented the necessity of learning their "miserable language."[29] In time, as Queen Victoria's reign bolstered confidence in British values, paternalism became more pronounced. Even the ordination of able Indians to the ministry, a common practice among Protestants in mid-century, gradually fell into disfavour. On the other hand, the church was by no means the only agency that found it difficult to decide whether to isolate the Indians and thus leave them unqualified to compete in a technological society, or to aid in their assimilation and thus destroy their traditional culture. Many Indians have at least paid the church the compliment of referring to it as the only institution whose contacts with them were always motivated by concern for their welfare.

## FRONTIERS OF FRENCH CANADA

Although the west offered sufficient room for expansion to Ontario Protestants, it did not do so for the Catholics of Quebec.[30] To those accustomed to the neighbourly intimacy of the *rang*, the emptiness of the west and the hostility of its multiplying Protestant settlers were even more forbidding than the legendary Manitoba cold. Unless Quebec were to lose the cream of its youth, however, there was clearly need for some alternative to a southward movement of population that was reaching alarming proportions in the 1860s. Colonization of unoccupied areas of the province was the preferred solution, popular enough in many quarters to be a serious obstacle to Taché's dream of a French Catholic northwest.

Colonization was not only, and perhaps not even primarily, a concern of the church. It was sponsored by successive provincial governments and to some extent born of economic necessity. In the speeches and writings of its apologists, however, it took on the attributes of a new crusade. On the Laurentian frontier, Catholic youth would be on their own soil, provided with the ministrations of their church, freed from the temptations of the city and from intermixture with other cultures, living in harmony on God's good earth. Father Antoine Labelle, the leading apostle of the movement, became so preoccupied with the provision of routes of access to the north that he was once reported to have absent-mindedly advised a penitent to say a *chemin de fer* instead of a *chemin de croix*.[31] Colonization did not bring back many *émigrés* from New England, as its promoters had hoped, but it resulted in the erection of many new parishes and made a lasting impression on the social policy of the church. The movement received its apotheosis in Louis Hémon's *Maria Chapdelaine*, the heroine of which exemplified all the virtues untiringly preached by "colonizing" priests.

Meanwhile the Acadians of the Maritime provinces, almost forgotten since *le Grand Dérangement* of 1755 and thereafter, were beginning to demand a place in the sun. Their awakening was inspired by the publication in 1847 of Longfellow's *Evangeline* and by the writings of the French historian Rameau de Saint-Père, from which many Acadians learned for the first time that they had a history and an identity. A seminary at Memramcook, New Brunswick, in 1844 was the first landmark of revival. An even more important event was the arrival there in 1864 of a French-Canadian priest, Camille Lefebvre. Exiled from Canada by the Congregation of the Holy Cross because his powers of oratory were regarded as dangerous to his soul, Lefebvre dedicated his talents to the rebirth of Acadia and for a time ruled the Canadian province of his order from Memramcook.[32] In 1880 Acadian delegates were honoured guests at a convention of the Society of Saint-Jean-Baptiste in Quebec, and their return to self-awareness was completed by a series of congresses on Acadian culture that began in 1881.

To the pious Acadians, whose corporate life was centred in their parish churches, renewal as a people seemed essentially a religious matter. When delegates to the first congress determined to assert an Acadian identity distinct from that of French Canada by choosing as their national festival the Feast of the Assumption rather than St. John the Baptist's Day, it seemed natural to mark the occasion with three cheers for the Assumption.[33] The difficult problem of choosing a national song was solved when Abbé François Richard, apparently on a sudden inspiration, began to intone the *Ave Maris Stella*. For such a people a place in the sun inevitably meant a place in the church. At that time there were no Acadian bishops, and even such important Acadian parishes as Edmundston were staffed with English-speaking priests. The Acadians began to demand French-language colleges, the ministrations of their own priests, and above all the appointment of an Acadian bishop. When the hierarchy showed no disposition to make concessions, Acadian leaders began a persistent campaign of passive resistance that anticipated many of the techniques of twentieth-century protest. A chain of Assumption Societies in the Maritimes and New England testified to the new Acadian self-consciousness, but not until 1912 would the first Acadian be appointed to a Maritime see.

## CHURCH STRUCTURES FOR A NATION

One of the most urgent tasks with which confederation confronted the churches was that of adapting to the needs of the new nation ecclesiastical structures that had been devised with small and isolated colonies in mind. Existing church bodies were insufficiently endowed with resources to match Canada's size, too closely identified with particular regions or ethnic groups to comprehend its diversity, or too dependent financially and psychologically on external support to satisfy its growing self-awareness. Most of them suffered from all three disabilities. Over the next few decades, therefore, almost all major denominations regrouped themselves to meet the new situation.

Roman Catholics chiefly needed to decentralize their administration. The whole of Canada west of the Maritimes constituted in 1867 a single ecclesiastical province under the jurisdiction of the Archbishop of Quebec. The creation of the civil province of Ontario suggested an ecclesiastical counterpart, and after confederation everyone accepted the inevitability of such a development. But then what was to become of the west? Taché himself regarded his establishment as scarcely ready for provincial status and feared that detachment from Quebec might result in some loss of French-Canadian interest. If a province of Ontario were formed, however, the west with its French-speaking clergy would on the basis of geography more naturally belong to it than to Quebec. Faced with this situation, the Canadian bishops

unanimously recommended that Toronto and St. Boniface should both become metropolitan sees. The former attained this status in 1870, the latter
in 1871. Montreal and Ottawa followed in 1886, and the number of dioceses
both east and west increased steadily. The formation of a Canadian hierarchy
would reach its culmination in 1908, when the more settled parts of the
country were removed from the missionary jurisdiction of the Congregation
for Propagating the Faith.

Anglicans had achieved a measure of coordination in their work by 1867
that provoked envious comments from a Methodist correspondent to the
*Christian Guardian*,[34] but they had little machinery for cooperation across
regional lines. Although the dioceses of eastern Canada were all technically
part of the ecclesiastical province of Canada, evangelical fears that church
assemblies would usurp the supposed prerogatives of the crown and of parish
vestries prevented the dioceses of Fredericton and Nova Scotia from sending
representatives to the provincial synod. Western Canada as far as the Rockies
constituted a single diocese directly dependent on Canterbury. The situation
gradually improved. By 1874 all eastern dioceses were taking part in provincial affairs. In the west, thanks to Machray's conviction that bishops
should have first-hand knowledge of every parish and mission within their
jurisdiction, one diocese after another was carved out of massive Rupert's
Land.[35] In 1875 these were grouped in the new ecclesiastical province of
Rupert's Land, furnished with unusual power over the dioceses in accordance with Machray's further conviction that a missionary operation requires
centralized direction. British jurisdiction over the area made it impossible,
for the time being, to carry Anglican reorganization beyond this point.

Presbyterians and Methodists, and to some extent Baptists, had to solve
even more complex organizational problems. None of these denominations
had an organization spanning the entire country. Each was also divided into
competing segments that represented divergent theologies, different polities,
or even diverse places of origin. If they were to hold their own in a united
Canada, these communions would need to end their internal competition
and consolidate their regional or sectarian fragments into national churches.

In 1867 the Presbyterians had already begun to move towards consolidation, Free Church and Secession elements having united regionally in the
Canada Presbyterian Church and the Presbyterian Church of the Lower
Provinces. By 1868 there were only four separate groups, these two and
corresponding bodies in connection with the Church of Scotland. Efforts
towards further union followed immediately.[36] George M. Grant introduced
a motion for union of the Maritime bodies at the first meeting of the regional
Kirk synod in 1868,[37] and in 1870 William Ormiston of the Canada Presbyterian Church proposed a wider union to Kirk leaders of the upper provinces. The promoters of union offered various arguments, but most of them
were variants on a common theme: the irrelevance in Canada of divisions

that had arisen out of controversies in Scotland. Within the larger and more aggressive Canada Presbyterian Church, especially among Montreal business men, there was much talk about opportunities for advance that a more efficient use of resources would make possible. Leaders of the Church of Scotland were aware that in some areas the Kirk was "hardly a native church at all, but rather a foreign mission,"[38] and feared that in separation it would have little future in Canada. Many in both churches hoped for an end to strife that had embittered relations between them.

The negotiating churches were practically identical in theology and polity, but two issues presented considerable difficulty. One was that of church and state. The former Seceders were strict voluntaries, the Kirk believed in religious establishments, and some representatives of the Free Church tradition demanded a strong declaration of the headship of Christ over national life. The issue had no practical bearing on the drafting of a constitution for a Canadian church, but tender Scottish consciences had to be satisfied that truth would not be compromised. The problem was satisfactorily resolved by applying the principle of forbearance, by which it was recognized that Presbyterians might conscientiously differ even on important matters while maintaining fellowship with one another. The other major hurdle was that the two churches in the upper provinces had between them no less than four theological colleges, each with partisans who argued that in the interests of economy at least one of the others ought to be closed. This was passed, in a typically Canadian spirit of compromise, by allowing all four to remain open. In 1875, after five years of negotiation, the Presbyterian Church in Canada came into being.

The Presbyterians set themselves an unhappy precedent by failing to achieve unanimity. During the conversations, there had been vigorous debate in the Canada Presbyterian Church, while the Kirk was relatively quiescent. Only in the latter, however, did any significant number of congregations refuse to enter the union. The arguments and tactics used in the ensuing debate would almost all be repeated in a later and wider church union: denial of the churches' right to unite, charges that the united church would be "creedless," parliamentary lobbying, and litigation over temporalities.[39] Whatever the defects of the union, all congregations of the Kirk except the revivalistic "Macdonaldites" of Prince Edward Island would eventually reconcile themselves to it.

One of the most significant fruits of union was the appointment in 1881 of James Robertson, minister of Knox Church, Winnipeg, as superintendent of missions for the northwest. Much has been made of the break with Presbyterian tradition this step represented, but the Assembly minutes contain no record of dissent from the terms of the appointment.[40] Its most unusual feature, perhaps, was that at the time there was only one Presbyterian mission on the prairies outside Manitoba. Robertson was on the ground, ready

in 1883 with a fund for erecting churches and manses, in time to anticipate
the great rush of settlers.

Sentiment for union had also appeared among Methodists before confederation. The New Connexion, itself the product of two earlier unions, expressed interest as early as 1854[41] and thereafter took a continuing initiative
in proposals for union. Efforts were concentrated at first on the union of
the smaller groups, which felt themselves somewhat overshadowed by the
Wesleyans, but in 1868 the English Wesleyans appointed W. Morley Punshon
as president of the Canadian Conference with instructions to promote
Methodist union. By 1871 denominational leaders were holding union tea
meetings.

Methodist arguments for union resembled those urged upon Presbyterians,
with perhaps less emphasis on reconciliation and more on the avoidance of
wasteful competition. The Methodists believed that in some ways they were
the most severely handicapped by division. They had the largest number of
splinter groups and the greatest amount of local overlapping. They suffered
most from the depopulation of rural Ontario, where many of their competing
circuits were located. Besides, union offered the best hope of ridding themselves of the sectarian label that still clung to them.

The groups differed chiefly in the relative authority exercised by ministers,
laity, and, in one case, bishops. These differing practices were seldom defended
on theoretical grounds, for Methodists typically took a pragmatic view of
church government, but they represented sharply contrasting styles of group
cohesion. The Methodist Episcopals were a highly disciplined body who
retained the quasi-military hierarchy although no longer the informality of
frontier days. The heart of Wesleyanism was its band of itinerants, who
continued the original conception of Methodism as a preaching campaign
and resisted any lay encroachments that might limit their freedom to
prophesy. The smaller groups of English background were intimate fellowships, knit by bonds of folk loyalty and more open to lay influence. Each
segment of Methodism naturally feared that union would mean the disappearance of its distinctive ethos.

By March 1871, representative leaders were able to agree on a basis of
union that incorporated into the Wesleyan system some lay representation
along with "superintendents" as a gesture to the Episcopal tradition. It was
soon evident that several groups were not ready for union. The Episcopals
nourished past grievances, the Bible Christians were offended because they
had not been sent an official invitation, and some Primitive Methodists were
reluctant to surrender their close cohesion as a group. In 1874, however, a
partial union brought together the Wesleyan Methodist New Connexion and
the Wesleyans of both sections of British North America, despite Maritime
suspicions of Upper Canadian dominance and in the face of opposition from
the mother church of the New Connexion in England.

Although partially checked, the project of a more general union would not die. Rural decline continued, and smaller groups either lost members or fell hopelessly into debt in an effort to compete. Meanwhile the needs of the west became steadily more urgent, and Methodists were not matching the efforts of the newly unified Presbyterians there. The Ecumenical Methodist Conference of 1881, which issued a strong appeal for Methodist solidarity, crystallized a growing sentiment for union. The remaining Methodist bodies, except the actively propagandist Free Methodists and the somewhat isolated Evangelical Association, joined in 1884 to form the Methodist Church.

The platform on which Methodists ultimately united was remarkably similar to the basis that had been formulated in 1871 and rejected then by several groups. The dominant Wesleyans appeared to have made the most generous concessions, admitting both superintendency and lay representation. There are strong indications that internal dissatisfaction with the Wesleyan constitution considerably reinforced the demands of the smaller groups. Many Wesleyan laymen were no longer content to submit to clerical control. Influential Wesleyan leaders, on the other hand, were convinced that only a strong central authority could arrest tendencies to regionalism and thus make possible a concerted witness to the nation. The recipe of union seemed to work. By 1886 the Methodists had appointed James Woodsworth to a position parallel to Robertson's in the west, and a period of denominational expansion ensued.

The Anglicans, envied in 1867 for their unity, had by 1884 fallen behind both Presbyterians and Methodists. Eastern and western provinces had no formal links, while the dioceses of British Columbia were still under the direct jurisdiction of Canterbury. From 1883 the Domestic and Foreign Missionary Society of the province of Canada existed to promote church extension, but it did little for the west and, according to Machray, not much more for its chosen field of Algoma.[42] In 1851 Bishop Edward Feild of Newfoundland had suggested an independent church for the whole of British North America.[43] His proposal was repeated by Bishop Fulford of Montreal in 1861, and in succeeding years there were many brave efforts towards consolidation such as the formation of the Canadian Church Union by a group of Sarnia laymen in the 1880s. Action was delayed by eastern fears of having to assume the burden carried by British societies in the west, and by western reluctance to exchange a functioning province for a connection with an area that had never shown much interest in its problems. It was finally agreed to retain existing provinces within a new national structure, and in 1893 a general synod was constituted. Mutual aid would not really become effective, however, until the foundation of the Missionary Society of the Canadian Church in 1902.

Other denominations would achieve similar consolidation only after long delay, and some have not yet achieved it. The Baptists tried hardest, largely at the prodding of their benefactor W. A. McMaster,[44] but they were hampered by internal tensions and by widespread fears of centralization. Among several attempts to create an agency that would channel aid from east to west, the most ambitious was the Dominion Board of Home Missions, founded in 1886, but it lasted only a year.[45] A single convention for Ontario and Quebec was achieved in 1888. Baptists were able to convene a national assembly in 1900, but an attempt in 1906 to form a Canada-wide union came to nothing. In that same year the Congregational Union of Canada was formed, but the number of Lutheran groups was still increasing.

## FROM FRONTIER MISSIONS TO NATIONAL CHURCHES

As churches acquired national organizations and began to plan on a national scale, they inevitably became more national in program and outlook. Presbyterian and Methodist unions accelerated this tendency by compelling several groups to sever their formal connection with British churches and thus to become more Canadian in orientation. The Presbyterians compiled an official hymn book in 1881 to replace Scottish collections then in use. Others soon followed their example, and in 1908 the Anglicans issued a Canadian prayer book. Protestant missionary organizations, pension funds, and publishing concerns led to the emergence of embryonic national secretariats, which tended to gravitate to Toronto.

Like other prominent Canadians, however, church leaders also saw the need of new links with the outside world to replace the vanishing ties of colonial dependence. They knew that Canadian expressions of Christianity would be sterile without continued fertilization from abroad, and they desired for themselves a larger sphere of influence than Canada alone could provide. The early years of Canadian nationhood coincided with the formation of world confessional organizations—the informal Lambeth conference of Anglican bishops in 1867, the World Alliance of Reformed Churches holding the Presbyterian System (later Order) in 1877, the Ecumenical (later World) Methodist Conference in 1881—and Congregationalists, Baptists, and Lutherans would follow in later years. These associations performed for the churches some of the functions for which secular leaders looked to the emerging British Commonwealth, and Canadian churchmen took them seriously. We have already noted that they contributed to the formation of one and acted on the advice of another. For the most part, however, their participation in international deliberations was still fairly modest.

Disseminating the civilization of metropolitan Europe had always been an important function of Canadian churches, and the process became more conscious as leaders sought to mould the citizenry of a new nation. Church colleges continued to be seedbeds of conversion and agencies of religious formation, but they also began to emphasize social polish and the appreciation of arts and letters. Informative lectures by the clergy on literary and scientific subjects attracted large crowds, although they would fall into decline before the end of the century. This enterprise of improving popular taste was often marred by sentimentality and preciousness, especially in denominations that lacked the tradition of an educated ministry, but it performed a necessary function in an adolescent society.

As churches became more self-consciously national they began to reflect on the process by which they had emerged out of frontier missions. Little work of scholarly merit resulted, but an examination of early studies of Canadian church history gives interesting clues to the mind-set of the Canadian churches during the decades immediately after confederation. Interest first turned, as in John Carroll's *Case and His Cotemporaries*,[46] to the recording of episodes in pioneer church life that might otherwise have soon been forgotten. The frontier was no longer part of the living present but already an olden time from which a more commonplace generation could draw inspiration and instruction. In similar vein, French-Canadian historians began to compose stylized accounts of the miraculous survival of their race and religion under alien rulers. Soon more formal denominational records such as William Gregg's *History of the Presbyterian Church in the Dominion of Canada*,[47] C. H. Mockridge's *Bishops of the Church of England in Canada*,[48] and the conference-sponsored *Centennial of Canadian Methodism*[49] began to appear. Their style was often wooden, but their self-conscious differentiation of humble beginnings from current achievement implied confidence that the faith was now firmly planted in Canada. Later churchmen would fit the events of their own times into the optimistic frame thus provided them.

### NOTES TO CHAPTER TWO

1. *Canadian Churchman*, February 28, 1866.
2. *Canadian Baptist*, November 2, 1865.
3. *Home and Foreign Record* of the Canada Presbyterian Church, January 1868, p. 65.
4. *Christian Guardian*, July 4, 1866.
5. Speech to the Confederation Resolutions, February 5, 1865. P. B. Waite, ed., *The Confederation Debates in the Province of Canada, 1865* (Toronto: McClelland and Stewart, 1963), p. 79.
6. *Presbyterian Witness*, September 17, 1864.
7. Robert Rumilly, *Histoire de la Province de Québec*, Vol. I, pp. 25-26.
8. The activities and attitudes of all the Quebec bishops are discussed in a series of articles in *Sessions d'Etude*, La Société Canadienne d'Histoire de l'Eglise Catholique, 1967.
9. For the attitudes of Bourget and Laflèche, see Walter Ullmann, "The Quebec Bishops and Confederation," *Canadian Historical Review*, Vol. XLIV, No. 3 (September 1963), pp. 213-234.

10. Connolly to Tupper, March 22, 1871. Letters of Archbishop Connolly, Archdiocesan Archives, Chancery office, Halifax, N.S.

11. "Si elle n'est pas sans défauts, si elle n'est pas tout ce qu'on aurait pu désirer qu'elle fût, rappelons-nous que rien n'est parfait dans ce monde, et que, dans un pays comme le nôtre, où tant d'intérêts divers sont en présence, il était impossible de se réfuser à des mutuelles concessions, et d'arriver à un arrangement qui pût donner satisfaction à tout le monde." Henri Têtu et C.-O. Gagnon, Mandements, Lettres Pastorales et Circulaires des Evêques de Québec, Vol. IV (Quebec: A. Coté et Cie, 1888), p. 581.

12. Mandement, June 13, 1867. Sessions d'Etude, 1967, p. 38.

13. A.-X. Bernard, ed., Mandements des Evêques de Saint-Hyacinthe (Montreal: 1889), Vol. II, pp. 422-423.

14. "une planche de salut." Lettre de Monseigneur Laflèche à Boucher de Niverville, Pointe-du-Lac, 2 mars 1865 (dated, in error, 1864).

15. A Canadian correspondent in the Guardian, July 17, 1867.

16. Toronto: James Campbell and Son, 1873.

17. A good example is a letter of Mgr Taché to Father Aubert, January 10, 1878. Paul Benoit, Vie de Mgr Taché, Archevêque de St-Boniface (Montreal: Beauchemin, 1904), Vol. II, p. 348.

18. Ibid., Vol. II, pp. 12, 16 and passim; Robert Machray, Life of Robert Machray, D.D., LL.D., D.C.L., Archbishop of Rupert's Land, Primate of All Canada, Prelate of the Order of St. Michael and St. George (London: Macmillan, 1909), p. 153.

19. George Young, Manitoba Memories, Leaves from My Life in the Prairie Province, 1868-1884 (Toronto: Wm. Briggs, 1898), p. 171.

20. Machray, op. cit., p. 205; Young, op. cit., p. 160.

21. A. Burnside, "The Contribution of the Rev. Albert Carman to Albert College, Belleville, and to the Methodist Episcopal Church in Canada, 1857-1884," M.Th. thesis, Victoria University, Toronto, 1962, p. 298.

22. Machray, op. cit., p. 161.

23. Norman Macdonald, Canada: Immigration and Colonization, 1841-1903 (Aberdeen: Aberdeen University Press, 1966), pp. 199-203.

24. A. G. Morice, History of the Catholic Church in Western Canada, Vol. II, p. 83.

25. Missionary Notices, May 1870, p. 102; quoted in J. E. Nix, Mission among the Buffalo (Toronto: Ryerson, 1960), p. 12.

26. S. Gould, Inasmuch (Toronto: MSCC, 1917), pp. 145-146.

27. Young, op. cit., p. 364.

28. Letter of George McDougall to D. D. Currie of Charlottetown, November 20, 1875. Hugh A. Dempsey, "The Lost Letters of George McDougall," Alberta Historical Review, Vol. 15, No. 2 (spring 1967), p. 21.

29. Young, op. cit., p. 301.

30. For a detailed analysis of the reasons, see A. I. Silver, "French Canada and the Prairie Frontier, 1870-1890," Canadian Historical Review, Volume L, No. 1 (March 1969), pp. 11-36.

31. Joseph J. Grignon, Le vieux temps (Saint Jerome: 1921), p. 76.

32. Robert Rumilly, Histoire des Acadiens (Montreal: the author, 1955), pp. 730, 743.

33. Conventions Nationales des Acadiens, Recueil des Travaux et Délibérations des Six Premières Conventions, compiled by Ferdinand J. Robidoux (Shediac: Imprimerie du Moniteur Acadien, 1907), p. 81.

34. Letter of James Gray in Christian Guardian, February 20, 1867.

35. Machray, op. cit., p. 165.

36. For a detailed account of negotiations leading to Presbyterian union, see J. A. Johnston, "Factors in the Formation of the Presbyterian Church in Canada," Ph.D. thesis, McGill University, 1955.

37. F. E. Archibald, "History of the Presbyterian Church in New Brunswick, from Its Earliest Beginnings to the Union of the Presbyterian Churches in Canada, 1784 to 1875," MS in the Archives of Pine Hill Divinity Hall, Halifax, p. 172.

38. W. L. Grant and Frederick Hamilton, Principal Grant (Toronto: Morang and Co., Ltd., 1904), p. 19.

39. J. T. McNeill, *The Presbyterian Church in Canada, 1875-1925* (Toronto: General Board of the Presbyterian Church in Canada, 1925), pp. 29, 227.

40. Acts and Proceedings of the 8th General Assembly of the Presbyterian Church in Canada, 1882, pp. 19, 20.

41. Minutes of the 26th Annual Conference of the Canadian Wesleyan Methodist New Connexion Church, 1854, p. 14. For a detailed account of negotiations leading to Methodist union, see J. Warren Caldwell, "The Unification of Methodism in Canada, 1865-1884," *Bulletin*, Committee of Archives of the United Church of Canada, No. 19 (1967).

42. Machray, *op. cit.*, p. 363.

43. Robert F. Rayson, "The Church of England in Newfoundland," *Journal of the Canadian Church Historical Society*, Vol. I, No. 3 (May 1954), p. 5.

44. Robert Hamilton, "The Founding of McMaster University," B.D. thesis, McMaster University, 1938, p. 81c.

45. Walter S. Ellis, "Organizational and Educational Policy of Baptists in Western Canada, 1873-1939," B.D. thesis, McMaster University, 1962, p. 18.

46. John Carroll, *Case and His Cotemporaries; or the Canadian Itinerants' Memorial: Constituting a Biographical History of Methodism in Canada, from its Introduction into the Province, till the Death of the Rev. Wm. Case in 1855* (Toronto: Samuel Rose, 1867-77).

47. William Gregg, *History of the Presbyterian Church in the Dominion of Canada, from the Earliest Times to 1834* (Toronto: Presbyterian Printing and Publishing Co., 1885).

48. C. H. Mockridge, *Bishops of the Church of England in Canada* (London: F. N. W. Brown, 1896).

49. *Centennial of Canadian Methodism* (Toronto: Wm. Briggs, 1891).

# THREE

# Extending the Frontiers

At the time of confederation the churches of Canada had been small, immature, and in some cases largely dependent on external aid. As they reorganized themselves to lay claim to an enlarged Canada, however, and as they struggled to fulfil its delayed promise, they acquired the skills and energies necessary for the undertaking of larger tasks. Even the old-fashioned circuit rider Joseph Hilts reckoned in 1892 that while the church was no more spiritual than in his youth, it had become increasingly missionary-minded and more venturesome in its planning.[1]

During the 1880s two developments combined to arouse the churches to a sense of heightened responsibility. One was the construction of the Canadian Pacific Railway, which at last united Canada effectively from sea to sea. The other was a renewal of missionary zeal within the churches of Europe and North America, both Protestant and Roman Catholic. The building of the railway was not sufficient in itself to account for the churches' lengthening of perspective, for scandals associated with railway politics were making many Canadians lose faith in their country. As Canadians were caught up in the general enthusiasm of Christendom for world-wide advance, however, they were challenged to assume a responsibility that seemed peculiarly theirs.

## THE CHALLENGE OF THE WEST

The land itself was big enough to absorb most of the expansive energies of the churches. The most urgent challenge was unquestionably that of the west, where in retrospect their efforts prior to 1885 would seem little more than the staking of claims on the future. During these years the line of settlement, and with it that of the churches' ministrations, had gradually been pushed westward through Manitoba. The energies of the churches during the next decades would be concentrated on the area between that line and the hitherto isolated fishing and mining camps of British Columbia, an area where in 1885 a few missionaries were enough to serve the tiny vanguard of white settlers. Beyond the homesteads of the newcomers, moreover, there were other calls upon the churches for pioneer work. Among the native Indians there were tribes that had not yet been reached, and effective missions to the Eskimos were still in the future. There would also long continue to be, as there are today, isolated pockets of settlement largely untouched by the church.

Strangely, most Canadians failed to recognize that their country was one of the great mission areas of the world. They normally thought of missions as institutions established in foreign lands, and their zeal was most readily stimulated by distance and exotic customs. James Robertson, the Presbyterian superintendent for western Canada, complained that his appeals could not compete in prestige and glamour with those of the foreign field.[2] Machray's dissatisfaction with eastern help has already been noted. Practically all major denominations had to seek aid in men and money from Britain, where the west was still regarded as a land of high adventure, although money at least should have been as readily available in Canada. Except for the persistent prodding of a few men of vision, the Canadian churches might have failed abysmally to rise to the western challenge.

Lack of enthusiasm was partly due to scepticism about the future of an area that never quite seemed to fulfil its promise. Seldom has a region waited so long or so impatiently on the verge of anticipated greatness. As early as 1830 the pioneer missionary of the west, J. N. Provencher, had written optimistically, "This wild country will become a great country, and your children will see it."[3] The first signs of fulfilment appeared in the mid-1860s, although in the form of settlers of a different language and religion. Then came grasshoppers and civil rebellion. In 1873 the Honourable William Morris assured the members of the first North-West Council,

> A country of such vast extent, which is possessed of abundant resources, is entrusted to your keeping; a country which, though at present but sparsely settled, is destined, I believe, to become the home of thousands of persons, by whose industry and energy that which is now almost a wilderness will be quickly transformed into a fruitful land where civilization and the arts of peace will flourish.[4]

In that same year, however, a serious depression ensued. Most Ontarians in search of new homes bypassed the Canadian prairies in favour of the American west, and others moved on when they discovered that much of the desirable land had already been alienated. Large areas of the Dakotas were peopled by Canadian immigrants, many of whom had tried Manitoba first.[5] "With us it is still the day of small things," the Presbyterians reported in 1877.[6] The arrival of the railway at the Red River in the following year brought settlers in large numbers, and many have accepted contemporary descriptions of tent cities hurriedly pitched to accommodate them as typical of the period. The boom did not last, however, and by 1883 Winnipeg lots were virtually unsaleable.

In 1885 the suppression of the Northwest Rebellion called attention to the availability for settlement of the entire west, and the spanning of the country by the CPR rendered it effectively open. In that same year, also, the development of Red Fife wheat added thousands of square miles to the potential growing area and pointed to the introduction of strains with an even shorter period of maturation. These events, although assured of an important place in Canadian history, did not bring an immediate flood of settlers. The mid-1880s were years of depression, and on the prairies of drought. There was some recovery in 1887, drought and depression again in the early 1890s. Scarcely a year seemed to measure up to expectations. In 1896 the Presbyterians were still reporting, "Complaints are sometimes heard of the slow growth of population in the west."[7] Only after the turn of the century, when the homesteads of the American west had been taken up, would the Canadian prairies come into their own.

Despite this succession of disappointments, western Canada was recording substantial gains of population in each decade. Manitoba increased from 65,000 in 1881 to 150,000 in 1891, and to 250,000 in 1901. Comparable figures for British Columbia were 50,000 in 1881 (of whom half were Indians), 100,000 in 1891, and 180,000 in 1901, for the intervening territories 55,000 in 1881, 65,000 in 1891, and 160,000 in 1901. This rate of growth, although impressive, was gradual in comparison with many states of the American west. Manitoba, British Columbia and the territories each contained more native-born residents in every census year than newcomers from all other parts of Canada combined. Most of the increase was the result of migration from eastern Canada, chiefly Ontario, although the proportion born in Britain, the United States, and China was much higher in British Columbia than on the prairies.

The delayed development of the west, although disappointing to boosters, had solid advantages both for Canada and for the church. It gave time to set up the institutions necessary for peaceful living together in advance of mass immigration. The foundation of the North West Mounted Police in 1874 was followed in 1883 by the beginning of municipal organization in the territories and in 1884 by provision for a school system and the establishment of a High Court of Justice, all before settlers were present in such numbers as to compel the adoption of such organs of mob rule as the deputy sheriff and the posse. The delay also gave time for what Machray described as "the blessed influence of the Church, which was here all ready to receive the tide of population when it came pouring in, and which moulded it as it came."[8] Despite some contemporary complaints to the contrary, the churches with their archbishops and superintendents were in a much better position to shape the mores of the region from the beginning than they had been in the early days of settlement in eastern Canada. Their task was not so much one of reclamation or even revival as of extension among people who in most cases had suffered no serious break in their habits of church-going and church support.

The situation in which the churches found themselves was highly competitive, offering great rewards to those who were able to greet the newcomers and great disappointments to those who offered their services too late or too intermittently. The churches did not begin with equal opportunities, some being already well established in the area while others were comparative newcomers. Each position had both advantages and drawbacks. The older churches could draw on long experience of the country and could count on the good will of its early settlers, but their prestige meant little to the new immigrants and the sites of their missions seldom proved strategic in the geography of the railway age. Newly introduced churches had to begin from nothing, but neither were they handicapped by the necessity of remodelling organizations that had been designed for an era that was passing away.

Roman Catholics had been longest at work in the area, and before the arrival of settlers from Ontario they had constituted a majority of the population. Their missionaries, especially those of the Oblate order, had achieved a remarkable reputation for adventurous pioneering and selfless dedication, and Grant was impressed on his western tour by their ability to maintain a high level of culture in the rudest mission stations.[9] In the new situation, however, they suffered from two serious disabilities. One was that while the Oblates manned the Indian posts effectively they lacked the resources to deal adequately with the influx of white settlers. The other was that most missionaries, whether Oblates or secular priests, spoke a language other than that of the great bulk of the immigrants. Taché and other bishops energetically sought English-speaking priests to meet the emergency, but they were unwilling to take the further step of turning over major responsibility to an English-speaking hierarchy. Their attitude, while understandable, contained the seeds of future conflict.

The Anglicans, who rivalled the Roman Catholics in seniority, shared some of their advantages and handicaps. They were well established in the Winnipeg area and had far more missionaries among the Indians than any other Protestant denomination. Their enterprise too had been formulated with the needs of the natives in mind, however, and the resources of the Church Missionary Society were available only for this purpose. For help in the new situation Machray had to appeal to the Society for the Propagation of the Gospel, which was responsible for church extension in the colonies, and his task was made no easier by the prevailing stereotype of

Canada as a land of mounties and Indians. At this juncture, too, the exclusively British connection of the province of Rupert's Land became a more serious handicap than ever. Many Canadian Anglicans assumed that its financial needs were taken care of, especially after the short-lived boom gave rise to rumours that the church owned real estate in Winnipeg of fabulous value. Machray complained repeatedly that eastern Anglicans neglected the west while Presbyterians and Methodists had "a marvellous supply of ministers."[10] Reliance on British support also inhibited the growth of local initiative among the Anglicans of the west. Students of overseas missions have noted the difficulty of transforming an enterprise managed and supported from abroad into one that is truly rooted in the soil. This phenomenon could easily be documented from Anglican history in the west, where even in the 1890s episcopal appointments went to English clergymen who had never set foot in Canada.[11]

The situation of the Presbyterians was radically different from that of either Roman Catholics or Anglicans. Comparative latecomers to the west, they had never committed themselves to extensive Indian work. They were thus able to devote their whole energy to the incoming settlers, uninhibited by the need of retooling an existing operation or by the nagging suspicion that in fulfilling one task they were neglecting a prior obligation. It proved of inestimable advantage, too, that their enterprise was based in Canada rather than Britain. Eastern Presbyterians were probably no more eager to give support than their Anglican counterparts, but they were constantly prodded both by Robertson and by an aggressive group of ministers in Winnipeg.[12] They knew, moreover, that they could turn to Scotland and Ireland only for supplementary aid.[13] They had the further advantage of being able to absorb western congregations into their existing structure, thus allowing them to participate responsibly in policy decisions from the outset.

The Methodists occupied an intermediate position. They had Indian work in Alberta and in what is now northern Manitoba, the maintenance of which continued to absorb some of their efforts. James Woodsworth became their superintendent of missions four years after the Presbyterians had appointed Robertson, and the time lag was to prove significant. Volunteers began to arrive in satisfactory numbers only after a meeting of the General Conference at Winnipeg in 1888 had stirred interest.[14] Robertson noted, too, that after this time "a better class of missionaries" were appointed.[15] Henceforth the Methodists kept pace with the Presbyterians for a while, although the latter maintained their early lead.[16]

Baptist missionaries had begun to arrive in the early days of Ontario settlement. Finding only one member of their denomination in Winnipeg in 1873, Alexander McDonald is reported to have said, "I did not come to find Baptists, I have come to make Baptists."[17] Despite this vigorous beginning, the Baptists were hampered for many years by their failure to secure a solid base of eastern support or to persuade anyone of stature to serve as their missionary superintendent for any length of time.[18] On the other hand, the Baptists of the west learned habits of self-reliance at a time when others were heavily dependent on aid from elsewhere. They peristed through many discouragements, and several attempts to enter the field of higher education culminated in the foundation of Brandon College in 1901.

The denominational pattern of western Canada changed considerably over the first decades of agricultural settlement. Roman Catholics, a majority in Manitoba in 1871 and still the largest single group in the entire west in 1881, were only third in 1901. Much of their strength was among the aboriginal inhabitants, whose numbers were then declining. The Presbyterians, a poor third in 1881, were first in 1901. The Anglicans were second in 1881, briefly first in 1891, and again second in 1901. The Methodists, in fourth place throughout, steadily increased their proportion of the population. The Mennonites were a signfiicant body in Manitoba. Other groups of substantial size in 1901 owed their importance to immigration that took place shortly before that census year and thus belong to a later phase of Canadian history.

These changes in the relative strength of denominations cannot be attributed to differences in the quality of the men who supervised their work. The leaders of all major communions were outstanding men who have been venerated by later generations. Taché and Machray were fathers of their people and founders of Manitoba. Robertson and Woodsworth were both highly effective superintendents, although Woodsworth lacked what today would be called Robertson's charisma. Alexander McDonald and Alexander Grant had comparable reputations among the Baptists, although the former left the area through lack of support in 1884 and the latter was drowned in 1897 at the height of his powers.

If the quality of leadership was uniformly high, the methods of the leaders varied tremendously. Machray and Robertson may fairly be selected as outstanding representatives of two contrasting approaches. Machray was an empire-builder in the finest traditions of Victorian England. At once a missionary, an educator, and a public man, he sought to mobilize the resources of church and state for the formation of a new society that would be an outpost at the same time of Britain and of Christendom. Robertson, who looked like a Scottish patriarch, brought to his task the dedicated efficiency of a North American executive. Like a successful salesman, he had a knack for coining striking phrases and an unlimited willingness to travel in search of contacts. He too was interested in education and in the general welfare of the west, but he concentrated his efforts on building churches and supplying them with ministers. Whether one regards Machray or Robertson as the more effective missionary will depend on one's criteria of judgment. Machray put his stamp on the institutions of Manitoba and of the prairies generally. Robertson made sure that no one would be unaware of the location of the nearest Presbyterian church.

Whatever the differences in approach, the changing denominational pattern of the west was basically set by the immigrants themselves. They took their loyalties with them, and, despite some wastage, the various denominations usually reached them before these loyalties had evaporated. What destroyed Taché's dream and awakened Machray's envy was simply that most of the settlers came from Ontario farms, where neither Roman Catholics nor Anglicans were relatively numerous. Why Presbyterians should have taken such a commanding lead is less easily explained, for Methodists outnumbered them in rural Ontario. It seems clear, however, that Presbyterians did move west in larger numbers. They may have done so because they were infected with Scottish wanderlust, because they had drawn inferior lands in Ontario, or because they were in the habit of reading George Brown's *Globe*. Whatever the reasons, Presbyterians were already confident at the time of Robertson's appointment that they were destined to become the largest church in the west.[19]

The religious ethos of eastern Canada was less easily transplanted than its denominations. It was only natural that children of the Ontario countryside should have little taste for stately rituals and ceremonies, especially in a pioneer setting. It was soon observed, however, that they had little more enthusiasm for the long expository sermons of the Presbyterians or for the class meetings, prayer meetings and camp meetings of the Methodists.[20] Westerners associated churches more with community spirit than with traditional forms of piety. They valued candour and approachability in their ministers more than scholarship or even spirituality, responding warmly to the all-round man who would roll up his sleeves, and suspecting the introvert of pretensions to superior dignity. So at any rate many early missionaries attested, and C. W. Gordon fixed the stereotype in *The Sky Pilot*.[21] The widespread employment of students on summer fields may have done more to set a distinctively western pattern of church life than has usually been recognized. Most Protestant congregations had in their formative years a type of ministry that was better adapted to organizing community activities and summer camps than to offering mature spiritual counsel, and the sacraments were sometimes not available at all.

## THE FRINGES OF CANADA

Christian missionaries among the native Indians continued to reach new tribes and to consolidate their efforts in areas they had entered at an earlier time. The Roman Catholics were well established in the Mackenzie valley, where Oblates and Grey Nuns were at work. In British Columbia the Catholic Indians, chiefly from the interior, demonstrated their visibility by converging on New Westminster each year to mark the Queen's Birthday with religious ceremonies and a display of temperance flags.[22] The Methodists had their most conspicuous success in the same province, where their pattern of revivalism gave scope for leadership to such outstanding native converts as W. H. Pierce and David Sallosalton. The Anglicans, although handicapped in British Columbia by the disaffection and eventual defection of William Duncan, were able to establish a strong presence in the Yukon in advance of the gold rush there. The number of Indians, presumably not Christian, who specified no religion to census takers declined by about half from 1881 to 1901. By this time missionary work was becoming highly institutionalized in the wake of treaties and the creation of reserves, and government agencies looked largely to the churches for community leadership. Local schools for Indian reserves were introduced by the Presbyterians at Prince Albert, but residential schools continued to be the pivots of most institutional programs.

Despite this continued advance, there were already signs of disenchant·ment with Indian missions. Efforts to serve the incoming settlers, whose needs so clearly called for immediate attention, overshadowed them in appeal both to the public and to church officials. The Indians, impoverished by the disappearance of the buffalo and the declining importance of the fur trade, ceased as helpless wards of church and state to have the glamour for missionaries that had been theirs as "noble savages." Missionaries who had been enlisted for their qualities as pioneers sometimes lacked the talent for organization that a more settled period required. Some institutions came under severe criticism for inefficiency,[23] and efforts to help Indians to adapt to the ways of the white man were hindered by a lack of economic opportunities on the reserves. Most discouraging of all to the missionaries were frequent reversions to pre-Christian practice among tribes that had at first seemed highly receptive to their message. They had not counted on what were really expressions of psychological revenge against a paternalism that negated indigenous cultural values. Serious slackening of effort would take place only after the turn of the century, when the flood tide of immigration suddenly made the Indians one of the smaller ethnic groups of the west; but as early as 1884 a committee of the Manitoba Methodist Conference found it necessary to deplore "the prevalent scepticism existing relative to the success of our Indian work."[24]

Meanwhile, however, Anglican missionaries were beginning to make re-markable progress among the Eskimos of the far north. Sporadic contacts had long been made with both eastern and western Eskimos, but until the late nineteenth century only the Moravians of Labrador were at work in Eskimo territory. Bishop Bompas was always interested in the Eskimos, but serious efforts to reach those of the west began in 1893 when I. O. Stringer went to the whaling station of Herschel Island near the Alaskan border.[25] Penetration of the eastern Arctic was a gradual process, arising naturally out of early contacts with Eskimos at the Cree mission at Moose Factory. It became a major enterprise when E. J. Peck arrived from England in 1876 to begin a missionary career that would stretch over forty-eight years.[26] From Fort George a series of missions along the eastern coast of Hudson Bay reached by 1899 to Fort Chimo on Ungava Bay. A remarkable feature of this mission from the beginning was the spontaneous response of the Eskimos themselves. Some groups embraced Christianity as a result of visits to mission stations and retained it for years until resident missionaries could be appointed. Peck, unlike many missionaries of the time, had the wisdom to encourage this self-reliance. He promoted literacy among the Eskimos, translated scriptures, prayers and hymns, and appointed Eskimos as teachers among their own people. It was largely the Eskimos themselves, however, who made their church a self-propagating religious community.

The impulse that drew some into Indian and Eskimo missions led others to seek out elements of the white population that had previously been neglected by the church. Chaplains of several denominations, including for a time the indefatigable Lacombe,[27] served construction workers on the CPR during the early 1880s. William Oliver, a shipbuilder who had been brought from Scotland by the Methodists to supervise the construction of a mission boat, was so impressed by the needs of the isolated loggers and lighthousekeepers of the British Columbia coast that in 1884 he began a long career as skipper and lay missionary.[28] John Antle, rector of an Anglican parish in Vancouver, was commissioned in 1904 to explore the islands and bays of the Gulf of Georgia. The upshot was that he too gave up his post and founded the Columbia Coast Mission.[29] George Pringle established the Loggers' Mission for the Presbyterians, and by the early twentieth century there were small fleets of mission boats on both east and west coasts.

One such effort became internationally known. Inspired by the preaching of Dwight L. Moody, a young Englishman named Wilfred Grenfell arrived in Labrador in 1892 as a medical missionary.[30] His commission was to the Newfoundland fishermen who summered in the area, but he was soon more concerned to relieve the poverty of the "liveyers" who had established homes there. He founded hospitals, schools, and especially small industries through which the people might learn to better their own condition. His work was not directly sponsored by any church organization, but he always regarded it as a Christian enterprise and expected his professional and voluntary helpers to be active laymen. Grenfell was at first a controversial figure, arousing the indignation of governments by publicizing the plight of the settlers and the opposition of traders by establishing cooperatives among them. He died honoured by all.

## OVERFLOWING THE BOUNDARIES

Missionary enthusiasm inevitably overflowed the boundaries of Canada to claim a share in the effort to propagate Christianity throughout the world that was then engaging the interest of Christians everywhere. The impulse to claim the globe for Christ had been revived among English-speaking Protestants by William Carey in 1792. It had never died out among Roman Catholics, but it was greatly stimulated during the nineteenth century by a general revival of religious ardour and by the formation of more new religious orders than ever before in a comparable span of time. Among Protestants the leading proponents of foreign missions were evangelicals, among Roman Catholics ultramontanes. Canadians could scarcely be immune to the contagion of a movement whose sponsors had contributed so much to their own church life. Even before confederation, as we have seen, some Canadian missionaries were at work abroad.

As the Canadian churches grew in strength and confidence, they naturally sent out more missionaries. The Methodists, aware that the acquisition of Rupert's Land had brought all their missions within Canada's borders, opened a field in Japan in 1873. In the following year the Baptists began a mission among the Telugus of India, where some of them were already at work under American direction. The Presbyterians tended to accept the inclinations of dedicated individuals and thus acquired a multiplicity of fields: Trinidad in 1868, Formosa in 1872, India in 1873. Canadian Roman Catholics had not yet been assigned specific areas of responsibility, but individuals were sponsored by French and other societies. Their fields of work ranged from India to Latin America.[31]

During the 1880s and 1890s the pace of missionary advance accelerated rapidly among both Protestants and Roman Catholics. For the sources of the new impulse we must look outside Canada. In the United States and Britain the revivalistic campaigns of Moody and Sankey, which had unusual success among university students, emphasized commitment to Christian service. At that time no form of service seemed so challenging as missionary work abroad, and the newly founded Student Volunteer Movement enlisted thousands in the cause. Roman Catholic enthusiasm for missions, although less spectacular in its expression, grew at a comparable rate. Among Protestants the new missionary breeze blew most strongly in the United States, among Roman Catholics in France. Once again, Canadians were bound to be among those most deeply stirred.

Within a few decades there was a tremendous scattering of missionaries out of Christendom. Churches and societies divided the hitherto non-Christian part of the world into mission areas, or in some cases competed for the same ground. They established evangelistic centres, schools, hospitals, orphanages, and industrial enterprises. Canadians fully shared in the expansion. In 1886 Congregationalists began work in Angola in cooperation with American colleagues.[32] The first Canadian Anglican missionary overseas was J. Cooper Robinson, sent to Japan in 1888 by the Wycliffe Missions. J. G. Waller went to the same country as an emissary of the official Domestic and Foreign Missionary Society in 1890.[33] Presbyterians and Baptists opened additional fields, and in 1892 the Methodists established in west China what would become one of the largest Protestant missions anywhere.[34] Roman Catholics, mostly French Canadian, found their way to an increasing number of countries. Many of them went to Africa, where the rise of the second French colonial empire gave abundant scope for the use of their language. Beginning with the White Sisters, who in 1885 commenced work in Algeria, Canadian congregations began to be assigned their own spheres of responsibility.[35]

As in earlier periods of missionary enthusiasm, a number of new enterprises stemmed from the initiative of individuals or small groups. Often the contagion spread from college students. William John McKenzie, a Presbyterian from Cape Breton, represented a tradition of conservative evangelicalism that was still very much alive in parts of Canada. One is not surprised that he sought to convert all his associates when one reads a prayer composed during his student days, "Lord help me to see the unbeliever, whatever his lot here, as going down to hell and a hater of Christ!"[36] He felt a definite call to preach in Korea, and friends helped him to go there independently in 1893 when his church declined to undertake new work on account of lack of funds. He died in 1895, and two years later the Presbyterians officially opened what became a very successful mission in Korea. Baptist work in Bolivia was initiated in 1896 through the enthusiasm of Archibald Reekie, who had long dreamed of South America but apparently underwent a definite conversion while a student at McMaster University.[37] John M. Fraser, a Roman Catholic from Toronto, felt an equally specific call to China. He went there in 1902 as a secular priest, at first without the sponsorship of any society. In contrast with McKenzie, he was to have a long missionary career. During the Second World War he suffered through the Japanese invasion of the Philippines, and after its end he helped to reconstruct an atom-bombed church at Nagasaki.[38]

The most conspicuous new feature of this phase of the Christian mission was the opening of practically the entire world to its influence. John R. Mott popularized the slogan, "the evangelization of the world in this generation," meaning not necessarily the conversion of the entire human race but at least the universal dissemination of the gospel. Missionaries of the period came remarkably close to their goal, and in harmony with the prevailing self-confidence of the west they furthered cultural as well as religious penetration. Despite their largely conservative motivation, therefore, missionary movements of the time contained within them the seeds of radical social change. Returned missionaries would later be influential in fostering social concerns within the Canadian churches.

## NEW PATTERNS OF ORGANIZATION

Missionary effort on the frontiers demanded new structures and procedures at the home base. As a nation at war finds itself compelled to submit to new disciplines, so the churches underwent significant changes as they prosecuted their militant although peaceful enterprises. Some of these changes resulted from efforts to mobilize the whole membership of the churches in support of missionaries on the field. Others were themselves expressions of mission, designed to make the services of the church available as effectively as possible to every age, sex, and interest group. Their most conspicuous result was to introduce the plethora of voluntary organizations, both local and national, that have become such a familiar aspect of Canadian church life. Most of these were based on American models, although French-speaking Catholics imported some of theirs from France.

Among Protestants, women were the first to organize for the furtherance of the missionary cause, and in Canada they have always been the chief instigators of enthusiasm for missions. Local women's auxiliaries existed from the early years of the nineteenth century. In 1876 Methodist Episcopal and Presbyterian women formed national societies, and those of most other denominations followed their example in the 1880s. Separate societies for home and foreign missions were sometimes established at first, but in all cases these eventually coalesced. Looking around for others to enroll, these dedicated women soon sponsored mission circles for older girls and mission bands for children of both sexes. Such groups, although largely dependent on mite boxes and voluntary projects, raised astonishing sums for missionary purposes.

A notable feature of all women's missionary societies from the beginning was the important place of education in their programs. National headquarters provided information to local groups in the form of printed letters from missionaries that could be read at meetings. Promotion was always emphasized more than analysis, but church women undoubtedly came to know and care more about distant countries than any other class of Canadians. From the first these societies sponsored work of their own both in Canada and abroad. Before many years, women's groups constituted large autonomous organizations that paralleled the official structures of the various denominations. They may have helped to perpetuate the segregation of women in church life, for men continued to dominate official church bodies, but along with local "ladies' aids" they made themselves indispensable to the work of the church.

Newly founded orders of deaconesses provided training and opportunities for women who wished to make church work their vocation. The Methodists imported this institution from the United States in 1887, and other denominations soon followed their example. The special field of deaconesses at that time was as social workers and evangelists in slum areas. Single women, whether in the employ of churches or of missionary societies, were often appointed to tasks for which it did not seem economically feasible to use men. Sometimes they opened up difficult areas for the church, only to see their work handed over to men when foundations had been laid and living conditions had become more tolerable.

Interest in the Christian mission was not confined to women, but men and young people proved more difficult to organize in support of it. During the late 1890s the Young People's Forward Movement stimulated some enthusiasm, especially for work in Canadian cities. The interdenominational Laymen's Missionary Movement, founded in 1907, attracted a number of prominent supporters and raised a considerable amount of money. These movements came on the scene late and soon vanished, leaving the women to carry the main burden of missionary promotion as they had in the past.

New programs of Christian education among youth were not only auxiliaries to the missionary enterprise but expressions of it, for the same considerations that led men and women to cross oceans to impart Christian instruction suggested the desirability of using the most efficient methods of education at home. The improvement of Sunday schools became for a time a missionary project of great priority, and Sunday school conventions were often occasions of high emotion. Horace Bushnell, an American Congregationalist who more than any other formulated the philosophy of the new Christian education, insisted that the aim of Christian nurture was to enable the child to grow into a place in the Christian community. It is not surprising, therefore, that Sunday schools introduced their pupils at an early age to the leading concerns of adult church members. In many localities they set aside one period each month for temperance, another for missions.

During the last decades of the nineteenth century several developments revolutionized Protestant programs of Christian education, which had previously consisted chiefly of the memorization of portions of scripture and of various catechisms. One of these was the introduction of regular curricula of lessons. In 1872 John H. Vincent, an American Methodist minister, persuaded a national Sunday school convention to authorize what became known as the International Lessons.[39] A major selling point of this curriculum was the concentration of an entire continent upon a single passage of scripture each Sunday. Teachers depended at first for help in presenting the material on commentaries that were written locally and published in the religious or often the secular press; many outstanding ministers achieved through such columns the fame reserved more recently for popular radio preachers. In time the denominations began to provide leaflets or books for teachers and pupils. Not until the twentieth century, however, would an attempt be made through graded lessons to meet the pedagogical needs of children of various ages.

The Methodists, who had their own publishing house, were pioneers in providing distinctively Canadian lesson materials. The churches also began to provide story papers as inducements to regular attendance at Sunday school, and incidentally as painless vehicles of spiritual and moral teaching. These ordinarily had catchy titles. *Happy Days* appeared in 1886, *Dew Drops* in 1897. *Onward*, a Methodist paper for senior students that was introduced in 1891, had for many years the largest circulation of any Canadian magazine.

Most young people who had graduated from or dropped out of public school regarded themselves as too old for Sunday school, so for them special midweek groups were formed. Germain Street Baptist Church, Saint John, had a young people's society as early as 1876.[40] Albert College, Belleville, sponsored a pioneer "Sunday School Parliament" that customarily met at the St. Lawrence camp ground of the Methodist Episcopals near the present Thousand Islands International Bridge.[41] The important movement in the field, however, was Christian Endeavour. Founded in the United States in 1880 and introduced into Canada in 1883, it offered to all Protestant churches a readily adaptable program that provided some form of active participation for every member at every meeting. Soon the various denominations formed their own associations—Epworth Leagues, Westminster Guilds, AYPAs or BYPUs—usually with Christian Endeavour as their basic ingredient. By the 1890s these societies were becoming regular components of church life. It is interesting to note, however, that almost from their inception they were reputed to be in decline. The church has never found its young people an easy constituency.

Those who have grown up in Canadian Protestant churches will recognize in these new developments of the 1880s and 1890s the formation of a pattern that has only shown signs of obsolescence within the last few years. Other equally familiar features were introduced at about the same time. Summer camping was promoted by the church, although normally in a family setting at such places as Berwick and Grimsby Beach and under more starchily religious conditions than would later prevail. Enthusiasm for adult religious education would prove more ephemeral, but at that time Bible classes and summer schools were in vogue, and literary institutes became a recognized feature of Methodism in Newfoundland. Christian education, which had hitherto been extremely informal, became as a result of these changes a highly structured activity. The aim of John H. Vincent was to enable the Sunday school to match the secular school in pedagogical effectiveness. It was only natural that Christian educators should come to lay more emphasis on method than on content and that in time many of them should adopt the approach of John Dewey.

Circumstances in the Roman Catholic Church forbade such a radical change in the style of parish life. The church was at that time too insistent on clerical supervision to allow the growth of an autonomous lay leadership and too decentralized in administration to provide the contacts needed for large-scale national organization. It lacked the resources in English Canada, and the inclination in Quebec, to emulate the streamlined programs then being developed in the United States. Nevertheless, Catholics successfully devised methods of their own for achieving similar ends. The religious orders, in line with the mendicant tradition established by St. Francis of Assisi in the thirteenth century, relied for the support of their missions on direct appeals to the public. In the twentieth century they would draw upon the skills of the advertising industry to develop these into sophisticated programs of direct mail. For the religious education of their children, Roman Catholics depended on day schools rather than on special Sunday classes. Their concern that these schools should receive tax support sufficient to maintain their efficiency thus had a very practical basis, and it is worth noting that Catholic interest in separate schools was increasing markedly at the time when Protestants were remodelling their educational practice.

Despite these differences, trends in church life often had a remarkable way of crossing denominational lines. The increasing prominence of women in missionary endeavours was equally notable among Protestants and Roman Catholics, expressing itself among the former in the rise of voluntary societies and the foundation of schools for deaconesses and among the latter in the growth of orders of nuns. The introduction to Canada in 1884 of the Anglican Sisterhood of St. John the Divine was a reminder that one communion was hospitable to both approaches. The provision of structured activity for the laity was likewise as typical of the period among Catholics as among Protestants. Men joined the Holy Name Society, while married and unmarried women had their separate sodalities. Young people were enrolled in the Catholic Youth Organization, or in Quebec from 1903 in l'Association Catholique de la Jeunesse Canadienne. These organizations, like their Protestant counterparts, encouraged their members to support the church's penetration of the world. Most of them, in those days of defensive Catholicism, were militant in outlook. Yet, again like their Protestant counterparts, they often served as little more than social and athletic clubs.

## INTELLECTUAL MOVEMENTS

New intellectual movements were beginning to affect Canadian Protestants in the latter part of the nineteenth century, although their impact on Roman Catholicism would be delayed for several decades. The liveliest academic centre of the period was Queen's University in Kingston, where, as principal, George M. Grant cultivated an atmosphere of hospitality to new ideas. The completion of a successful financial campaign in 1887 enabled him to assemble a staff of extremely able teachers, and the foundation of the *Queen's Quarterly* in 1893 was an important milestone in Canadian intellectual history. Even before Grant's time, however, Principal William Snodgrass had established a tradition of academic excellence. John Watson, one of his appointees, was known to fellow-scholars as a leading Kantian and to his students as an unusually stimulating teacher. Queen's in the late nineteenth century combined religious and moral earnestness with a spirit of free inquiry, emphasizing philosophical idealism in its undergraduate course and introducing Presbyterian theological students to the latest developments in German biblical criticism. Its period of eminence represented not so much an indigenous development as a transplantation to Canada of Scottish intellectual vigour. It had an immense influence, however, in awakening students to questions that had seldom interested Canadians before.

Queen's was only the most conspicuous example of a change in mental climate that gradually affected the education of all Canadian Protestants, including their ministers. Victoria University began in 1865 to appoint to its staff selected graduates who had been encouraged to study in Germany, first in arts and science but later also in theology.[42] George Paxton Young of Toronto, whose deviations from orthodoxy compelled him to move from Knox College to the nonsectarian University College, won a formidable reputation among theological students not so much for his realist philosophy as for his ability to compel freshmen to rethink the orthodox assumptions they had imbibed in Sunday schools.[43] There arose a generation of able teachers, especially in universities and arts colleges, who regarded it as an important part of their duty to help students to come to terms with biblical criticism and Darwinism without abandoning their Christian commitment. The theological colleges offered greater resistance to change, but by the end of the century almost all of them had quietly accepted many of the findings of the new scholarship. They did so, mainly, because students were familiar with the questions raised by critics and sought help in resolving their own doubts. There was little desire to abandon accepted doctrine, but rather a sense that intellectual honesty in the face of new discoveries compelled the reappraisal of much that had been regarded as fundamental. More corrosive of Protestant orthodoxy than uncertainties about biblical authorship, perhaps, was a widespread conviction that for the religious person moral imperatives carry more weight than revealed doctrines.

These changes in the Protestant outlook were related to each other and to the prevailing evangelical tradition in complex and sometimes ambiguous ways. D. C. Masters has called attention to the disintegrating effects of liberal ideas on the beliefs that undergirded evangelical Christianity.[44] The critical approach was resisted much more stubbornly by such evangelical colleges as Knox and Huron than by such representatives of old state-church traditions as Trinity and Queen's. It was evangelical opposition, indeed, that led to the practical separation of Queen's from the Presbyterian Church in 1875.[45] Similarly, the new emphasis on gradual education into church membership left little room for the old crisis experience of conversion. Those who sought to save the heathen from a literal hell might well conclude that the new theology and the new methodology were equally designed to cut the nerve of missionary motivation.

On the other hand, churchmen of evangelical background contributed a great deal to the emergence of the new liberal concept of the church. Their leadership in the formulation of new programs was too obvious to be doubted. The dates of new curricula, educational periodicals, and organizations for women and youth all tell the same story. Methodists, Presbyterians, and Anglicans almost invariably appear in that order, with Baptists ranging between first and third place. Conspicuously, too, those who took the lead in campaigns for temperance and missions were usually also prominent at Sunday school conventions. The most telling evidence of all for continuity between the old evangelism and the new pedagogy is provided by changes in the meaning of a few key words. The class meeting gave way before the Bible class. The camp meeting became the summer camp, with undiminished emphasis on the sentinel campfire that provided illumination and inspiration at night. The band, a witnessing group that became progressively younger with the years, ended up as the mission band.

The contribution of evangelicals to theological change was less decisive, but it should not be underestimated. Victoria's early welcome to biblical criticism has been noted, and Canadian Methodists and Baptists at one period held a large proportion of Old Testament chairs in the United States. Whatever hesitations evangelicals may have had about the new theological trends, what ultimately emerged from them was in effect a somewhat secularized evangelicalism—less certain about the need for individual rebirth but still aggressively missionary, moralistic, and socially concerned. Later controversies between modernists and fundamentalists would largely be internal struggles among heirs to the evangelical tradition.

The desire for more effective witness and the incursion of new theological ideas were not the only factors making for change in the late nineteenth century. The increasing importance of small-scale industry, with the consequent transformation of a rural into a town and small-city culture, also had important effects on church life. Buildings became more ornate, if not always more tasteful. Gowns were donned by choirs and ministers—usually the former before the latter—in line with a North American tradition that attaches social prestige to formality in worship. Fellowship groups assumed an air of gentility, and the more spiritual complained that young people's societies were too often merely means of making suitable matches. Despite the superficial character of some of the changes, they were part of the process by which a frontier society accustomed itself to civilized manners. It was only natural that such a stage should also be marked by an increasing awareness of metropolitan influences that manifested itself most conspicuously in a desire for closer ties with the motherland. It may have been significant that Grant, the sponsor of advanced theological ideas, frequently spoke on behalf of the Imperial Federation League and believed in the divine mission of the Teutonic peoples.[46]

## STRAINS OF ADJUSTMENT

The acceptance of new ways inevitably provoked controversy and sometimes division. The nervousness of the churches when confronted by change was most conspicuously illustrated by a series of attacks on churchmen who were regarded as theological radicals. In 1876 commissioners to the Presbyterian general assembly raised questions about a sermon in which D. J. Macdonnell, a prominent minister of Kirk background, had expressed doubts about the existence of an unconditional and conscious eternity of punishment. Church leaders did not wish to imperil the newly achieved union, and a compromise was eventually arranged by which doubt about a section of the Westminster Confession was distinguished from denial of it.[47] In 1893 John Campbell, a professor at the Presbyterian College at Montreal, was accused of heresy on the same subject by his two colleagues on the faculty. His synod ultimately accepted a statement that really retracted nothing.[48] George Workman of Victoria University was not so fortunate. After returning from the customary period of graduate study in Germany, he was attacked by several leaders of the Methodist Church, including general superintendent Albert Carman, for denying the accepted view that certain passages in the Old Testament could be regarded as conscious predictions of the coming of Christ. He lost his theological chair at Victoria, and in 1907 he was forced out of the Wesleyan College at Montreal on a variety of charges. A similar attack in 1909 on George Jackson, a British import who was under appointment to the chair of English Bible and Homiletics at Victoria, had the contrary effect of leading in 1910 to the drafting of a somewhat ambiguous declaration on academic freedom that brought Methodist heresy hunts to an end.[49] By this time the Baptists were also having troubles, but that story and its climax must be left to another chapter. F. J. Steen, who was compelled to resign from the staff of the Montreal Diocesan College in 1901, seems to have been the only Anglican to lose his post for liberal views.

Dramatic as some of these incidents were, they represented a much easier transition than took place in either Britain or the United States. They aroused comparatively little interest at first among the laity, although the foundation of the Toronto Bible College in 1894 indicated the appearance of uneasiness in some circles. Charges were usually pressed by fellow-ministers or officials, and in the case of the Methodists they may have been motivated as much by prejudice against a highly educated ministry and by hostility to wealthy sponsors of the new learning as by serious theological questioning. Unfortunately, concern for the peace of the church or the freedom of its teachers almost completely overshadowed consideration of the substantive issues involved. As a result of excessive caution the new learning remained practically an arcane possession of the clergy, and laymen who were not let into the secret would become increasingly uneasy about it.

More immediately troublesome to Protestant churches than theological controversy within the ministry, however, was dissatisfaction with their total programs among elements of the rank and file. During the 1880s two important sectarian movements appeared in Canada, the Salvation Army and the "Hornerites." The two were to have markedly different careers, but they had much in common at the outset. They were both offshoots of Methodism, and appealed chiefly to discontented Methodists. They both owed their existence to an impulse to "holiness" that appeared in Britain and the United States about the middle of the nineteenth century. They both characteristically proclaimed the possibility of complete sanctification. In the Maritimes, during the same period, the Free or Arminian Baptists suffered from the inroads of the Salvation Army and of new revivalist Baptist groups.[50]

When it was introduced into Canada by Jack Addie in 1882, the Salvation Army had not begun to establish its present reputation as an ultra-respectable social service agency. Joseph Hilts reported that its revivals were more disorderly than any camp meetings he could recall from his youth,[51] and hostile rowdies added to the disorder. The Army was highly competitive, especially with the Methodists, and the cacophany of rival bands could be heard from the Newfoundland outports to the Indian mission at Port Simpson, British Columbia. Then as now, however, the Army made its chief impact upon the inner city.

Ralph Horner began his career as a Methodist minister, although at Victoria University he had already been disillusioned by a lack of holiness among his fellow-students. From 1886 he conducted holiness campaigns largely on his own, chiefly through large tent meetings which he introduced into Canada. He was soon expelled from the Methodist ministry, and indeed no respectable denomination could long have endured his frankly competitive methods and his claims to "cyclones of power" capable of converting the most obdurate sinner in an instant. In 1895 he founded the Holiness Movement Church, and after breaking with it he began the Standard Church of America in 1916.

These movements owed their appearance neither to theological novelty nor to any difference of opinion over moral standards. Their attraction was rather to those who felt ill at ease in the rarefied atmosphere of the conventional churches, and their rise was symptomatic of the churches' difficulty in working both sides of the tracks in an increasingly stratified society. Their clientele might also be described as consisting of those who could not share the churches' dream of a christianized Canada because they felt themselves to be cut off from meaningful participation in national life. The Salvation Army appealed especially to recent immigrants from Britain, the Hornerites to impoverished Protestants of Irish background.

Despite such minor setbacks, the morale of the churches was higher than ever. Their strength rested on a solid base of popular piety, partly inherited from the old world and partly stimulated by enthusiastic movements. They were building larger edifices, devising more effective programs, and successfully shaping the moral values of the nation. They were penetrating new frontiers of the faith, both within and beyond Canada's borders. They were becoming accustomed to statistics that showed constant and even accelerating growth. Here and there, it is true, there were signs of future trouble for those who could read them. The new programs did not appeal to all Canadians, and internal tensions were beginning to appear. In time the fissures would widen, but they were not yet sufficiently alarming to shake the confidence of the churches in their capacity to meet the Canadian challenge.

## NOTES TO CHAPTER THREE

1. Joseph H. Hilts, *Experiences of a Backwoods Preacher* (Toronto: Methodist Book Room, 1892), p. 354.

2. Acts and Proceedings of the 15th General Assembly of the Presbyterian Church in Canada, 1889, Appendix 1, p. xxii.

3. Quoted by Adélard Langevin, Archbishop of St. Boniface, in Paul Benoit, *Vie de Mgr Taché*, Vol. I, p. v.

4. Quoted in E. H. Oliver, *His Dominion of Canada* (Toronto: The Board of Home Missions and the Women's Missionary Society of The United Church of Canada, 1932), p. 37.

5. Norman Macdonald, *Canada: Immigration and Colonization, 1841-1903*, p. 194.

6. Acts and Proceedings of the 3rd General Assembly of the Presbyterian Church in Canada, 1877, Appendix, p. iii.

7. Acts and Proceedings of the 22nd General Assembly of the Presbyterian Church in Canada, 1896, Appendix 1, p. xxiii.

8. Robert Machray, *Life of Robert Machray*, p. 334.

9. G. M. Grant, *Ocean to Ocean*, pp. 182-185.

10. Machray, *op. cit.*, p. 341.

11. T. C. B. Boon, *The Anglican Church from the Bay to the Rockies*, p. 187.

12. George Bryce, *John Black: the Apostle of the Red River, or, How the Blue Banner was Unfurled on Manitoba Prairies* (Toronto: Wm. Briggs, 1898), p. 119.

13. C. W. Gordon led a delegation to Britain in 1893 to recruit ministers. Acts and Proceedings of the 20th General Assembly of the Presbyterian Church in Canada, 1894, Appendix 1, p. xviii.

14. J. H. Riddell, *Methodism in the Middle West*, p. 165.

15. Acts and Proceedings of the 18th General Assembly of the Presbyterian Church in Canada, 1892, Appendix 1, p. xvi.

16. Like the Presbyterians, the Methodists found it necessary to turn to Britain for help. James Woodsworth was sent to England in 1894 on a mission similar to Gordon's. Riddell, *op. cit.*, p. 231.

17. J. Gordon Jones, *Greatness Passing By! Biographical Sketches of Some Canadian Baptists, Emphasizing Their Contribution to Our National Life from 1867 to 1967* (Toronto: Baptist Federation of Canada, 1967), p. 50.

18. C. C. McLaurin, *Pioneering in Western Canada: A Story of the Baptists* (Calgary: the author, 1939), p. 215.

19. "The great bulk of the immigrants coming into the country are Presbyterians." C. B. Pitblado in Acts and Proceedings of the 7th General Assembly of the Presbyterian Church in Canada, 1881, Appendix, p. xiii.

20. Riddell, *op. cit.*, p. 146.

21. Ralph Connor (C. W. Gordon), *The Sky Pilot* (Toronto: Westminster, 1899).

22. A. G. Morice, *History of the Catholic Church in Western Canada*, Vol. II, p. 327.

23. See Maurice H. Lewis, "The Anglican Church and its Mission Schools Dispute," *Alberta Historical Review*, Vol. XIV, No. 4 (autumn 1966), pp. 7-13.

24. Minutes of the Proceedings of the First Session of the Manitoba Annual Conference of the Methodist Church, 1884, p. 44.

25. F. A. Peake, *The Bishop Who Ate His Boots* (Toronto: Anglican Church of Canada, 1966), p. 22.

26. See Arthur Lewis, *The Life and Work of E. J. Peck Among the Eskimos* (London: Hodder and Stoughton, 1905).

27. Benoit, *op. cit.*, Vol. II, p. 415.

28. See R. C. Scott, *My Captain Oliver: A Story of Two Missionaries on the British Columbia Coast* (Toronto: Committee on Missionary Education of The United Church of Canada, c. 1947).

29. W. E. Taylor, *Our Church at Work: Canada and Overseas*, 2nd ed. (Toronto: MSCC, n.d.), p. 59.

30. See Wilfred Grenfell, *A Labrador Doctor* (Boston: Houghton, c. 1919).

31. Lionel Groulx, *Le Canada Français Missionnaire* (Montreal and Paris: Fides, 1962), p. 81.

32. See John T. Tucker, *Old Ways and New Days in Angola, Africa* (Toronto: The Committee on Young People's Missionary Education, n.d.).

33. C. W. Vernon, *The Old Church in the New Dominion* (London: SPCK, 1929), pp. 178-180.

34. See *Our West China Mission*, by the missionaries on the field (Toronto: Missionary Society of the Methodist Church, 1920).

35. Dominique de Saint-Denis, comp., *The Catholic Church in Canada*, 6th ed. (Montreal: Thau, 1956), p. 265.

36. E. A. McCully, *A Corn of Wheat* (Toronto: Westminster, 1903), p. 20.

37. Jones, *op. cit.*, p. 75.

38. Alphonsus Chafe, sfm, "Missionary Apostolic," *Scarboro Missions*, Vol. XXXII, No. 6 (June 1951), pp. 12-17, 22-32.

39. W. C. Barclay, *History of Methodist Missions* (New York: The Board of Missions of the Methodist Church, 1957), Vol. 3, p. 100.

40. George E. Levy, *The Baptists of the Maritime Provinces, 1753-1946*, p. 224.

41. D. C. Masters, *Protestant Church Colleges in Canada: A History* (Toronto: University of Toronto Press, 1966), p. 104.

42. C. B. Sissons, *A History of Victoria University* (Toronto: University of Toronto Press, 1952), *passim*.

43. There are hints that his presence at the University of Toronto may have been responsible for some Baptist opposition to the federation of McMaster University with it. *Memorial of Daniel Arthur McGregor, Late Principal of Toronto Baptist College*, published by the Alumni Association of Toronto Baptist College (Toronto: Dudley and Burns, 1891), p. 38.

44. Masters, *op. cit.*, p. 89.

45. W. L. Grant and Frederick Hamilton, *Principal Grant*, p. 433.

46. *Ibid.*, pp. 178-179, 399-400.

47. J. T. McNeill, *The Presbyterian Church in Canada, 1875-1925*, pp. 204-207.

48. *Ibid.*, pp. 207-209.

49. For a detailed account of the Workman and Jackson cases, see George A. Boyle, "Higher Criticism and the Struggle for Academic Freedom in Canadian Methodism," Th.D. thesis, Victoria University, 1965.

50. Edward M. Saunders, *History of the Baptists of the Maritime Provinces* (Halifax: John Burgoyne, 1902), pp. 406, 407.

51. Hilts, *op. cit.*, p. 69.

# FOUR

## Causes and Controversies

The missionary thrust that was such a conspicuous feature of Canadian church life during the decades immediately after 1867 had not only geographical and cultural but also moral and spiritual dimensions. The prevalent desire to claim the world for Christ, which impelled some Canadians to the far west or the Far East, impressed on others who remained at home the urgency of ensuring that Canada itself should be a genuinely Christian nation. Confederation made Canada larger and promised to make it more prosperous, but it set no standards of conduct and provided no structure of values. Determining these intangibles was a role the churches readily accepted for themselves.

The task of impregnating Canada with Christian ideals was made more urgent, in the minds of church leaders, by the predominance of commercial values in the years after confederation. Preoccupation with money-making was by no means peculiar to Canada, but it was intensified by the need to work out the logistics of nationhood in a hurry. Conservative politicians praised railway promoters as nation-builders of the highest order. Those who founded the Canada First movement in 1871 were more aware of an unpatriotic scramble for spoils, and their leader W. A. Foster asked for "some bond more uniting than a shiftless expediency; some lodestar more potent than a mere community of profit."[1] The churches inclined to the more sceptical evaluation and were prone like most North Americans of the time to suppose that "economic and social problems . . . could be solved by simple moral judgments."[2] Their interest in Canada's future, however, was not inspired merely by a negative reaction to commercialism. With a record of successful evangelization behind them, they regarded the effective christianization of Canada as an uncompleted but not impossible task. Before they could possess the promised land, they would have to drive out the Canaanites who infested it.

The identification of Israelites and Canaanites naturally varied from denomination to denomination and from one school of theology to another.

The thrust towards active Christian intervention in Canadian life was largely supplied by the movements described in Chapter One: continental ultramontanism and English tractarianism, Scottish and American voluntaryism and evangelicalism. Confederation gave these movements new opportunities in Canada while deflecting some of their energies into new channels. In particular, the decades after 1867 were dominated by a crusading ultramontane Catholicism and a crusading evangelical Protestantism. They were inevitably decades of ardour and of conflict: ardour as churches formulated programs of spiritual improvement, conflict as these programs collided with one another and with the secularizing effects of commercial enterprise.

## THE ULTRAMONTANE *PROGRAMME*

During Canada's first years ultramontane sentiment was at its peak throughout the Roman Catholic Church. Pope Pius IX, who had shown favour to liberal reforms upon his accession in 1846, turned against the forces of change when nationalists demanded that the papal states should be incorporated into a united Italy. The defence of the beleaguered pontiff became a sacred duty to fervent Catholics, including Canadian Catholics of all ethnic origins. In 1868 a band of young French-Canadian volunteers sailed to Rome to join the papal zouaves, and in 1870 Connolly was the only Canadian bishop at the first Vatican Council to oppose the promulgation of the dogma of papal infallibility.[3]

Within Canada, however, ultramontanism took hold as an organized movement only in Quebec. There it had opportunities for public influence that existed in no other part of the world. On the continent of Europe, where it had originated, ultramontanism was a movement of protest against secularistic governments. In Canada as a whole, and in provinces with a Protestant majority, it could hope for influence only within the church itself. In the newly formed province of Quebec, however, it had a unique opportunity to determine the ideology of a political unit. Many *québecois* felt the need of a political philosophy that would distinguish them from the alien culture by which they were surrounded. The most obvious source of such a philosophy was the Roman Catholic Church, to which they already had a much closer emotional attachment than to the political institutions of their conquerors. Confederation, which constituted Quebec as a separate province, thereby made political ultramontanism possible.

Long a pervasive attitude in French Canada, ultramontanism acquired a public identity in 1871 with the organization of the Union Allet and the publication of the *programme catholique*.[4] The *programmistes* sought to implement the ideals of Pius IX without compromise. The church, purged of the sceptical and the half-hearted, was to rally around its embattled pontiff. The state was to become its willing servant in areas, such as education and moral legislation, to which the church's teaching authority applied. The *programmistes* were laymen, some of them alumni of the zouaves. Their leader was a senator, F.-X. Trudel, and several others would become prominent in Quebec politics. In private they were men of prayer and ascetic practice, in public devotees of a holy cause. Their chief advisers were Bishops Bourget of Montreal and Laflèche of Trois-Rivières, and they were in touch with the conservative ultramontane leader Louis Veuillot in France. For most other bishops they had little regard. Rumilly describes them as "a group of laymen, more ultramontane than the pope, claiming to represent the church and to interpret its words, and not hesitating when necessary to give a lesson to the bishops."[5]

A crusade of such intensity would have languished without formidable infidels to combat. On hand to play the role of Saracens were members of the *Institut canadien* of Montreal.[6] Founded in 1844 to raise the cultural standards of French Canada, the Institute had enjoyed at the outset the support of all segments of the community. The books and periodicals in its library naturally reflected current European thinking, however, and a flurry of revolutionary activity in 1848 caught the enthusiasm of some prominent members. Ultimately the Institute became a bastion of political Liberalism and a hotbed of religious liberalism, although it continued to include among its members a fair number of practising Catholics who merely liked to think for themselves. Bishop Bourget became alarmed and persuaded the Roman authorities to condemn the Institute.

The most dramatic encounter between the two antagonists was the celebrated *affaire Guibord*, which held the attention of the province over five years.[7] In 1870, when members of the Institute were under a blanket excommunication, one of them named Joseph Guibord died. His widow requested that he be buried in consecrated ground, which the church authorities refused. Members of the Institute arranged for temporary disposal. Then, being able to muster a considerable array of legal talent, they went to court and ultimately secured a favourable judgment from the Privy Council. At last in 1875 they were able to escort Guibord's overdue remains to the Catholic cemetery under the protection of an escort of English-speaking soldiers. Fearing that the grave might be tampered with, they then ordered cement poured around the coffin. They had failed to reckon with ecclesiastical ingenuity. On the day of the funeral, Bourget issued a pastoral letter that declared the plot in which Guibord had been buried to be forever unconsecrated ground. Apart from its comic aspects, the chief significance of the episode was that it seemed to rule out the possibility in Quebec of a cultural élite independent of clerical control.

In the eyes of ultramontanes the intellectuals of the Institute were merely the avant-garde of a larger and more formidable enemy, the Liberal party. Liberalism was naturally suspect to nineteenth-century ultramontanes. In continental Europe many liberals were freemasons and sceptics, and all liberals were advocates of the secular state and strong opponents of papal claims. In Quebec itself the Liberals were damned by their past record, having been associated since the days of Papineau with republicanism and free thought. Although by 1870 the *rouge* tradition was in decline, its fatal fascination seemed to induce some Liberal editor to refurbish the old anti-clerical slogans immediately before each election. Parish priests sympathetic to ultramontanism would thereupon warn their people that voting for a Liberal candidate would involve them in the mortal sin of apostasy. When the validity of some elections was challenged on the ground of "undue influence" by the clergy, ultramontane periodicals condemned as blasphemers not only the candidates who brought such charges but the lawyers who pressed them and the judges who upheld them. With such aid the Conservatives easily won the provincial election of 1875, although in many ridings by surprisingly small margins.

The ultramontanes operated most effectively, however, as a pressure group within the church and within the Conservative party. In opposing the Liberals they were merely following in the footsteps of generations of faithful Catholics. Their special mission was to establish truth within the Conservative fold. Sir George-Etienne Cartier, until his death in 1873 Sir John A. Macdonald's lieutenant in Quebec, was closely associated with commercial interests and mingled readily with English-speaking Canadians. Intent chiefly on the profitable exploitation of Canadian resources, he had no desire to hand over any of his prerogatives to clergymen. To the ultra-faithful he and his followers were little better than traitors to Catholicism, and the ultramontanes accordingly set out to capture the Conservative party. At times, however, their hatred of Liberalism enabled the Conservative leadership to exploit the support of the church while giving little in return. In 1875 Laflèche instructed the faithful not to vote for Conservative candidates who failed to support clerical control of education, but he could not advise them to vote Liberal.

The keenest shafts of the ultramontanes were reserved for those within the church who showed insufficient zeal for their program. Their most notable target was Elzéar A. Taschereau, the former rector of Laval University who had now become archbishop of Quebec and metropolitan of the Roman Catholic Church in the province. Taschereau had behind him in Quebec City a tradition different in many respects from that of the upstart diocese of Montreal. No one but a *programmiste* would have called this tradition radical or dangerous. Rather it was austere and conservative, in keeping with the classically scholastic curriculum of Laval. To the committed counter-revolutionary, however, the moderate conservative often appears shifty and unreliable. The Quebec establishment was not really harbouring dangerous thoughts, but it wished to remain politically disengaged to an extent that scandalized the extremists of Montreal. The prominence of several members of the Taschereau family in the Liberal party did not help to smooth over the rift.

The most contentious issue was the desire of the ultramontanes for an independent university at Montreal. Arts colleges of the classical tradition were scattered throughout the province, but *québecois* could obtain professional education for their children only by exposing them to the contagion of heterodoxy at Laval. The prospect became intolerable when one of the law professors at Laval consented to act as legal counsel to a Liberal candidate in a prosecution for "undue influence." For some reason, feelings were most bitter among medical men. Balked by the Laval monopoly in Quebec, Montrealers turned to the Methodists of Ontario and secured from them the right to confer degrees of Victoria University on graduates of their own French-language course. It was one of the medical instructors at *l'Ecole Victoria* in Montreal who wrote after Bourget's retirement a pamphlet entitled *The Catholic conscience outraged and the rights of intelligence violated by the two defenders of Laval University, His Grace Monseigneur Taschereau, Archbishop of Quebec, and His Highness Monseigneur Fabre, Bishop of Montreal.*[8] No Methodist at Cobourg could have written more scathingly about the Roman hierarchy.

### RESPONSES TO ULTRAMONTANISM

Ultramontane agitation was showing tangible results by 1875. In that year the victorious Conservatives passed a bill that abolished the ministry of education and turned over its powers to autonomous Roman Catholic and Protestant sections of the Council of Public Instruction. Towards the end of the year, in the aftermath of the Guibord incident, it was possible to persuade all the bishops of the province to issue a *mandement* denying that there could be such a thing as a liberal Catholic and insisting on the right of the clergy to intervene in politics when the teachings of the church were challenged.[9]

The *programmistes* soon discovered, however, that beyond certain limits they were balked by the higher authorities of the church. In 1876 the Holy Office issued an instruction to the Canadian bishops ruling that papal condemnations of liberalism were not intended to apply to all political parties "which by chance call themselves liberal,"[10] and successive appeals by Laflèche for Roman intervention only evoked cautions against excessive zeal. In the same year the bull *Inter varios sollicitudines* granted a papal charter to Laval, which was further permitted to establish a branch in Montreal. Discouraged and ill, Bourget submitted his resignation. He soon recovered his health and spirits, but not before his resignation had been accepted and a more pliable successor appointed. Since all these developments took place during the pontificate of Pius IX, the most ultramontane of popes, the disappointment of the *programmistes* can readily be understood. In dealing with Protestant countries such as Britain and Holland, however, Pius always respected the principle of separation which he reprehended in Catholic states.[11] He was obviously aware of the Protestant fact in Canada.

On June 26, 1877, a young Liberal politician named Wilfrid Laurier addressed the Canadian Club of Quebec. In his remarks he carefully distinguished political Liberalism from the ideological liberalism of Europe that had so often been condemned by the church, emphasizing the dependence of the Canadian party on the innocuous Whig tradition of England. Evidently aware of the ruling of the Holy Office in the previous year, he had taken the precaution of ensuring that a copy of his speech would reach the hands of Bishop Conroy, a special papal emissary then in the province. Rome accepted the proffered olive branch, and at Conroy's behest the bishops issued a circular instructing the clergy to restrict themselves to statements of principle while leaving their application to the conscience of individual voters.[12]

Laurier's appeal has been variously appraised as a master-stroke of practical statesmanship and as a final surrender of the *rouge* position under ultramontane pressure. Both interpretations can be defended, and both have their defenders today. There can be no doubt, on the one hand, that the Liberals were hungry for power, and that their chances seemed negligible so long as as they courted the displeasure of the church. Their reconciliation with the ecclesiastical authorities was thus politically opportune, and in its wake the venerable anticlerical tradition of Louis-Joseph Papineau was to vanish almost without a trace. On the other hand, Laurier and his colleagues do not seem to have betrayed any personal convictions in abandoning the memory of the French Revolution, which in any case had ceased to be relevant to the Quebec situation. Certainly they made possible a gradual disengagement of politics from religion in Quebec and thus eventually in the rest of Canada.

The Liberals reaped no immediate fruits from Laurier's speech, for in the provincial election of 1878 the clergy were almost as active as ever in threatening their supporters with hell fire. Quebec politics took a radically new turn, however, after the Northwest Rebellion of 1885. The Protestants of Ontario, seeing in the rebellion merely one more example of French Catholic disloyalty, vehemently demanded the execution of its leader Louis Riel. French Canadians, who knew that by this time Riel's paranoid visions had estranged him completely from the church, nevertheless bitterly resented an agitation so pointedly directed at them. Riel was tried and convicted, whereupon Ottawa was deluged with contradictory appeals for clemency and for the application of the full rigour of the law. The Macdonald administration, more confident of solid support in Quebec than in Ontario, declined to intervene. The result was to place the ultramontanes, and indeed most of the Quebec clergy, in an awkward position. Despite their disgust with the government they could not bring themselves to support the Liberals. The people of Quebec noted their attitude and began to lose faith in the political judgment of the clergy. Further blows to the ultramontanes were the bestowal of a cardinal's hat on Taschereau by the conciliatory Pope Leo XIII in 1886 and the passing over of Laflèche's Trois-Rivières when Montreal and Ottawa were given the status of archepiscopal sees.

The man who was to take advantage of Quebec's disenchantment was Honoré Mercier, a Liberal who formed the Parti National on a double appeal to loyalties of race and religion. Losing the support of Laurier but gaining that of an ultramontane group known as *castors* or "beavers," he swept into power in the provincial election of 1887. The result was to initiate a concept of French Canada that has survived until the present, although today in a demythologized and secularized form. Church leaders had long recognized the importance of keeping their people isolated from the corrupting influences of Anglo-Saxondom, but they had shrunk from outright French-Canadian nationalism on account of its association with the sceptical and republican tradition of Papineau. Now some of them took the further step of claiming for French Canadians, as holy people with a special mission to maintain the faith, the right to determine their destiny without interference. Mercier was the first premier of Quebec to act like the head of a national state. Laflèche had an even more ambitious dream, that of a sovereign French Canada extending into parts of New England where emigrants had settled.

Thus ultramontanism was in the end to bear strange fruit. It set forth a program of resistance to secularizing tendencies that was to be carried through in part by those whom it regarded as its natural enemies. Many ultramontanes took little satisfaction in the result, and the clergy lost much of their political influence in the process. By 1896, however, when Laurier became prime minister in the first strong Liberal government of Canada since confederation, Quebec had become both in ideal and in reality the theocratic society that ultramontanes had desired and Protestants had feared.

## THE EVANGELICAL PROGRAM

The ultramontanes were matched in crusading zeal by the leaders of what was commonly known among English-speaking Canadians as "evangelical Protestantism." The evangelical strain in Canadian Protestantism represented the convergence of several streams of influence—voluntaryism native and imported, the missionary vigour of the Free Church of Scotland, the militant anti-Romanism of Irish immigrants, above all North American revivalism and the reforming activism that issued from it. Its representatives varied widely in their presentation of the gospel, which ranged from the unrestrained revivalism of some Methodists to the sober insistence on sound doctrine and plain worship of evangelical Anglicans. They also differed, as we shall see, in the rigidity of their moral taboos. Such diversities were outweighed, however, by significant common features that enabled evangelicals to recognize each other without difficulty.

Basic to the evangelical position was insistence on the necessity of a definite experience of personal conversion to Christ. In Canada during the late nineteenth century, most Protestants expected to have such an experience, and zealous attempts were made to cultivate it. In 1884 John E. Hunter, released by the Methodist Conference for evangelistic work, joined Hugh T. Crossley to form a team whose exploits are still recorded in Canadian folk memory. In the following year a mission to Toronto by Dwight L. Moody was sponsored by all leading Protestant denominations,[13] and the *Christian Guardian* regularly reported successful camp meetings. Mass evangelism was by no means a monopoly of Methodists and Baptists. Knox Canada Presbyterian Church, Galt, was the scene of revival in 1869.[14] Even George M. Grant, who was repelled by the sensationalism and fanaticism of some evangelicals, preached a sermon at River John, Nova Scotia, in 1875 that set off a county-wide revival.[15]

To the typical Canadian evangelical, conversion was merely the first step in a process of continued growth in grace towards sanctification or holiness. Methodists had always exhorted their people to seek the "second blessing" of perfect love, and an intensified search for holiness in the United States after the moral slackness of the Civil War period affected Canadians of several denominations. This impulse to sanctity, although essentially religious in motivation, readily overflowed into enthusiasm for the improvement of society. Involving not merely a specialized class of "saints" but ideally the total membership of the church, it encouraged a large measure of lay initiative and leadership. By the time of confederation, indeed, there had emerged in Canada an élite of evangelical laymen whose names could be counted on to appear on the subscription lists of worthy causes and on the boards of directors of such institutions as the YMCA. In Toronto, evangelical Anglicans were leading patrons of education and culture as well as of religion. Notable in Montreal were the Dougall family, Congregational proprietors of the *Witness*, who sank a fortune into the sponsorship of spiritual and moral causes over more than a century. Such men recognized a basic kinship, and some of them even speculated about the possibility of Protestant union.

Evangelicals of all communions shared a vision of a more completely christianized Canada that resembled in some respects the ultramontane dream but differed from it markedly in others. What they sought was essentially a sanctified nation—moral, enlightened, and devoted to the principles of the Protestant Reformation. Between evangelical Anglicans and the leaders of most other Protestant denominations, however, there was a wide and growing divergence with respect to the proper method of implementing this program. Most Anglican evangelicals insisted that the transformation of society could come about only through the conversion of individuals. They encouraged voluntary participation in schemes for social betterment, but resisted attempts to commit the church to any kind of social program. Other Protestant denominations, despite strict taboos against involvement in party politics, moved towards the acceptance of direct responsibility for inculcating patriotism into their members and for imparting a Christian character to national life. Differences in situation help to explain this divergence in approach.

## CONTROVERSIES WITHIN THE CHURCH OF ENGLAND

Evangelical ideas met formidable opposition within the Church of England, where the contrasting churchmanship of the Oxford Movement was steadily gaining ground. Anglo-Catholic views were most conspicuously represented by some of the bishops, but they also affected many of the clergy and were beginning to shape the practice of a number of parishes. Evangelicalism was well entrenched, however, and it was powerfully reinforced by Irish immigration and by its affinity with the mainstream of North American Protestantism. The evangelicals had strong lay support and lay leadership, and a number of wealthy men were prepared to contribute generously to their cause.

By 1867 Anglo-Catholicism had become associated with "advanced" practices of worship, which were sometimes based on antiquarian research and sometimes copied from the baroque style then fashionable in the Roman Catholic Church. Anglican services in Canada had previously been marked by a rather cut-and-dried formality, and had been distinguished from those of other denominations by their inhospitality to emotional display rather than by any lack of plainness. Dramatic ceremony and colourful costume were so unfamiliar, therefore, that even slight innovations were capable of scandalizing many Anglicans. In 1868, for example, the Provincial Synod of Canada condemned the use of candles and wafers.[16] Another bone of contention was the assertion of episcopal claims to authority. Congregations had been accustomed to a large measure of autonomy and resisted attempts to bring them within a centralized diocesan administration. The two issues often coalesced, for hostility to what bishops stood for was easily translated into opposition to episcopal prerogatives as such.

Opponents of Anglo-Catholicism, both within and without the Church of England, tended to regard it as merely a variant of the aggressive Roman

Catholicism that was then represented by the ultramontane movement. Popery and Puseyism were frequently pictured as twin salients of a gigantic pincer movement that threatened to overwhelm Canadian Protestantism and extinguish its liberties. There was, in fact, no such threat. Tractarians were not papists, and in Canada they showed no inclination to seek political influence. Their emphasis on priests and sacraments awakened suspicions, however, which occasioned defections to Rome seemed to confirm. Undoubtedly fears of a Catholic conspiracy were responsible for much of the bitterness of a controversy that might otherwise have been conducted with greater gentility.

Controversy was endemic throughout the 1860s and 1870s, coming to public notice most prominently in a series of local skirmishes. In Halifax a group of evangelical Anglicans had leased a Congregational meeting house named Salem Chapel. Their chaplain, Canon J. C. Cochran, customarily wore a black preaching gown during services. Bishop Hibbert Binney, a high churchman, ordered him to wear a surplice. Cochran refused to take what he described as a first step towards Rome, and in 1866 Binney dismissed him from his post.[17] Ill feeling continued to simmer in Halifax for some time. In 1872 the rector and wardens of St. Paul's Church refused to admit the bishop's staff, although they assured the bishop that he would be welcome if he came without it.[18] Evangelicals also complained of romanizing tendencies in the bishop's organ, the *Church Chronicle*.

A more serious conflict broke out in Victoria in 1872.[19] The Venerable W. S. Reese, guest preacher at the consecration of the cathedral there, took the occasion to commend a measure of formality and ceremonial in the church. Edward Cridge, the evangelical dean of the cathedral, was so horrified that he protested publicly before announcing the next hymn. An acrimonious correspondence ensued between him and his bishop, George Hills, who has been described as a moderate tractarian. Victoria in those days was a somewhat stagnant frontier town, and Cridge as an old Hudson's Bay Company chaplain was very much an insider. Claiming that the bishop had no authority over the local church, he was able to secure the election of a sympathetic body of officeholders and refused to admit not merely the bishop's staff but the bishop. Eventually Hills had to go to court to get his cathedral back, while most of the congregation deserted to organize a Reformed Episcopal parish.

Toronto was the scene of a more prolonged struggle. The evangelicals, with strong lay backing, concentrated throughout on organizing their forces. In 1868 they formed the Evangelical Association of the United Church of England and Ireland. In 1873 this became the Church Association, pledged to maintain the principles of the Protestant Reformation against ritualism and rationalism. Its membership included some of the most prominent men in the city. Chief Justice W. H. Draper was its president, and others who belonged were Robert Baldwin, son of the well-known Reformer, and Sir Daniel Wilson, president of the University of Toronto.

In 1871, evangelicals almost succeeded in carrying through the synod of the diocese of Toronto a regulation giving parishes the right to nominate their own clergy.[20] In 1873, however, they suffered a crushing defeat. Finding themselves handicapped in recruiting clergy by the high church atmosphere of Trinity College, they fought back in 1877 by founding the Protestant Episcopal Divinity School. Renamed Wycliffe College, this institution quickly became a rallying point for the movement. So tense was the situation that for two years Principal James P. Sheraton was forbidden by Bishop A. N. Bethune to officiate at services within the diocese.

Sincerely as it was fought on both sides, the conflict diverted much of the energy of the Church of England from missionary advance and weakened its public influence during a critical period of national development. Anglicans found it necessary to maintain parallel sets of theological colleges, missionary societies (until 1904), hymn books (until 1908), and even Sunday school lessons (until 1920). They had to ensure a balance of forces on boards and committees that often prevented imaginative innovation. They were sometimes compelled by deadlocked elections to pass over men ably qualified for the episcopate. Some Anglican leaders of the time played outstanding roles in Canadian life, but they could obviously have contributed more if they had been less distracted by domestic turmoil. A further result of internal division was to inhibit Anglican participation in the evangelical campaign for the transformation of Canadian life. Unable to make full use of the machinery of the church or to mobilize its entire membership, evangelicals were confirmed in their preference for individual initiative and in their distrust of official pronouncements. It would, in the end, be left to others to stir the social conscience of Anglicanism.

## COMMITTED PROTESTANTS

In most denominations of undiluted Protestantism, the evangelical program encountered little serious resistance. There were some exceptions. The Lutherans, who differed from other Protestant denominations in language and doctrinal emphasis, showed little interest. Many Presbyterians of Kirk background distrusted enthusiasm and resisted attempts to rally them behind evangelical campaigns and moral crusades. Some Baptists under the influence of premillenarianism regarded attempts to improve this world as misguided and even faithless. In both communions there were still a few pockets of hyper-Calvinism where predestination was taken seriously enough to inhibit fervent preaching to the unregenerate. Generally, however, the support of both Baptists and Presbyterians for current evangelical causes could be assumed. The Methodists were, of all communions, most predisposed by their perfectionist theology and their centralized polity to projects of spiritual and moral improvement. Although in the years immediately after confederation they were not too well endowed with imaginative leadership, they found it relatively easy to concentrate their forces. The Congregationalists, while scarcely counting as a denomination, contributed more than their share of dedicated individuals.

Internal controversies within Protestant denominations, although sometimes lively, were seldom on issues that called into question their commitment to an evangelical program. Most of them arose out of conservative resistance to the increasing sophistication of denominational life. The introduction of organs and hymns set off a wave of local upheavals in Presbyterian congregations, especially in those of Free Church background.[21] The Free Methodists, who first appeared in Canada in 1876, had freedom from organs as one of their reasons for existence along with free grace and free pews. Among Methodists, especially the smaller groups, there was also some opposition to the introduction of such "unspiritual" means of raising money as tea meetings.[22] Such objectors did not hinder their denominations from exerting their full weight on issues of national concern.

The declared social aim of the evangelicals was to make Christian principles the foundation of Canadian life. They conceived this aim chiefly in moral rather than political terms, and in practice they stressed the negative more than the positive aspects of morality. The Christian Canada they so often prophesied in glowing terms would be one from which, within the limits of human possibility, sin both public and private had been expelled. The list of moral evils to be eradicated varied somewhat from denomination to denomination. Presbyterians were most disturbed by the desecration of the Lord's day. Methodists inveighed with special force against undesirable literature, in which they commonly included all novels. Baptists took a strong stand against dancing and occasionally passed resolutions against enticing posters in front of theatres. Anglicans were particularly upset by the deeply ingrained Canadian habit of taking the Lord's name in vain. Against all of these practices, however, as well as against the use of tobacco, there was a widespread evangelical sentiment that transcended denominational lines.

## DRIVING OUT EVIL SPIRITS

None of these vices, nor all together, could arouse a fraction of the indignation that was vented on the consumption of booze. Such families as the Gooderhams and the Worts could hold honoured places in evangelical congregations of the Church of England, despite their connection with the distilling industry, and Presbyterians were never unanimous in their condemnation of the bottle. Without question, however, the war against alcohol was the evangelical cause *par excellence* of the late nineteenth century. To be a Methodist or Baptist was almost automatically to be enlisted in it, and every evangelical denomination contributed a quota of warriors.

The temperance movement was no novelty in Canada in 1867. The demon rum had been fought for many years by sermons and resolutions, temperance societies and demands for repressive legislation. As the century advanced, however, there was a distinct tendency to increased rigour. Emphasis gradually shifted from the discipline of church members for drunkenness to education in the evils of drinking, then to agitation for the abolition of the liquor trade. As the years passed, too, temperance steadily overshadowed other concerns, until in the minds of some it superseded faith, hope, and love as the touchstone of Christian discipleship. It is not easy to understand this obsessive concentration, for while drunkenness was always a serious problem in an immature society, it does not seem to have become noticeably more common in the late nineteenth century. One factor may have been the presence in such denominations as the Methodist and Baptist of a growing number of "unconverted" members who ignored disciplinary rules on the subject.[23]

A striking illustration of the trend was the evolution of Methodist attitudes towards beer and wine.[24] In the early decades of the nineteenth century the use of these beverages was acceptable, and brewers were prominent in the Methodist ranks. In later years it became a commonplace of temperance propaganda that alcohol in any form was equally reprehensible, and there was a natural desire to enforce total abstinence on church members. At this point, however, the Methodists were hampered by a conflict of principles. On the one hand they were fervent teetotalers. On the other they were bound to make no alteration in the rules laid down by John Wesley, and although Wesley had forbidden "ardent spirits" he had also expressed concern lest the substitution of tea for beer should sap the manhood of English workers. In the end the Methodists solved their problem neatly by deciding, against all the historical evidence, that "the General Rules are to be understood as forbidding the buying and selling, or using intoxicating liquors as a beverage."[25] In the meantime they had brought about a change in their communion practice. In 1867, the Wesleyans amended a rule requiring the use of port wine to permit the use of wines of Canadian manufacture.[26] By 1883, however, the General Conference of the Methodist Church was urging official boards to use only "the pure, unfermented juice of the grape."[27] Other denominations took the same step, and the introduction of the individual cup almost inevitably followed.

By the late decades of the century, legal prohibition rather than voluntary abstinence was the main objective of the temperance forces.[28] The word "prohibition," like "temperance," has had a great variety of meanings. Prohibition could be local, provincial, or national. It might or might not include beer and wine, and many pious farmers were horrified by any suggestion that it should include cider. Sometimes it implied no more than the abolition of the public bar. Use for medicinal purposes was always allowed. Hence the prohibition movement consisted, in practice, of a series of attempts to secure and enforce legislation of varying and often overlapping types. Most early laws, such as the Dunkin Act of 1864 in the united province of Canada and the federal Scott Act of 1878, merely allowed localities to prohibit the sale of liquor by licence within their bounds. Such statutes were always followed by attempts to secure widespread adoption of their provisions.

Local option seldom achieved the results expected of it. An intensive campaign in 1884 and 1885 induced many Ontario counties to adopt the Scott Act. Within a few years the people of Ontario seem to have worked up a rare thirst, however, and by 1889 every county had voted repeal. Even areas where prohibition was maintained were usually within reach of legal liquor. Most of Newfoundland went dry under the provisions of an act of 1887, but prohibitionists complained that the whole province was supplied from St. John's.[29] The goal accordingly became dominion-wide prohibition. A referendum in 1898 resulted in a substantial majority for prohibition, although voters in Quebec rejected it by a margin of more than four to one. The Laurier government cited the fact that less than one-quarter of registered voters had approved the measure as a justification for taking no action.

Churches as such did not take a prominent part in the early stages of the campaign for prohibition, although they readily expressed their sympathy and ministers were actively involved. The initiative was taken largely by lodges, notably the Sons of Temperance and the Independent Order of Good Templars, and by the Women's Christian Temperance Union. Proponents always felt, however, that they were engaged in a great Christian cause. Probably never in Canadian history have so many lay people, both men and women, engaged themselves so actively in public affairs out of conscious Christian conviction.

In time, especially after organized opposition to prohibition had appeared, the churches began to intervene more directly. The Presbyterian General Assembly in 1886, and the Methodist General Conference in 1890, urged members to vote for candidates who were committed to prohibition.[30] Ministers who had been accustomed to speaking at temperance rallies found it natural to move on to political platforms when the same issue was at stake. Alexander Sutherland, the Methodist missionary secretary, launched in 1888 the short-lived New Party dedicated primarily to the achievement of prohibition.

Although prohibitionists made much of the harm done by liquor, it would be a mistake to regard the movement as essentially negative. Its advocates had in mind not the eradication of a single evil but the formation of a new type of man and thereby the creation of a new type of society. A sober Canada would be an approach to Methodist perfection, an updated version of the Scottish covenanted nation. Prohibition could be regarded either as the keystone of a broad program of reform or as a reform sufficient in itself to usher in utopia. Sutherland included in his party's program universal suffrage for men and women, an elected senate, civil service reform and, more vaguely, "Righteousness and Truth in public affairs as well as in private business, and no compromise with wrong."[31] The Nova Scotia Prohibition party, on the other hand, was content to wait until it should come to power to consider "the minor issues affecting the welfare of the country."[32]

"Let us go up and possess the land, for we are able," was a favourite slogan of temperance organizations. Clearly implied in it was a belief in the validity and possibility of imposing Christian standards of conduct on all Canadians regardless of religious affiliation. This confidence in repression as a method of building a righteous nation gave the whole prohibition movement a somewhat authoritarian flavour. The founding convention of the New Party was open only to those who would signify in advance their adhesion to every plank in its platform.

## CRUSADES IN COLLISION

Ultramontanism and evangelicalism, each the militant expression of an exclusive claim to Christian truth, could scarcely coexist in Canada without colliding. Suspicion between Roman Catholics and Protestants, already a well-known phenomenon of Canadian life, was readily fanned into overt hostility by local irritations or by deliberate agitation. During the late nineteenth century a series of inflammatory incidents marked the hot phases of a continuing cold war. Feelings were embittered in 1869 and 1870 by the Red River incident, the Vatican declaration of papal infallibility, and the Italian occupation of Rome; in 1877 by rioting in Montreal that followed a provocative Orange parade; and again in 1885 by the trial and execution of Louis Riel. There were larger issues, however, from the working out of which such embroilments were merely distractions.

Most Protestants of the period had a very low opinion of the Roman Catholic Church, which they identified with ignorance, semi-pagan religious practice, and hostility to free institutions. They were also deeply suspicious of Roman Catholic motives, regarding the church as a monolithic machine whose priests were all agents committed to a deliberate plan of world domination.[33] To evangelicals who dreamed of the achievement of a Christian Canada, its entrenched position was an offence comparable only to the existence of the nefarious liquor traffic. They deemed it their duty, therefore, not only to resist further encroachments of Roman power but to rescue those who were already under its bondage. It is perhaps significant that

Protestants made no systematic attempt to convert English-speaking Catholics but concentrated their evangelistic efforts in the province of Quebec. Since the aim was not merely to convert individuals but to assert the lordship of Christ over the nation, it was necessary to penetrate the very heart of darkness and destroy the citadel of Antichrist.

The evangelization of French Canada, an enterprise that had received relatively little publicity for some years, became a major issue again in 1875 when Charles Chiniquy commenced a series of missions in Montreal and throughout eastern Canada. At one time a French-Canadian folk hero as the result of his impassioned appeals for temperance, Chiniquy became a Presbyterian in 1860 after being defrocked in Illinois for various irregularities.[34] His stock in trade as a Protestant evangelist was highly coloured exposure of Roman malpractice, which he also offered in many pamphlets and in two enormously popular books.[35] He created a sensation, and riots erupted wherever he went. Chiniquy lacked the stability to lead a significant movement. Some of the French-speaking ministers of Montreal soon tired of his eccentricities, and the long-established Baptist mission at Grande-Ligne reported no unusual accession of converts during the period of his ministry.[36] Undoubtedly, however, his mission stimulated fresh interest among Protestants in the conversion of French Canada. The Presbyterians, who already had an ambitious program of colportage in Quebec, set up a Board of French Evangelization in 1875. The Montreal *Witness* published Chiniquy's addresses in French, and Principal D. H. MacVicar of the Presbyterian College maintained a lifelong interest in the enterprise.

Roman Catholics naturally saw the religious situation from a different point of view. A minority in Canada, and a distinctly smaller one in North America as a whole, they were concerned not to eliminate Protestantism but to ensure the survival of the Catholic faith. They pictured Protestants not as conspirators but as bigots whose insuperable prejudice would suffer no institutions incompatible with their own to exist. They were less afraid of direct attacks than of subtle pressures, especially in English-speaking areas where Protestants set the tone of society. Catholics who were set amid such temptations looked chiefly to the separate school to ensure the continuance of their tradition.[37] Clergy and laity might disagree about the running of such schools, as Archbishop Lynch of Toronto found to his chagrin, but they united to defend them against Protestant attack.[38] Roman Catholics held up their fair treatment of Protestant schools in Quebec, where the Chauveau Bill of 1869 set up two autonomous school systems, as an example to others.

The first encounter on the issue after confederation had results disquieting to Roman Catholics. In 1870 a prominent Methodist, George King, led the Liberals of New Brunswick to power on a promise to give the province a system of free public education in place of the few existing confessional schools. An act passed in 1871 forbade tax-supported schools to teach religion or to continue the use of French as their language of instruction. Roman Catholics protested that the British North America Act guaranteed to religious minorities the educational rights they had enjoyed in 1867, but the Privy Council ruled that this protection applied only to rights conferred by law and that in New Brunswick confessional schools had merely been allowed in practice. An appeal to the Macdonald government for federal disallowance was no more successful. In 1873 many Catholics refused to pay their school rates in protest, and a number of pieces of property, including the carriage of Bishop Sweeny of Saint John, were seized in consequence.[39] Some of the Catholic demands were eventually met in 1875, but meanwhile the Cartier Conservatives and the more accommodating bishops of Quebec had come under severe attack for failing to take a stronger stand in defence of their co-religionists. The New Brunswick school issue, indeed, was the immediate occasion for the formulation of the *programme* of the Union Allet.

Ontario, the heartland of militant Protestantism, was remarkably quiescent for almost twenty years after confederation. Separate schools were constitutionally guaranteed, and few on either side were disposed to test the strength of the other. Catholic schools were chronically impoverished, however, and in 1886 the Liberal government of Oliver Mowat gave an opening to the opposition by amending the law to allow the allocation to separate schools of taxes paid by Catholic tenants and Catholic shareholders in corporations. The Conservative party did not oppose the amendments when they were presented to the legislature, but at the prompting of the Toronto *Mail* it awakened to their enormity in time for the next election. Conservative orators then recalled other evidence of collusion between Mowat and Archbishop Lynch. One item that seemed to justify "trotting out the Protestant horse" was the use for scripture readings in school of the notorious "Ross Bible"[40] from which certain passages had been expurgated because Archbishop Lynch had suggested that they would be offensive to Roman Catholics. A Protestant trustee was quoted as having exclaimed at a board meeting, "We want the whole d——d Bible, and nothing but the Bible!"[41] With such ammunition, the Conservatives fought successive elections in 1886, 1890, and 1894 on the cry of "no popery."

The Jesuit Estates agitation of the late 1880s raised no major substantive issue but created an immense furor. The government of Honoré Mercier, desiring to erase the stigma of anticlericalism from Quebec Liberalism, agreed in 1888 to compensate the Jesuit order for property that had been confiscated by the crown after its temporary suppression in 1773. The measure was controversial in Quebec.[42] Protestants had no particular grievance, for their schools received increased grants in return. Archbishop Taschereau believed that he had a grievance, however, arguing that the property of a suppressed order should have reverted to the church as a whole. Such subtleties were lost on most Protestants, for whom the calling in of the pope to adjudicate among rival Catholic factions raised the spectre of imminent papal control of the whole of Canada. Militant Protestants rallied under the leadership of D'Alton McCarthy, who unsuccessfully demanded federal disallowance of the Mercier bill. In 1889 Ontario supporters formed the Equal Rights Association, with Principal William Caven of Knox College, Toronto, as chairman. This was soon succeeded by the Protestant Protective Association, a secret society of American origin that openly sought to drive Roman Catholics out of public life.[43] By this time, however, the separate school question held the centre of the stage in Ontario once more.

The most celebrated of all Canadian religious struggles was precipitated in 1890 by the Liberal government of Thomas Greenway in Manitoba. The newly elected administration swept away the dual school system that had prevailed in the province since its formation, replacing it with a single nondenominational structure and withdrawing the right of instruction in minority languages. Protestant settlers had complained against denominational schools ever since they had become a substantial majority in the province, but the agitation that led to their abolition was imported by McCarthy as an overflow of Ontario anti-papal zeal. Feelings in what had been a relatively tranquil province were soon embittered by the controversy. Archbishop Taché felt betrayed, arguing that minority rights were guaranteed by the Manitoba Act of 1870 and insisting that Greenway had solemnly undertaken before his election to make no change in educational arrangements.[44] Machray and other Anglican leaders, who favoured parallel systems of denominational schools, saw considerable justice in his position. Spokesmen for militant Protestantism, on the other hand, regarded any interference with the will of the majority as evidence of sinister manipulation behind the scenes.

Opposition to the provincial authorities proving futile, the Roman Catholics appealed to the Conservative federal government for remedial legislation. Prime Minister Sir Mackenzie Bowell, who was a prominent Orangeman, promised this. Wilfrid Laurier, the Roman Catholic leader of the Liberal party, expressed sympathy but declared his unwillingness to intervene in a provincial matter. Laurier won the election and in 1897 arranged the compromise customary in such cases. Some measure of relief was afforded to the Catholics of Manitoba, and Pope Leo XIII advised the faithful in the encyclical *Affari vos* not to refuse "partial satisfaction of their claims."

## THE LIMITS OF RELIGIOUS CONTROVERSY

Despite their inability to see much good in one another, ardent spokesmen for the two religious traditions appear in retrospect to have had a great deal in common. They both insisted on the enforcement of rigid moral standards, the sabbatarianism of evangelical Protestants finding its counterpart in a ban by the relatively moderate Taschereau on Sunday excursions by boat or train.[45] Roman Catholics rivalled Protestants in their commitment to temperance, if not to total prohibition. Lynch exacted from candidates for the priesthood a vow of abstinence for several years after ordination,[46] and Bourget in a letter to Chiniquy during the latter's Roman days had deplored "the harm that the pretended moderate use of strong drink does in Canada."[47] *Programmistes* were as ardent as evangelicals in exposing public scandals, even when the Conservatives were the culprits as in the Tanneries affair of 1874. Protestant and Roman Catholic leaders alike were hostile to the advent of organized labour, which they interpreted as a new form of corporate selfishness. George Brown invoked religious principles in opposing a typographers' strike in 1872, although his position as one of the employers concerned should warn us against regarding his views as typical of Canadian Protestantism. In 1884, when the Knights of Labour had gained some support among Quebec workers, Taschereau secured from the Holy Office a ruling that those who took part in their activities committed grave sin.[48]

Such similarities in program reflected an even more fundamental resemblance in motivation and temper between Protestant and Roman Catholic zealots. Both were animated by the crusading sense of mission that permeated the church in the nineteenth century, and both assumed the mores of an agrarian society to be normative for a Christian nation. Even the ultimate aims of the two groups were not altogether different. Widely as they disagreed in their theoretical view of the relation of the church to the state, both expected governments to legislate in accordance with Christian principles and neither hesitated to apply pressure when they failed to do so.

For both contenders, the nineteenth century ended ambiguously. Ultramontane attempts to punish Laurier at the polls in 1896 for his failure to intervene in the Manitoba school crisis failed ignominiously, while the prohibitionists were able to derive little more satisfaction from their pyrrhic victory in the referendum of 1898. In both cases, however, success more than outweighed failure. The ultramontanes had eliminated religious liberalism as a credible alternative for the province of Quebec. The evangelicals had destroyed the respectability of alcohol in the rest of Canada. Both achievements would endure almost to the present.

In the course of achieving these victories and sustaining these defeats the churches provoked suspicions that would ultimately contribute to the secularization of Canadian life. Their aggressive campaigns kept the nation constantly agitated, while their quarrels seriously threatened the fragile bonds that held it together. Public men found that concessions to one denomination inevitably led to demands from others and drew the obvious conclusion that the safest course was to keep as clear as possible of religious issues. The Manitoba School Act, however unfair it might seem to Catholics, was the result of a genuine fear of papal aggression that extreme ultramontane claims had done much to foster. Protestant leaders, after spearheading this attack on Roman Catholic influence, would in turn find the credibility of their campaign for the christianization of Canadian life seriously damaged by the anticlerical suspicion that resulted. Similar effects were already evident in British Columbia, where a government that was determined not to become embroiled in sectarian struggles forbade clergymen to become either teachers or trustees in the public school system. John Robson, a Presbyterian who more than any other man shaped British Columbian school laws, did not intend to exclude Christian influence from education. The ultimate result, however, was to nourish an attitude of religious neutrality that could easily pass over into hostility to the church and its programs.

Looking back over the record of controversy, one might wonder how Canada held together through the first decades of confederation. A religious atmosphere in which Protestants could adopt Chiniquy as a star performer and in which saintly Oblates could find no good word to say about Protestant missionaries who showed zeal remarkably similar to their own contained extremely explosive possibilities. Even within denominations, constructive dialogue was made difficult by Protestant fanatics who deluged with letters of abuse any minister who ventured to query the wisdom of total prohibition and by Roman counterparts who did not scruple to call the Archbishop of Quebec a bad Catholic. Fortunately for the nation, if not for religious absolutism, there were also powerful forces aiding coexistence.

Within the churches themselves there were some men who sought mutual understanding, although their voices were not always heard above the tumult. In Halifax, Archbishop Connolly and George M. Grant worked together for confederation and maintained a close personal friendship even when they differed on ecclesiastical issues.[49] In Manitoba, largely through the mediation of Archbishop Machray, the clergy of all denominations respected each other throughout the Red River troubles and for some years were able to work together in harmony. At Quebec, Archbishop Taschereau represented a resilient tradition of nonpartisan Catholicism. It was beyond the power of such men to prevent the sectarian temper from occasionally getting out of hand. Grant could not carry a Presbyterian general assembly against the fiery evangelical MacVicar on an issue that had already inflamed passions, the Winnipeg accord did not survive the educational controversies of the 1890s, and Taschereau was helpless to curb ultramontane hysteria in such crises as the Guibord affair. No men were more highly respected in their denominations than Grant, Machray and Taschereau, however, and along with others of like mind they represented a leavening influence of considerable significance.

A fair portion of credit for Canada's survival must go to public men who recognized that a country composed of various religious and ethnic groups cannot be governed without compromise. The motives of conciliatory politicians were not always admirable, often arising out of a mere desire to construct a coalition of interests that would ease their way to power. George Brown strained the credibility of his ultra-Protestant profession when he supported separate schools in New Brunswick to embarrass a Conservative government, and the Quebec bishops displayed little courage when they played the issue down to avoid embarrassing the same government. Nevertheless, such incongruities helped to make Canada a viable nation.

Most telling of all, perhaps, has been the silent resistance of Canadians to divisive forces. If appeals to race and religion have been a conspicuous feature of Canadian politics, their failure to produce the dividends expected of them has been equally striking. Quebec Liberals may have owed their crushing defeat in 1875 to clerical opposition, but they took a worse beating in 1881 when the clergy were silent. The Conservatives of Ontario relied on the "no popery" cry over three elections. They lost all three of them, and their appeal to religious passions may have cost them as many votes as it gained. The federal election of 1896 furnished some striking examples of apparent indifference to religious issues. The Manitoba school question was probably the chief issue of the campaign. The Conservatives promised relief to the Roman Catholics, while the Liberal platform conceded Manitoba's right to settle its own problems. When the votes were counted, however, the Conservatives had taken a majority of the seats in Manitoba while the Liberals had swept Quebec. Canadians of the time evidently deserved more credit for tolerance than they have sometimes received, or perhaps they took their party loyalties more seriously than their religious affiliations.

Appeals to religious prejudice, long a stock in trade of Canadian politics, tapered off rapidly towards the end of the nineteenth century. Ontario Conservatives, stunned by an unexpected by-election defeat in the Protestant city of London, dropped their campaign against separate schools overnight. Soon the parties were accusing one another of keeping old animosities alive, and before long even this indirect appeal to prejudice had lost its effectiveness. A similar truce followed the federal election of 1896. However dissatisfied both religious groups may have been with the compromise of 1897, neither church leaders nor politicians had the stomach for a continuation of strife. Many of the controversies of the nineteenth century had already become obsolete, although as yet few Canadians were aware of their demise.

NOTES TO CHAPTER FOUR

1. W. A. Foster, *Canada First; or, Our New Nationality* (Toronto: Adam, Stevenson, 1871), pp. 29-30.

2. H. F. May, *Protestant Churches and Industrial America* (New York: Harper, 1949), p. 44.

3. Cuthbert Butler, *The Vatican Council, 1869-1870* (London: Collins Fontana Library, 1962), p. 402.

4. In *Le Journal de Trois-Rivières*, 20 avril 1871.

5. "un groupe de laïcs plus ultramontains que le pape, prétendant accaparer l'Eglise et interpréter ses paroles, et ne craignant pas, au besoin, de faire la leçon aux évêques." Robert Rumilly, *Histoire de la Province de Québec*, Vol. III, p. 86.

6. See Philippe Sylvain, "Quelques aspects de l'antagonisme libéral-ultramontain au Canada français," *Recherches sociographiques*, Vol. VIII, No. 3 (septembre-décembre 1967), pp. 275-298.

7. See Théophile Hudon, sj, *L'Institut Canadien et l'Affaire Guibord* (Montreal: Beauchemin, 1938).

8. Elzéar Paquin, *La conscience catholique outragée et les droits de l'intelligence violés par les deux défenseurs de l'Université Laval, sa Grâce Monseigneur Taschereau, archevêque de Québec, et sa Grandeur Monseigneur Fabre, évêque de Montréal* (Montreal: 1881).

9. Lettre pastorale (No. 47) des évêques de la province ecclésiastique de Québec, 22 septembre 1875, Henri Têtu and C.-O. Gagnon, *Mandements, Lettres Pastorales et Circulaires des Evêques de Québec*, nouvelle série, Vol. I, pp. 320-336.

10. *Ibid.*, n.s., Vol. II, pp. 268-271.

11. E. E. Y. Hales, *Pio Nono* (London: Eyre, 1954), p. 146.

12. Circulaire (No. 68) des évêques de la province ecclésiastique de Québec au clergé de la dite province, 11 octobre 1877. Têtu and Gagnon, *op. cit.*, n.s., Vol. II, pp. 44-49.

13. *Canadian Methodist Magazine*, Vol. XXI (1885), pp. 75-77.

14. J. A. Johnston, "Factors in the Formation of the Presbyterian Church in Canada, 1875," p. 68.

15. W. L. Grant and Frederick Hamilton, *Principal Grant*, p. 171.

16. Journal of the 4th Session of the Provincial Synod of the United Church of England and Ireland in Canada, 1868, p. 56.

17. *Correspondence between the Bishop of Nova Scotia and the Reverend Canon Cochran, M.A., touching the dismissal of the latter from the pastoral charge of Salem Chapel, Halifax, N.S.* (Halifax: Macnab and Shaffer, 1866).

18. *The Staff Question, Letters of the Bishop of Nova Scotia and the Rev. Mr. Fitzgerald's replies thereto, etc., etc., etc.* (Charlottetown: Laird and Mitchell, 1873).

19. F. A. Peake, *The Anglican Church in British Columbia*, pp. 79-84.

20. Spencer Ervin, *The Political and Ecclesiastical History of the Anglican Church of Canada* (Ambler, Pa.: Trinity Press, 1967), p. 57.

21. For a detailed account of the organ controversy, see Fred Rennie, "Spiritual Worship on a Carnal Instrument," M.Th. thesis, Knox College, Toronto, 1969.

22. A. Burnside, "The Canadian Wesleyan Methodist New Connexion Church, 1841-1874," pp. 164-165.

23. S. D. Clark, *Church and Sect in Canada* (Toronto: University of Toronto Press, 1948), pp. 255, 258.

24. For a detailed account, see C. R. Wood, "The Historical Development of the Temperance Movement in Methodism in Canada," B.D. thesis, Victoria University, 1958.

25. The Doctrine and Discipline of the Methodist Church (Toronto: 1886), p. 16.

26. Minutes of the 44th Annual Conference of the Wesleyan Methodist Church in Canada, 1867, p. 78.

27. Journal of Proceedings of the First United General Conference of the Methodist Church, 1883, p. 156.

28. For a full account of the movement, see Ruth E. Spence, *Prohibition in Canada* (Toronto: The Ontario Branch of the Dominion Alliance, 1919).

29. *Ibid.*, p. 496.

30. Journal of Proceedings of the 3rd General Conference of the Methodist Church, 1890, p. 341; Acts and Proceedings of the 13th General Assembly of the Presbyterian Church in Canada, 1886, p. 59. Such resolutions, although usually unanimous in the Methodist Church, were not always so among Presbyterians.

31. Spence, *op. cit.*, p. 143.

32. *Ibid.*, p. 149.

33. E. R. Norman traces the image of Roman Catholicism current among Protestants of both Canada and the United States to English sources. *The Conscience of the State in North America* (Cambridge: Cambridge University Press, 1968), p. 90.

34. For a well documented, although highly unsympathetic account, see Marcel Trudel, *Chiniquy*, 2nd edition (Trois-Rivières: Editions du Bien Public, 1955).

35. *The Priest, the Woman and the Confessional*, first published in French in Montreal in 1875, eventually in at least fifty editions in many languages. *Fifty Years in the Church of Rome*, first published in 1885 and also issued in many editions. For a full bibliography, see Trudel, *op. cit.*, pp. xvii-xxiii.

36. Theodore Lafleur, "A Brief Historical Sketch of the Grande Ligne Mission from its Beginning in 1835 to 1900," *Baptist Year Book*, 1900, pp. 302-303.

37. During the same period, Roman Catholic schools in the United States multiplied for the same reasons. J. H. Nichols, *History of Christianity, 1650-1950*, p. 202.

38. See Franklin A. Walker, *Catholic Education and Politics in Ontario* (Toronto: Thos. Nelson and Sons, 1964), Chapters 2, 3.

39. Robert Rumilly, *Histoire des Acadiens*, pp. 753, 765.

40. George W. Ross was minister of education in the Mowat government.

41. *The Globe*, February 8, 1886.

42. For the immediate background of the controversy, see Roy C. Dalton, *The Jesuit Estates Question, 1760-1888* (Toronto: University of Toronto Press, 1968), Chapters 9, 10.

43. James T. Watt, "Anti-Catholic Nativism in Canada," *Canadian Historical Review*, Vol. XLVIII, No. 1 (March 1967), pp. 45-58.

44. A. A. Taché, *Une page de l'histoire des écoles de Manitoba*, p. 89; quoted in Paul Benoit, *Vie de Mgr Taché*, Vol. II, p. 641.

45. Mandement (No. 91), 26 avril 1880. Têtu and Gagnon, *op. cit.*, n.s., Vol. II, p. 207.

46. H. C. McKeown, *The Life and Labors of the Most Rev. John Joseph Lynch, D.D., Cong. Miss., First Archbishop of Toronto* (Montreal and Toronto: James A. Sadlier, 1886). p. 261.

47. Letter of September 26, 1846; quoted in Trudel, *op. cit.*, p. 76.

48. Têtu and Gagnon, *op. cit.*, n.s., Vol. II, p. 455.

49. Grant and Hamilton, *op. cit.*, p. 81.

# FIVE

## The Dawn of Canada's Century

A disappointment to its citizens during the first three decades after confederation, Canada seemed by the end of the nineteenth century to be at
last on the verge of national fulfilment. A severe depression that had lasted
throughout the early 1890s gave way to unprecedented prosperity. A long-
standing drift of youth to the United States was reversed as American settlers
took up homesteads in the Canadian west. The Klondike gold rush of 1898
added a touch of colour that helped Canadians to believe in their future.
Between 1890 and 1910, according to a reputable estimate, the gross national
product increased by 122.7 per cent.[1] Nor was optimism founded on Canadian developments alone. To many English Canadians these were local manifestations of a wider imperial destiny that promised vicarious greatness to
loyal dominions. The diamond jubilee of Queen Victoria in 1897, the sense
of kinship inspired by participation in the South African War, and the
popularity with the public of schemes for imperial federation all became
linked in imagination with the prospects before Canada. In this interlude of
euphoria, when hitherto staid citizens spoke of breathing ozone rather than
common air, Prime Minister Laurier predicted without tongue in cheek that
the twentieth would be "Canada's century." The churches took advantage
of the general optimism to launch successful "Twentieth Century Funds"
for missionary expansion at home and abroad.

### THE CHALLENGE OF CANADIAN GROWTH

Although Canadian development was furthered by a new sense of purpose
that came with the Laurier administration, by the inauguration of a definite
policy to sell Canada to potential immigrants and by the adoption of imperial preference and penny postage, it came about mainly through natural
causes. Business was good in the United States under McKinley, and prosperity followed its usual course across the border. The world price of gold
rose, and with it that of natural products including wheat. The building of

larger ocean-going ships reduced freight rates and opened new markets to Canadian goods. Beginning in 1899, a cycle of wet years brought good harvests to the west. Sophisticated techniques of farming prairie land had already been developed, and in 1908 the introduction of the rapidly maturing Marquis wheat pushed the limits of agriculture farther north. Most significantly of all, the free land of the American west had been taken up and Canada's position as a second choice began to pay off.

The deluge of settlers for which western Canada had waited so long arrived at last; in the decade from 1901 to 1911 more than a million people came to the three prairie provinces. Unlike earlier arrivals, most of them were newcomers to Canada. In 1896 less than 17,000 immigrants had entered Canada. the smallest number since confederation. In 1901 more than 50,000 arrived, however, and in 1906 more than 200,000. Most of them spoke English, having come from the United States or Britain. More conspicuous, however, were those who came from countries of which most Canadians had scarcely heard and brought customs with which they were completely unfamiliar. In the 1880s the passion for emigration had shifted from northern to eastern Europe, and it was from the latter area that Canada most readily attracted settlers. Many immigrants were members of religious minorities in Europe who sought greater freedom in the new world,[2] often sectarians such as Mennonites and Doukhobors who had proved impossible to assimilate even in their countries of origin. In their eagerness to people the country, the authorities sold large blocks of land to religious and ethnic groups who wished to maintain their way of life, thus giving added visibility to the intrusion of alien customs. Most conspicuous of all were Ukrainians from what was then the Austrian province of Galicia, "stalwart peasants in sheepskin coats" whom Interior Minister Clifford Sifton regarded as ideal settlers.[3] More often than not, contemporary descriptions of immigrants referred to them.

During the same decade, Canadians began to feel the effects of modern urbanism. Between 1901 and 1911 the proportion living in cities and towns rose from 37.5 to 45.4 per cent of the population. More significant, however, was the appearance of cities in which the opportunities of urban living became real and its problems acute. Many of the new city dwellers were immigrants, so that the problems of urbanism and of assimilation often coalesced. Others came from small towns and from the countryside, accelerating a process of rural decline that many deplored but few sought to remedy.

The initial reaction of the churches to the new situation was one of concern and even alarm. Canadian church life had always been competitive, and immigration altered the denominational balance. Roman Catholics could justifiably feel threatened, for among the immigrants their proportion was distinctly lower than in the existing Canadian population. Protestants had their worries too, for movements of population were bringing Catholics and

Orthodox into areas where they had hitherto been rare and many of the Protestant immigrants belonged to denominations other than those which had dominated the Canadian scene. Equally upsetting were changes in the ethnic composition of the nation. All Canadian churches had deep roots in national traditions, and the preservation of ethnic patterns often took on quasi-religious connotations. Protestants—Methodists and Presbyterians almost as much as Anglicans—identified their mission with that of the British peoples. Among Roman Catholics a delicate balance between French and Irish leadership was upset by the intrusion of new ethnic groups.

An even more serious effect of immigration and urbanism was to undermine the rural values which the churches had so painstakingly cultivated. Just when Canadians were settling into approved patterns of belief and behaviour, it seemed, they would be severely tempted to depart from them. Protestants were aghast to discover that continental Europeans were indifferent to their taboos against liquor and Sunday labour and that under urban conditions native Canadians often lost their scruples on these matters. Roman Catholics were troubled by the anticlericalism of many eastern Europeans and by the secularism that readily developed in the cities. The ideals most seriously threatened were, indeed, precisely those of the evangelicals and ultramontanes who had done so much to set the nation's standards. It was generally agreed that the peril was greatest in British Columbia because of the presence of orientals who were regarded as impossible to assimilate,[4] because of official toleration of gambling and prostitution, and because of a secular spirit bequeathed by early speculators. Even in the Maritimes, however, there were complaints that tourism was destroying the sanctity of the sabbath.[5] John Stark warned the Baptist Convention of Ontario and Quebec, "All that is choicest and best in our national life is trembling in the balance."[6]

On the other hand, the churches welcomed the new opportunities for service that were inherent in national growth. Having sent men and women to the ends of the earth in the name of Christ, they were not likely to recoil from a similar challenge at home. As on many occasions in the past, they seemed to have neither the resources nor the skills required for the new situation. They had successfully overcome obstacles before, however, and they would only gradually discover that their familiar prescriptions were not always specific to twentieth-century ills.

## THE CHURCHES AND IMMIGRATION

The most familiar aspect of the challenge, and the one most successfully met, was that of reaching immigrants whose mother tongue was English or French. The physical task was colossal, for in the western provinces and in northern Ontario the population grew at a rate unprecedented in either

Canada or the United States. The churches had the great advantage of being on the ground already and of having at their disposal the institutions of an orderly society. Their problem was that of keeping pace with the progress of settlement, and as a network of railway branch lines fanned out over the prairies they found their resources taxed to the limit. The churches were no longer able to anticipate railway construction as in earlier days, and they never succeeded in occupying all of the hinterland. A survey conducted just after the First World War indicated that half of the children in rural Alberta were growing up in entire ignorance of the Christian religion.[7] In the towns and villages the churches became centres of community life, while students and other lay preachers ranged the countryside on horseback to provide energetic if not always experienced leadership.

The more Protestant groups, having the advantage of strong ties with eastern Canada, mainly continued their earlier methods. Whatever their official polity, they relied heavily on missionary superintendents whose knowledge of their territory gave them practically autocratic authority. The Presbyterians, who extended Robertson's territory in 1890 to include British Columbia, benefited from the foundations he had laid and made even more rapid progress after his death in 1902. Between that year and 1910 the number of their western missions increased from 258 to 503.[8] The Methodists did not fare so well, receiving fewer members by immigration than in the years of Ontario settlement and having to contend with a growing shortage of ministers. In all western provinces their proportion of the population fell dramatically despite a reorganization of mission work in 1902. The same was true of the Baptists, although they achieved greater continuity of leadership than in the past and began to consolidate their position.

The Anglicans, who increased rapidly in numbers through immigration, had great difficulty in securing support for their enterprise. The Society for the Propagation of the Gospel, which was responsible for aid to colonial missions, initiated in 1896 a policy of gradual withdrawal on the reasonable assumption that the new general synod would rally the support of the whole Canadian church behind the western provinces. Then in 1902 the Church Missionary Society began to reduce its grants to native work. Unfortunately the Missionary Society of the Canadian Church was founded only in 1902 and was becoming effective only by about 1905. During the most crucial years of western development, therefore, the Church of England had to contemplate retrenchment rather than advance. In 1905 Bishop J. A. Newnham of Saskatchewan reported "churches closed, missions vacant, the support of your clergy promised by the people, yet withheld."[9] During the same period, the Rev. G. E. Lloyd took charge of a group of English settlers who had been brought by a well intentioned clerical promoter to the area around what is now Lloydminster and established about thirty-five centres of worship among them.[10] Towards the end of the decade English churchmen, becoming aware of the magnitude of the crisis, began to sponsor a variety of projects. The most important of these was the Archbishops' Western Canada Fund, set up in 1909, which sponsored railway missions and built churches and vicarages that were affectionately known as Canterbury Cathedrals and Lambeth Palaces.[11] Another important innovation was the inauguration in 1908, on Lloyd's initiative, of Sunday School by Post.[12]

The Roman Catholic Church was prepared to serve French-speaking immigrants to the west, but ill-equipped for those of any other language. The church in Ontario was still in the pioneer stage and had few surplus priests for export. Even those who might have been available were less than eager to serve under French-Canadian bishops, and they objected strenuously to such French customs as the wearing of the *soutane* or cassock at all times. Archbishop Adélard Langevin of St. Boniface was able to point out in 1913 that in eighteen years he had tripled the number of priests in his archdiocese and established twenty-five educational institutions, but of 164 priests only nine had English as their mother tongue.[13] Archbishop Fergus P. McEvay of Toronto had already taken steps to remedy this situation. In 1908 the Catholic Church Extension Society was founded in that city, and in 1913 St. Augustine's Seminary at Scarborough began to train priests for service in all parts of Canada.[14] The church in western Canada soon began to lose its exclusively French appearance.

Work among immigrants of nationalities other than British or French called for new approaches by all churches. The first need was to welcome them to Canada and to help them to establish themselves. Most denominations maintained chaplains at ports of entry. Neil McNeil, Roman Catholic archbishop of Vancouver from 1910 to 1912, set up a Catholic Immigrants' Information Office in that city.[15] At Winnipeg a Catholic Immigrant Aid Society was under the direction of the Oblates, who despite their generally French orientation were tireless in their efforts to reach newcomers.[16] By the beginning of the first war most churches had established regular procedures for meeting immigrants and helping them through their initial period of adjustment.

All churches undertook pastoral work in immigrant communities. A number of them did so in the normal course of seeking to provide for their own members. Lutheran work came almost entirely within this category. Its direction was at first almost exclusively in American hands, but the foundation of a Lutheran seminary at Edmonton in 1913 made possible the recruiting of Canadian pastors. Most Roman Catholics of western Canada also came from the continent of Europe. Poles were the largest group, but St. Peter's Abbey at Muenster, Saskatchewan, became the spiritual centre of an important colony of German settlers. The Presbyterians had a natural constituency among the Dutch and the Hungarians. The Baptists, who were represented in most European countries as a result of energetic proselytizing in the nineteenth century, had a German-speaking minister in Manitoba by 1885 and were soon working with several nationalities. Several denominations became involved in work with Chinese and East Indians through contacts that had been made by missionaries abroad. Churches did not limit their efforts, however, to groups with which they had a natural ecclesiastical affinity. The first Methodist pastorate among immigrants was in a Ukrainian community in 1901. Congregationalists specialized in work among Swedes and Germans. The Anglicans, although heavily committed to Indian and Eskimo missions, provided teachers for non-Anglo-Saxon areas through the Fellowship of the Maple Leaf. The Japanese deserve a special word. Almost alone among immigrant groups, they took the initiative throughout in organizing their own churches.

In many cases the churches found the immigrants unresponsive to their pastoral approach, or else they discovered that people unaccustomed to Canadian ways had needs that were not met merely by the provision of church services. They were soon drawn, therefore, into more institutional types of work. In rural areas the crying need was for hospitals, since immigrant communities offered few financial inducements to doctors. These led to contacts with families, and as a result school homes were established to teach children English and prepare them for life in Canada. In the cities, where unskilled immigrants naturally drifted into slums, All Peoples' Missions were founded. The prototype of these, and the laboratory in which methods of approach were worked out, was the Methodist All Peoples' Mission in north Winnipeg. J. S. Woodsworth, who loved the immigrants although he deplored their attitudes and habits, was its superintendent from 1907 to 1913.[17] Among Roman Catholics a similar function was performed by Friendship Houses, which were founded by the Baroness de Hueck on the advice of Archbishop McNeil and were run, contrary to custom, by lay sisters.[18]

The Protestant churches embarked on a large-scale missionary enterprise among immigrants of varied nationalities without a clear view of what they were attempting to accomplish. At least three motives drew them into it. The first, and perhaps the most powerful, was a simple recognition of the needs of strangers in a strange land. Another was a natural desire to offer the gospel to those who seemed to be without it, a category within which Protestants tended to include Roman Catholics and Orthodox. A third motive, which became increasingly powerful as naturalization bestowed the franchise on more and more immigrants, was a desire to implant Canadian ideals of citizenship. "Canadianism" became a favourite word in Protestant circles, and it invariably implied both loyalty to British institutions and conformity to Victorian moral standards.

Protestant leaders regarded these aims as complementary, for they believed that evangelism and Canadianization were forms of service to the immigrants.[19] In practice it was no easy matter to keep the three in balance. Churches learned that they had to refrain from proselytizing if they were to make Canadianism palatable to immigrants who already had religious affiliations, and that even their offers of service were unacceptable when ulterior motives were suspected. On the whole they came down on the side of citizenship, while gradually learning to value the cultural contributions the newcomers could make. The distance they travelled between 1909 and 1917 is marked by the difference between Ralph Connor's well-intentioned but patronizing portrayal in *The Foreigner* and W. T. Gunn's genuinely appreciative attitude in *His Dominion*.[20] The results of Protestant effort cannot readily be assessed in terms of success or failure. Although they gained relatively few members for their churches, they eased the way of many immigrants into Canadian society.

To Roman Catholics the social assimilation of immigrants was of less concern than their harmonious integration into church life. Until 1896 most Catholics of western Canada were French-speaking, and so was the entire hierarchy that governed them. The new cosmopolitan immigration completely altered the ethnic balance. The French remained the largest single group, but the Catholic community ceased to be predominantly French. Catholic immigrants, relatively more numerous than their counterparts in the major Protestant communions, were proportionately more vocal in ecclesiastical affairs. Bishops soon found that the only remedy for local contention was to set up separate parishes on ethnic lines.

The most controversial issue was the composition of the hierarchy in the west. When new ethnic strains appeared, it was still possible for a time to justify the French monopoly with the argument that English-speaking Catholics were only one of many minorities within the church. It soon became evident, however, that the newcomers were learning English rather than French. The Irish of Winnipeg began to agitate for a bishop of their own, and the apostolic delegate Mgr Sbarretti was convinced that the west was destined to be an English-speaking area.[21] In 1912 an English-speaking bishop was appointed to the newly erected see of Calgary, and in 1915 a long struggle ended in the division of the archdiocese of St. Boniface and the appointment of A. A. Sinnott as archbishop of Winnipeg. The ultimate result was to secure harmony at the price of considerable ethnic fragmentation. Greater Winnipeg has now the unusual distinction of being the seat of three Catholic archbishops, including one of the Ukrainian rite.

The Ukrainians constituted a special problem that attracted the attention of several denominations. Most of them were Greek Catholics, owing allegiance to the pope but accustomed to a married priesthood and a modified Orthodox liturgy. Few of their own clergy were able to follow them to Canada, for in 1894 a Vatican ruling had forbidden married priests outside

Europe. The clergy who were available, being mainly French-speaking and entirely of the Latin rite, were unacceptable to many of the settlers. The Canadian church authorities did what they could. Father Lacombe sought single Ukrainian priests in Austria, and several Latin priests were permitted to change their rite. Despite such exertions the Ukrainian community remained dissatisfied, and its future ecclesiastical allegiance was very much in doubt.

This confused situation was the setting for an unusual experiment on the part of the Presbyterian Church in Canada. Shortly after the turn of the century, a number of disaffected Ukrainians in Manitoba turned for help to an American breakaway group led by an eccentric bishop named Seraphim. J. A. Carmichael, the local missionary superintendent, arranged for the Presbyterians to sponsor this Independent Greek Church.[22] Its leader, Ivan Bodrug, was a man of evangelical sympathies who had already studied some theology at Manitoba College. The church was organized on Presbyterian lines but was allowed to retain an expurgated Orthodox liturgy. At one time it had fifty-one missionaries and seemed about to win the allegiance of most Ukrainian settlers. Neither the Presbyterian authorities nor the Ukrainian priests, however, had clearly determined whether the Independent Greek Church was to represent a modified Orthodoxy or merely a first step towards Presbyterianism. After Carmichael's death the enterprise broke down, and in 1913 the Presbyterian Church absorbed its protegé. Meanwhile in 1912 Nykyta Budka had been appointed as a Catholic bishop of the eastern rite,[23] and Protestantism soon ceased to be an option for the Ukrainian community.

## THE CHURCHES AND URBANIZATION

In swollen cities the churches sought to adapt their appeal to people who themselves were adjusting to unaccustomed styles of living. They had a fair measure of success. The adult Bible class was in its heyday, popular preachers drew crowds to downtown churches, and the more evangelistic denominations were pleased with the success of a revivalist mission to Toronto by Torrey and Alexander in 1906. The main appeal of such methods was to single young men and women from churchgoing homes in the country, and one of their primary purposes was to help these young people to maintain their faith and their standards among the temptations of the city. It was already clear, however, that the regular ministrations of the church were failing to attract or to help large new classes of city-dwellers. For these it would be necessary to devise new approaches.

The poor had always weighed heavily on the Christian conscience, and during this period the proliferation of slums accentuated their squalor and their isolation. Since they did not feel at home in the regular fellowship groups of the conventional churches, their needs seemed to call for the creation of special institutions of rescue. This type of work was no novelty to Roman Catholics, who had a venerable tradition of organized charity. Toronto had a House of Providence by 1857, and the Catholics of Quebec had long maintained orphanages and homes for the aged. D. J. Macdonnell, whom we have met as an alleged heretic, was one of the first Protestant ministers to take a special interest in the working class. He was already planning educational programs for them in the 1870s, and in 1890 he founded an institute at St. Andrew's Church, Toronto, that featured night classes and a reading room as well as a savings bank.[24] In 1894 a gift from Hart A. Massey enabled the Methodists to open the Fred Victor Mission in Toronto,[25] and in the early years of the century such institutions multiplied.

Varying traditions of social work had already been established in more highly industrial countries, and Canadian denominations tended to adopt the patterns with which they were most familiar. Presbyterians looked to the work of Thomas Chalmers and Norman Macleod in Scotland, Methodists to Jane Addams' Hull House in Chicago, Anglicans to settlements in London's east end. In the 1890s the Salvation Army began to sponsor hospitals and rescue centres, and its influence affected all the churches. Downtown congregations of various denominations compensated for the deterioration of their surroundings by casting about for new forms of service. There was also a proliferation of undenominational centres, often founded by concerned individuals. It has been claimed that Canadian Protestants, despite their late start, became more deeply involved in social projects during this period than those of the United States.[26] The explanation may be that they still held the allegiance of a larger proportion of slum-dwellers.

Recognizing that these good works only relieved some of the results of poverty, churchmen also sought to eliminate its causes. Protestants, especially those of evangelical persuasion, found it natural to attribute all forms of social malaise to moral failure and therefore to seek their cure by eliminating opportunities for vice. This diagnosis, which was already generally accepted in church circles, was rendered more plausible than ever by the resurgence under urban conditions of traditional forms of disapproved behaviour and by their increased exploitation for commercial purposes. The churches pursued their familiar campaign against sin with renewed vigour, and when education proved insufficient they increasingly sought to enforce legal sanctions. A favourite target was gambling, which became more popular with growing affluence. Another was prostitution, an abomination that could only be named as "the social evil."

The protection of Sunday became a vital issue only with the rise of cities. In 1895 the Lord's Day Alliance was founded at the instigation of J. G. Shearer, a Presbyterian whose name figured prominently in all social causes. At first it had comparatively little to do, for by this time most provinces had enacted protective laws. In 1903, however, the Privy Council ruled provincial legislation on the subject *ultra vires* and there was considerable opposition to the passage of a strong federal act. Shearer campaigned tirelessly, and in 1906 Parliament passed a Lord's Day Act satisfactory to the churches. Two aspects of the struggle greatly encouraged the advocates of moral reform. One was that they had achieved a clear-cut victory despite the hostility of powerful commercial interests and of large sections of the press. The other was that they had been able to form a broad coalition that included not only organized labour but the Roman Catholic hierarchy.[27]

On the temperance issue, which they regarded as even more crucial, the century began badly for reform leaders. In 1902 the voters of Ontario endorsed prohibition by an almost two-to-one margin, but the vote fell slightly short of the absolute majority of eligible voters which the government had demanded as a condition of legislation. In that same year, however, S. D. Chown began an aggressive career as president of the Temperance Legislation League and as secretary of a newly established Methodist board of Temperance, Prohibition and Moral Reform. In 1905 Archbishop Bruchési of Montreal launched a crusade for temperance and asked the Franciscans to promote it, although he declined to endorse total prohibition.[28] Encouraged by these developments, and elated by the passage of the Lord's Day Act, church leaders pressed for the final outlawing of the liquor traffic. They were able to mount aggressive campaigns in every province, although they nowhere attained their objective before the outbreak of the First World War. The Ontario election of 1914, in which almost unanimous prohibitionist support for the Liberals under N. W. Rowell resulted in no significant swing of votes, was a particular disappointment.

Although the Roman Catholic clergy of Quebec stopped short of the absolute stands of some Protestants, contenting themselves with appeals for voluntary abstinence from liquor and allowing occasional compromise on Sunday labour, their response to industrialization was equally moralistic. In line with their tradition of church-sponsored colonization, they endorsed the virtues of the simple rural life even more explicitly than evangelical Protestants. Specially designated agricultural missionaries extolled its merits, and Bishop Laflèche described farm work as "the normal state of man here below."[29] The real motive of this glorification of agriculture was to keep French Canadians isolated from secularizing influences and thus to maintain a viable Catholic society in Quebec. The clergy were not hostile to industrialization when it encouraged French Canadians to remain in the province, as in the boom years from 1896 to 1912. They were not even averse to technical education, as has often been alleged, although they lacked the resources to sponsor it themselves and opposed it when it was separated from religious instruction. "Back to the land" was a standard remedy for economic crisis, however, and even in industrial communities the church attempted to perpetuate the style of life and the moral values of rural Quebec.

The church's preoccupation with agriculture had at least the merit of encouraging rural priests to promote better methods of farming. The same motive led to the sponsorship of agricultural organizations, beginning with *le Syndicat Central des Agriculteurs du Canada* in 1893. Cooperative buying and selling were also first attempted in rural areas, usually on the initiative of parish priests. Alphonse Desjardins, official reporter of the House of Commons, made the cooperative idea the basis of a popular movement. Beginning at Lévis in 1900, he organized a chain of *caisses populaires* or credit unions that would spread to New England and ultimately back to the English-speaking parts of Canada.[30] Such enterprises of self-help accorded well with the desire of the church to keep cash transactions as far as possible within the French-Canadian family.

## THE SOCIAL GOSPEL

Although the churches were slow to admit the inadequacy of their traditional remedies, it soon became obvious that these were at best partial solutions to the problems of the city. Quebec priests, even while insisting on the superiority of the country life, were sensibly handing out recommendations for industrial jobs to needy parishioners and sometimes actively encouraging industries to locate in their parishes. The pressures of urbanism similarly compelled the Methodists, at the height of the prohibition movement, to relax their long-standing rule of total abstinence for their members.[31] It was clear that the city had come to stay, and that urban problems would have to be solved in urban terms.

Protestant social concern represented in the main an overflow of the "social gospel" that had come to maturity in the United States about 1895, although there was a constant fertilization of British ideas as well. Social radicalism gained a foothold during the depression years of the early 1890s, but it was stimulated even more by Canada's later crisis of growth. Canadians continued to respond to developments elsewhere, and such American books as Walter Rauschenbusch's *Christianity and the Social Crisis* (1907) and *The Social Creed of the Churches* issued by the Federal Council of Churches (1908) were equally influential on both sides of the border. Nevertheless, the Canadian version of the social gospel had some distinctive features. It continued the main emphases of earlier campaigns of moral reform, which it supplemented but did not replace. It also absorbed a somewhat nationalistic flavour from its association with efforts to assimilate foreign immigrants, and All Peoples' Missions became seedbeds of advanced social thought.

During the 1890s the social gospel won enthusiastic support only from a relatively small number of ministers, although it was beginning to flavour a good many sermons and editorials. By the 1900s it had become a pulpit commonplace in several Protestant denominations. It played a major role in the lay Brotherhood Movement, which had been introduced from England in the early 1890s. It was taken up by student YMCAs and, through the organizing activities of N. W. Rowell, by the Epworth Leagues of Methodist young people.[32] It was prominently featured at the Ecumenical Methodist Conference at Toronto in 1911 and at a pre-Assembly congress of Presbyterians in 1913. It reached its pre-war peak at a social service congress that brought representatives of many religious and secular organizations to Ottawa in 1914, its most influential long-term embodiment in denominational boards of evangelism and social service that began to take definite shape in the early years of the same decade.

The program of the social gospel was at first relatively innocuous. It proposed the conversion of industrial leaders, the consecration of their wealth to the good of others,[33] and the impregnation of society with the teachings of Jesus. Early social gospellers shrank from any suggestion of class conflict, which was inconsistent with their dream of a perfect order. Later statements were bolder, although not always more explicit. In its 1906 report, the Methodist Committee on Sociological Questions characterized the existing social order as "far from being an ideal expression of Christian brotherhood" but diagnosed its chief malady as selfishness and proposed no remedies more startling than individual conversion and—of course—temperance.[34] Many ministers moved towards a theology that practically identified the teaching of Jesus with a program of social regeneration and correspondingly played down the importance both of traditional doctrine and of individual experience. A more radical group, of which Salem Bland was the outstanding representative, ranged itself on the side of labour and moved towards direct political action. The ranks of the social gospel were still solid in 1914, but it was already clear that some were prepared to go far beyond the generalities that satisfied most preachers.

Although all major communions interested themselves in social problems, Methodists welcomed the social gospel with a fervour unmatched elsewhere. Presbyterians shared its concern for social righteousness but seldom its confidence that a changed environment would mean a transformed humanity. Anglicans discussed socialism at a congress at Halifax in 1910, but they borrowed their ideas and rhetoric mainly from Britain rather than the United States. Baptists were affected, but their tradition of individualism acted as a brake. Methodists were less troubled by such reservations. Several important denominational offices that fell vacant in 1906 were filled by ardent social gospellers,[35] and by 1914 the new Board of Social Service and Evangelism could assert as a matter of accepted principle that "it is the business of the

Church to set up on earth the Kingdom of God as a social organization based on the Golden Rule of Christ."[36]

This enthusiasm on the part of Methodists calls for some explanation, for in earlier years the North American segments of the denomination had shown comparatively little interest in social questions. In part it can be understood as a redirection to urban problems of the energy that had re-shaped the Upper Canadian frontier, with unchurched workers taking the role once played by unchurched pioneers. In part it can be explained as a compensation for the fading of evangelistic fervour, for many Methodists embraced social activism with the zeal of devotees of a new evangel. What-ever its immediate motivation, the social gospel had authentic Methodist roots in Wesley's doctrine of Christian perfection. One could say of Cana-dian Methodists, as Elwyn A. Smith has suggested of social gospellers gen-erally, that they "seized the machinery of eschatology" in order to bring about an immediate millennium in this world.[37] The link between the earlier and later Methodism was the prohibition movement, which shattered inhibi-tions against political involvement and awakened the hope of enforcing the sanctification of Canadian society.

Despite its insistence on concern for labour and the poor, the social gospel was essentially a bourgeois phenomenon. Its rise coincided with the emer-gence to leadership of a generation of ministers whose religious experience owed as much to such organizations as Christian Endeavour as to revival meetings and whose theological studies had made them aware of the critical approach to the Bible. Its support came from professionally trained clergy, especially in denominations in which professional training was a novelty, and to a lesser degree from forward-looking businessmen. Its leaders, them-selves the products of organizations, were by temperament organizers and builders of ecclesiastical bureaucracies. On the whole, the social gospel failed either to change the attitudes of the business community or to retain the allegiance of working men to the church. Its greatest achievement, per-haps, was its decisive role in shaping the ideology of Canadian agrarian movements, whose leaders resembled those of the social gospel itself in representing a transitional stage between the old rural moralism and the new urban sophistication.

## LEO XIII AND SOCIAL CATHOLICISM

Whereas Protestant social activists followed the bent of their own think-ing, Roman Catholics were guided by Pope Leo XIII's encyclical *Rerum Novarum* of 1891 on the condition of the working classes. They were thereby enabled to formulate a more clearly articulated program, although they were naturally also somewhat circumscribed in their speculations. In his encyclical, Leo defended private property against socialist attacks, opposed the unnecessary extension of state intervention, and warned against the danger of strikes to public peace. On the other hand he called upon employers to pay fair wages and to establish working conditions conducive to morality and health, and asserted the natural right of workers to organize unions. His most explicit positive suggestion was that Catholics should form their own unions, through which workers might both obtain material benefits and receive instruction in the application of Christian principles to social problems. The general tone of the encyclical was sympathetic to workers, who were described as "surrendered, all isolated and helpless, to the hardheartedness of employers and the greed of unchecked competition."[38] It assumed, however, the continued existence of a hierarchical society in which workers would practically be identified with the poor.

The Quebec clergy were slow to respond to *Rerum Novarum*, and when they did respond they seized first on its conservative aspects. The encyclical reinforced ultramontane suspicions of socialism, encouraged the prevalent moralism by tracing exploitation largely to individual greed, and contained an implicit condemnation of secular international unions. Sometimes it was invoked to defend French-Canadian workers from alien domination. On other occasions, *curés* turned Leo's attacks on usury against small Jewish, Syrian, and even French-Canadian merchants, while exempting from criticism the American industrialists who wielded real power. The most conspicuous immediate result of *Rerum Novarum* was to stimulate the formation of Catholic unions, beginning with *la Fédération Ouvrière* founded at Chicoutimi in 1903 by Mgr E. Lapointe. These were almost invariably organized on the initiative of the clergy rather than of the workers themselves, were always closely advised by chaplains, and at first devoted more attention to instruction in Catholic social doctrine than to bargaining on behalf of the workers. They avoided strikes and extravagant demands, boasted of preserving industrial peace, and often acted like company unions.

On the other hand, *Rerum Novarum* gave several openings to the development of an outlook not unlike that of the Protestant social gospel. While restricting the state to a limited role in society, the encyclical acknowledged that the state exists not merely to ensure the liberty and security of the church but also to promote the general welfare. Merely by calling attention to the plight of the poor, moreover, it encouraged Catholics to devote themselves to the amelioration of social ills. Although Leo did not call specifically for the formation of cooperatives, his appeal for self-help through mutual association suggested their suitability and his denunciation of avaricious middlemen became part of their ideology. It could easily have been a Methodist but was in fact Archbishop McNeil of Toronto who wrote, "The prominence of the Kingdom of Heaven in the New Testament showed that it is by association and cooperation that individuals are to be saved."[39]

Among those who took it seriously, *Rerum Novarum* lent itself to two divergent lines of development. Those who took to heart its reassertion of the traditional condemnation of usury blamed the major ills of society on financial institutions and moved towards a radicalism of the right that would ultimately take the form of Social Credit. Those who heeded its admonition to become directly involved with the problems of the worker took an active part in labour organizations, increasingly identified themselves with the proletariat, and moved haltingly towards a radicalism of the left. For the time being, however, conservatism predominated over radicalism of either strain.

## COOPERATION AMONG THE CHURCHES

One of the most conspicuous features of the early years of the twentieth century was a desire for closer relations among the churches. This was inspired less by a conscious commitment to ecumenicity than by the emergence of problems for which individual denominations had no ready solutions and in the face of which their isolated endeavours seemed inadequate. The problems raised by the new cities seemed to call for a sharing of experience and resources, the presence of immigrants for the strengthening of unitive forces, the moral crisis for concerted pressure on governments and on public opinion. The result was a search for consensus among the churches that coincided with the growth of a sense of Canadian nationhood. It was aided by a concurrent breaking down of old barriers. Many churchmen became less interested in old quarrels of Calvinist and Arminian or even of Protestant and Catholic than in the triumph of virtue over vice or of nationalism over divisive old-country loyalties.

Some individual Christians had always succeeded in breaking through denominational lines, but now churches began to work together officially. Anglicans, Presbyterians, Methodists, and Congregationalists instituted co-operative theological teaching at Montreal in 1912. Work among immigrants was often cooperative, and mutual consultation was frequent. Service projects such as the Maritime Home for Girls at Truro, Nova Scotia, were inaugurated on an interdenominational basis. In no field, indeed, was joint action more conspicuous than in that of social service. It led in 1907 to the formation of the Moral and Social Reform Council, which in 1913 became the Social Service Council and later the Christian Social Council of Canada. Social action was an area in which even Protestants and Roman Catholics could cooperate. In Vancouver, Archbishop Neil McNeil worked readily with Protestants in moral campaigns,[40] and in several provinces temperance delegations to governments included representatives of Roman Catholicism as well of various Protestant denominations.[41]

Old sources of division remained, however, and Canadians continued at times to exercise their talent for religious controversy. The admission of

Saskatchewan and Alberta as provinces in 1905 was the signal for a quarrel over separate schools reminiscent of that in Manitoba a decade earlier. Relations between the two language groups deteriorated as English Canadians became enthusiasts for imperial federation and Henri Bourassa responded by calling French Canadians to look to their own interests. Strife between French and Irish troubled the Roman Catholic Church not only in Manitoba and New Brunswick but also in Ontario, where the two groups contended for the control of the University of Ottawa. The search for national unity could itself be divisive. Protestant opposition to separate schools in Saskatchewan and Alberta arose not only from traditional anti-Catholicism but from a desire that the children of various nationalities should be educated together, while renewed demands that French-speaking minorities should learn English were in part an echo of similar pressures on immigrant groups.

## MOVING TOWARDS A UNITED CHURCH

An era favourable to cooperation was also hospitable to proposals for consolidation and union. After years of negotiation the Regular and Free Baptists of the Maritimes came together in 1905 and 1906 to form the United Baptist Convention. The logical next step was the formation of a national federation, but successive attempts during the years from 1907 to 1914 foundered on opposition within the Convention of Ontario and Quebec. Around 1906 there were also a number of experiments in local union between the Baptists and the Disciples of Christ, although these too proved ephemeral.[42] The Congregationalists, having achieved their own national union in 1906, absorbed in 1907 a small group of American origin known as the United Brethren in Christ. These minor unions were significant straws in the wind, but meanwhile a much larger union had been projected that would issue in 1925 in the formation of The United Church of Canada.

The union of at least the major Protestant churches was a live issue in every English-speaking country in the late years of the nineteenth century and the early years of the twentieth. In England, the Home Reunion Society was founded in 1888. In Scotland, to which many Canadian Presbyterians still looked for precedents, the Free Church and the United Presbyterians came together in 1900. In the United States, ambitious schemes of union were put forward by Philip Schaff of the Reformed Church and by the Episcopalian William Reed Huntington. In other British dominions, there were union proposals similar to the one eventually adopted in Canada. Three factors were mainly responsible for this surge of interest in church union. One was the appearance of new theological interests, such as biblical criticism and moral idealism, that made traditional denominational lines seem less meaningful than they had before. Another was an increasing church-consciousness, partly stimulated by the Oxford Movement, that hardened some positions but also awakened a bad conscience about sectarianism. A third was a growing concern for the mission of the church, which made denominational competition seem wasteful and frivolous. Missionary zeal seldom gave rise directly to proposals for union, but its presence or absence usually determined whether there would be a sufficient sense of urgency to overcome the inertia of separation.

Church union in Canada across major denominational lines was first proposed officially by the Anglicans, who were always most conscience-stricken about division. In 1889, on the initiative of the provincial synod of Canada, Anglican, Presbyterian and Methodist representatives held an exploratory meeting at Toronto.[43] The response of most Methodists was lukewarm. Presbyterians showed greater interest, but their union committee reported to the general assembly in 1890 their conviction that "incorporate union" was unattainable.[44] The Lambeth Conference of 1888 had made the acceptance of the historic episcopate a condition of Anglican participation in union, and the churches had little experience in dealing with the thorny issues thus raised. The Presbyterians also thought that the Nicene Creed, on which the Anglicans insisted, was not sufficiently explicit as a statement of doctrine. Interest soon turned to plans that would include only nonepiscopal churches. Congregationalists and Presbyterians flirted briefly in 1893, the Methodists proposed a federal union in 1894, and in 1899 these three churches agreed not to build churches within six miles of each other in the west. By the end of the century, however, interest in serious steps towards union had faded, and church union committees had ceased to meet. Continuing activity was largely confined to Anglicans, notably Herbert Symonds who helped to found the Church Union Society in 1898.[45]

The dormant issue came to life suddenly in 1902, when Principal William Patrick took advantage of his position as a Presbyterian fraternal delegate to the Methodist general conference in Winnipeg to propose the union of the two denominations.[46] The Methodists responded warmly, the Congregationalists asked to be included, and by early 1904 committees of the three were able to report their unanimous conclusion that organic union was "both desirable and practicable."[47] Patrick's initiative had been only one of many similar proposals, but the time was apparently ripe and a joint committee was charged with the task of preparing terms of union.

The preparation of a basis of union proved to be the easiest part of the process. Committee members did their work without the benefit of the sophisticated ecumenical discussions of the twentieth century, a circumstance that simplified and perhaps even oversimplified their task. Their only serious difficulty in determining the doctrinal conditions of union arose from Congregational resistance to the imposition of credal tests. They surmounted it by requiring ministers not to sign a statement of belief but to convince a regional conference of their "essential agreement" with the standards of the Basis of Union.[48] Even in polity, which gave them greater trouble, they decided that the several systems were more compatible in practice than they had seemed on paper. The most ticklish problem proved to be that of determining how ministers should be appointed to congregations. Methodists had stationing committees, while Presbyterians and Congregationalists relied on calls from individual congregations. The difference was one of ethos even more than of principle, symbolizing contrasting concepts of the church as constituted by the preaching of dedicated ministers or by the faith of believing congregations. The framers of the Basis compromised by giving the right of appointment to settlement committees while defining their functions in such terms that they have usually merely ratified calls from congregations.[49]

The Basis was on the whole a conservative document, juxtaposing a mild Calvinism with a mild Arminianism in its statement of doctrine and balancing the powers of various church courts in its polity. Its lack of novelty has been attributed to the advanced age of the committee members,[50] but it may have owed more to their preoccupation with the forging of a new instrument for social betterment. Theology was then at a discount, and even young people of the time were more interested in social involvement than in theological restatement. In one important respect, however, the framers of the Basis would admit no compromise. Despite the current popularity of schemes of federation in the United States, they insisted that union should mean a complete merging of denominational identities. Earlier unions of Presbyterians and Methodists in Canada had been organic, and they had worked well. An amendment in favour of federation obtained few votes at the Presbyterian general assembly of 1906,[51] although the idea would be revived later.

By 1908, the Joint Committee had completed the preparation of the Basis of Union, and the negotiating churches set out to secure the approval of their constituencies. Authority among the Congregationalists was vested in local churches, and by 1910 such an overwhelming majority of these had voted in favour that the denomination was ready to proceed. The Methodist general conference approved the Basis in that same year, referred it both to regional bodies and to a popular vote, and was satisfied by 1912 that it could enter union without a schism. The Presbyterians soon discovered that their situation was more difficult. Their general assembly approved the Basis in 1910, and the majority of presbyteries necessary under Presbyterian law was easily obtained. When a plebiscite showed almost one-third of the membership opposed, however, the assembly of 1912 decided to postpone consideration in the hope of securing eventual unanimity. The result was to delay the consummation of union to a later period.

In 1906, meanwhile, Baptists and Anglicans had been invited to join the negotiations. The Baptists, who were hampered by the lack of a national consultative body, eventually accepted the negative verdict of the Convention of Ontario and Quebec. The Anglicans replied that they were prepared to negotiate along lines approved by a recent Lambeth conference. Although this response does not seem to have been intended as a refusal, it was interpreted by the Joint Committee as making Anglican participation impracticable.[52] Thus within a few years the probable boundaries of the proposed church were fairly clearly drawn.

Union across denominational lines, although promoted in every English-speaking country, was seriously attempted only in Canada. The difference was primarily due to some basic facts of Canadian life. For effective mission in the Canadian setting, a church needed to be large enough to serve an expanding frontier, comprehensive enough to appeal to a great variety of communities, and sufficiently identified with national aspirations to overcome nostalgia for old-world patterns. These considerations had been powerful incentives to earlier unions within denominations, and each measure of consolidation had been a signal for proposals of wider union. As early as 1874, George M. Grant had raised the possibility of a union broader than any that has yet been proposed officially in Canada, in which even Roman Catholics would "seal with their consent that same unity, the image of which they so fondly crave."[53] Until the end of the century, however, the major denominations remained confident of their ability to surmount the difficulties inherent in the Canadian situation. It was the challenge of the new urbanism and the new cosmopolitanism that tipped the scale and gave Patrick a hearing that had previously been denied to equally eloquent pleaders for union.

Church union was, from one point of view, an aspect of the liberal evangelical drive to sanctify Canadian society. Although the motives that led individuals to support or oppose union were so complex as to baffle anyone who attempts to analyze them, its general affinity with movements of social reconstruction was always obvious. Presbyterians, who were pioneers in propagating a Christian Canadianism, contributed more than their share of early proposals for church union. The Methodists, who at a later stage most wholeheartedly supported the social gospel, were eventually almost unanimous in their support of union. So were the Congregationalists, who usually put the weight of their small numbers behind reformist causes. The Baptists, whose individualism held them somewhat aloof from controversial social issues, were not greatly interested in union. The Anglicans, along with many Presbyterians who represented the rather different social approach of the old established churches, could not be included. The typical unionist was also an advocate of prohibition, overseas missions, advanced Sunday school methods, the involvement of the church in social betterment, and the promotion of good citizenship among new Canadians.

Once the Basis of Union had been formulated in 1908, members of small town and village churches began to arrange local amalgamation without waiting for denominational action. The organization of community churches was a direct consequence of the union movement, becoming popular only after the national bodies had demonstrated their serious intent and involving almost exclusively congregations of the negotiating communions. It was a largely spontaneous development, however, and often embarrassed officials who feared the loss of denominational loyalties and missionary contributions. Local unions were not limited to any region, taking place in the Maritimes and rural Ontario as well as in the newer parts of the country.[54] It was in the west, however, and especially in Saskatchewan, that the movement developed a distinctive ethos. In most parts of Canada, the churches were able to contain the desire for consolidation by persuading union congregations to affiliate with existing denominations. In Saskatchewan there was a widespread desire to anticipate union by organizing in terms of the new Basis. Ultimately the General Council of Local Union Churches would become one of the constituent units of The United Church of Canada.

The churches had established too many congregations in the west because each was afraid of being anticipated by others, and some congregations that at first seemed sufficiently strong were later weakened by the proliferation of new towns along the lines of branch railways. This overextension, with the economic hardship that resulted from it, was probably the principal cause of a rash of local unions in the early 1910s. It was not the only factor, however, and it contributed little to the ideology of the movement. To many of its proponents the community church came to symbolize a way of life. It was a natural expression of the general desire to unite people of many origins in a comprehensive fellowship, of the mentality that welcomed the wheat pool and the agricultural cooperative, above all of the self-conscious Canadian nationalism that first achieved general acceptance on the plains.[55] Even more than the original official proposal of union, this people's movement represented the optimistic Canadianism of the era. Through the community churches, this optimism and this Canadianism would become part of the fabric of The United Church of Canada.

### NOTES TO CHAPTER FIVE

1. O. J. Firestone, *Canada's Economic Development, 1867-1953, with Special Reference to Changes in the Country's National Product and National Wealth* (London: Bowes and Bowes, 1958), p. 68.

2. I. F. Mackinnon, *Canada and the Minority Churches of Eastern Europe, 1945-1950* (Halifax: The Book Room, 1959), p. 20.

3. Quoted in J. W. Dafoe, *Clifford Sifton in Relation to His Times* (Toronto: Macmillan, 1931), pp. 142, 319.

4. But in 1894 the Presbyterian Church in Canada objected to official discrimination against Chinese immigration. Acts and Proceedings of the 20th General Assembly, 1894, p. 35.

5. E. M. Saunders, *History of the Baptists of the Maritime Provinces*, p. 409.

6. *Baptist Year Book*, 1900, p. 47.

7. W. G. Smith, *Building the Nation* (Toronto: Canadian Council of the Missionary Education Movement, 1922), pp. 182-183.

8. Acts and Proceedings of the 28th General Assembly of the Presbyterian Church in Canada, 1902, Appendix, p. 4; Acts and Proceedings of the 36th General Assembly of the Presbyterian Church in Canada, 1910, Appendix, p. 14.

9. Quoted in T. C. B. Boon, *The Anglican Church from the Bay to the Rockies*, pp. 289-290.

10. For sharply contrasting views of this episode, see G. E. Lloyd, *The Trail of 1903* (Lloydminster: the Lloydminster *Times*, 1940) and Helen Evans Reid, *All Silent, All Damned* (Toronto: Ryerson, 1969).

11. D. J. Carter, "The Archbishops' Western Canada Fund," *Alberta Historical Review*, Vol. 16, No. 1 (Winter 1968), pp. 10-17.

12. Boon, *op. cit.*, p. 314.

13. John M. Reid, jr., "The Erection of the Roman Catholic Archdiocese of Winnipeg," M.A. thesis, University of Manitoba, 1961, pp. 54, 75.

14. See Richard J. Dobell, ed., *Fifty Golden Years, 1913-1963* (Scarborough: The Librarian of St. Augustine's Seminary, n.d.).

15. George Boyle, *Pioneer in Purple: The Life of Archbishop Neil McNeil* (Montreal: Palm, 1951), p. 114.

16. Jean Hulliger, *L'Enseignement Social des Evêques Canadiens de 1891 à 1950* (Montreal: Fides, 1958), p. 72.

17. See J. S. Woodsworth, *Strangers within Our Gates, or Coming Canadians* (Toronto: Missionary Society of the Methodist Church, 1909) and *My Neighbor: A Study of City Conditions, a Plea for Social Service* (Toronto: Missionary Society of the Methodist Church, c. 1911).

18. Boyle, *op. cit.*, pp. 114, 203.

19. Brown, one of Ralph Connor's clerical heroes, sought to make the Galicians in his charge "good Christians and good Canadians, which is the same thing." Ralph Connor (C. W. Gordon), *The Foreigner* (Toronto: Westminster, 1909), p. 253.

20. W. T. Gunn, *His Dominion* (Toronto: Canadian Council of the Missionary Education Movement, 1917).

21. Reid, *op. cit.*, p. 25.

22. For a detailed account of the whole experiment, see Michael Zuk, "The Ukrainian Protestant Missions in Canada," unpublished thesis in the Library of McGill University, 1957.

23. Paul Yuzyk, *The Ukrainians in Manitoba* (Toronto: University of Toronto Press, 1953), p. 71.

24. J. F. McCurdy, *The Life and Work of D. J. Macdonnell* (Toronto: Wm. Briggs, 1897), pp. 23-24, 289, 309.

25. Minutes of the Toronto City Missionary Society of the Methodist Church, December 29, 1894, in the Archives of Victoria University and The United Church of Canada.

26. C. E. Silcox, *Church Union in Canada* (New York: Institute of Social and Religious Research, 1933), p. 233.

27. For a thorough and illuminating discussion of the struggle, see A. M. C. Waterman, "The Lord's Day in a Secular Society: A Historical Comment on the Canadian Lord's Day Act of 1906," *Canadian Journal of Theology*, Vol. XI, No. 2 (April 1965), pp. 108-123.

28. Ruth E. Spence, *Prohibition in Canada*, pp. 357, 359.

29. "l'état normal de l'homme ici-bas." "Discours de Mgr L.-F. Laflèche au congrès des missionaires agricoles à Oka, le 9 août 1895," quoted in W. F. Ryan, sj, *The Clergy*

*and Economic Growth in Quebec (1896-1914)* (Quebec: Les Presses de l'Université Laval, 1966), p. 93.

30. Yves Roby, *Alphonse Desjardins et les Caisses Populaires, 1854-1920* (Montreal: Fides, 1964), Chapitres 4-7.

31. Journal of Proceedings of the 8th General Conference of the Methodist Church, 1910, pp. 88-89.

32. Richard Allen, *The Social Passion: Religion and Social Reform in Canada 1914-28* (Toronto: University of Toronto Press, 1971), p. 339.

33. Pamphlet in honour of Hart A. Massey, *Why Save Money?* insert in the Minutes of the Board of Management, Fred Victor Mission, April 13, 1897, in the Archives of Victoria University and The United Church of Canada.

34. Journal of Proceedings of the 7th General Conference of the Methodist Church, 1906, pp. 274-278.

35. William H. Magney, "The Methodist Church and the National Gospel, 1884-1914," *Bulletin*, Committee on Archives of The United Church of Canada, No. 20 (1968), pp. 70-71.

36. Journal of Proceedings of the 9th General Conference of the Methodist Church, 1914, p. 407.

37. Elwyn A. Smith, "Theological Second Thoughts on Social Involvement," *Christian Century*, January 15, 1969, p. 78.

38. Anne Fremantle, ed., *The Papal Encyclicals in Their Historical Context* (New York: Mentor, 1956), p. 167.

39. Boyle, *op. cit.*, p. 191.

40. J. W. Grant, *George Pidgeon: A Biography* (Toronto: Ryerson, 1962), p. 46.

41. Spence, *op. cit.*, pp. 411, 430.

42. C. C. McLaurin, *Pioneering in Western Canada*, p. 153.

43. T. R. Millman, "The Conference on Christian Unity, Toronto, 1889," *Canadian Journal of Theology*, Vol. III, No. 3 (July 1957), pp. 165-174.

44. Acts and Proceedings of the 16th General Assembly of the Presbyterian Church in Canada, 1890, p. 60.

45. W. L. Grant and Frederick Hamilton, *Principal Grant*, p. 494. See also Herbert Symonds, *Lectures on Christian Unity* (Toronto: William Briggs, 1899).

46. *Manitoba Free Press*, September 9, 1902.

47. Acts and Proceedings of the 30th General Assembly of the Presbyterian Church in Canada, 1904, p. 297.

48. *Basis of Union Together with a Brief Historical Statement* (Toronto: 1921), p. 26.

49. *Ibid.*, p. 24.

50. Silcox, *op. cit.*, p. 127.

51. The vote was 179 to 22. Acts and Proceedings of the 32nd General Assembly of the Presbyterian Church in Canada, 1906, p. 39.

52. The correspondence suggests an almost incredible degree of mutual misunderstanding. The Joint Committee, writing on December 12, 1908, understood the Anglicans to have insisted on the Lambeth resolution as "a prior condition of union." Bishop A. Hunter of Quebec, in his reply of April 29, 1909, assumed that the Anglicans were being asked as "a prior condition of union" to abandon the Lambeth resolution. On behalf of the Joint Committee E. D. McLaren then suggested, in a letter of June 16, 1909, "a frank discussion of the whole question of Church Union, unfettered by any restriction on either side and without authority to commit in any way the Churches they respectively represent." There the correspondence ended, perhaps on account of the death of the secretary of the Anglican committee. See Journal of Proceedings of the 6th Session of the General Synod of the Church of England in the Dominion of Canada, 1911, pp. 247-249.

53. Quoted in Grant and Hamilton, *op. cit.*, p. 155.

54. In 1923 union churches were reported as numbering 1,244, of which 229 were in eastern Canada. Silcox, *op. cit.*, p. 227.

55. See G. M. Morrison, "The United Church of Canada: Ecumenical or Economical Necessity?" B.D. thesis, Victoria University, 1956, especially p. 100.

# SIX

# The Failure of Consensus

In 1914, when events beyond her borders drew Canada into a major world war, the churches rallied without hesitation to the national cause. They did not all do so for precisely the same reasons. To Anglicans, who included many recent immigrants from Britain and who in any case had always maintained close ties with the motherland, the war represented an appeal to elemental sentiments of kinship. From the outset they proved readiest of all to enlist. Liberal evangelicals, with their commitment to social involvement, saw in the war a defence of the Canada they were seeking to create and into which they were seeking to integrate immigrants of non-Anglo-Saxon origin. Catholic bishops endorsed participation in what they regarded as a just war. Bishop Fallon of London and other Irish Catholics set aside memories of British oppression to become ardent supporters, and even such Quebec nationalists as Henri Bourassa at first took the same position. Behind these varied arguments one can discern a common motivation. Churches that had had so large a part in establishing the norms of Canadian life could not be indifferent to an enterprise that involved the nation so deeply.

## THE CRUSADE AGAINST THE KAISER

One result of the general enthusiasm was to betray churches into measures of support for the war they would later have cause to regret. It was only to be expected that they would seek to bolster the morale of their people in a time of crisis by providing chaplains for the troops and pastoral comfort for relatives, perhaps even by offering prayers for victory. They went far beyond such traditional roles. Ministers urged enlistment from their pulpits, and some of them became official recruiting agents for the government. Church periodicals became organs of war propaganda, and membership rolls were scrutinized for potential soldiers. In their commendable eagerness to share in the national ordeal, the churches made little attempt to delineate the proper spheres of Caesar and Christ.

No denomination more conspicuously laid itself open to criticism than the Methodist. J. S. Woodsworth's description of a recruiting service at St. James' Church, Montreal, on October 4, 1915, has often been quoted. There was no New Testament lesson, Woodsworth observed, but there were addresses by a business man, a general, a university president, and the minister of the congregation in which "a deliberate attempt was made through a recital of the abominable acts of the Germans to stir up the spirit of hatred and retaliation." Woodsworth continued:

> The climax was reached when the pastor in an impassioned appeal stated that if any young man could go and did not go he was neither a Christian nor a patriot. No! the climax was the announcement that recruiting sergeants were stationed at the door of the church and that any man of spirit—any lover of his country—any follower of Jesus—should make the decision then and there.[1]

Since the minister of St. James', C. A. Williams, was later put in charge of recruiting for the province of Quebec, it would probably be misleading to generalize from this experience. Yet the Methodists did recommend the pulpit as the most effective recruiting agency, and in 1917 every conference resolved in favour of conscription and national government. The Methodists failed so notably to exercise discrimination not because they were more ardent patriots than others but because they lacked a clearly defined tradition of the proper roles of church and state. Their position on war had always been ambiguous. As early as the War of 1812, Methodists whose convictions were solidly pro-British had been known to refuse to take human life, and this pacifist sentiment persisted. On the other hand, Canadian Methodists were always sensitive to accusations of disloyalty based on their American background, and as a result they tended to overcompensate. Mere nationalism, however, could never justify participation in war. In order to overcome their scruples, Methodists had to convince themselves that every war in which they fought was "a holy war."[2] To a greater or lesser extent, however, Christians of all denominations did the same.

Enthusiastic support for the war did not distract interest from social concerns. On the contrary, wholehearted support rested on the conviction that tremendous moral and social issues were at stake. The war provided an occasion for applying the social message of the churches both as law and as gospel. On the one hand, its prosecution demanded a total dedication of the self that fitted well with the current emphasis on national conversion, and indeed churchmen experienced some exhilaration in being able to press their calls for self-discipline on a public made responsive by crisis. On the other hand, its successful conclusion seemed to promise the age of peace and plenty to which social gospellers had long looked forward. The hope of a "war to end war" had almost universal appeal precisely because minds were already receptive to the vision of a secular millennium of which the current struggle seemed to be an appropriate Armageddon. On no other terms can one explain the tremendous popular interest in Allenby's Palestine campaign.

Total commitment demanded, by a logic that had already become familiar, the enforcement of moral probity. The more Protestant churches automatically welcomed such measures of wartime austerity as a government crackdown on racetracks. Alcohol continued to be the main issue, and under war conditions it was possible to mobilize the support of Anglicans, French Canadians and trade unionists behind demands for prohibition. Abstinence became a form of patriotism: Judge Eugène Lafontaine, president of the Anti-Alcohol League of the Roman Catholic Church, "denounced beer as an unsanitary and mischievous beverage, pointing to the brutality of the German nation as an evidence of its ill effects."[3] The temperance movement at last attained the success that had hitherto eluded it. Prohibition was adopted by province after province, beginning with Manitoba in 1916, until by 1919 it was possible to publish a map showing Canada as totally dry.[4] The federal government adopted even more stringent regulations than the provinces, although the Senate demonstrated its scepticism about the millennium by refusing to extend them for twelve months after the end of the war.

The desire for a world that would offer greater satisfactions to most of its inhabitants was also growing during the war years, and the social gospel was already available as a theological basis for it. Canada's most important agrarian movement germinated during these years, and its most influential leaders were religiously motivated. The most explicit statements of social Christianity ever issued by Canadian churches were formulated towards the end of the war, when chaplains returned to make known the aspirations of the fighting men and their dissatisfaction with existing conditions. Methodists, Presbyterians and Anglicans all issued statements favouring measures of socialization and better terms for labour,[5] and in 1919 the Maritime Baptists set up a Social Service Committee.[6] Significantly, however, the most radical document was not the report of a board of social service but that of the Methodist Committee on the Church in Relation to the War and Patriotism to the general conference of 1918. This report called for the abolition of the existing economic system, and although it was passed by a depleted house on the final day of conference it was widely endorsed by the denominational press and officials.[7] During these years almost every public man felt obliged to advocate radical changes in society. The Progressives elected sixty members to Parliament in 1921 by promising a new approach to politics, and even the old-line parties borrowed many of the slogans of the social gospel.

## TENSIONS OF THE TWENTIES

Although the war seemed to have advanced the moral and social programs of the churches, it is obvious in retrospect that it set in motion forces
that would recoil upon those who had supported it and taken advantage of
the opportunities it offered. The enlistment of ministers as chaplains, and
of both ministers and theological students as combatants, resulted in a
neglect of rural congregations that would not quickly be repaired.[8] When
the churches were able to supply clergy again they often met local resentment, especially in the west. Even more serious was a weakening of the moral
sanctions on which all the churches had depended. Soldiers brought back
to Canada the relaxed standards of their barracks, and meanwhile women
in war jobs had enjoyed a freedom unknown in pre-war Canada. Canadians
had never been quite as strict in their morals as was sometimes supposed,
but for the churchgoing middle class the wartime revelation of what the
common folk did meant a traumatic loss of innocence. The shock to the
young J. S. Woodsworth in 1899 of discovering that English Congregationalists provided playing cards and ash-trays at their settlement in east London would have been incomprehensible to the next generation.[9] Before long,
too, there would be a revulsion against the war and against those who had
associated themselves with it. Some of the earlier expressions of this reaction
were within the church. In 1923, pacifism became the chief issue at a North
American conference of the Student Volunteer Movement.[10] By 1924, the
Presbytery of Sydney had declared itself against war, and resolutions against
high school cadet corps would agitate church courts throughout the decade.
Inevitably, however, the institutional church was itself suspect.

Although varying rates of enlistment gave rise to some recriminations
among the denominations in the later years of the war, the Canadian religious
consensus was still sufficiently intact in 1918 that a number of Protestant
churches were able to cooperate in the promotion of an Inter-Church Forward Movement. This emphasized personal commitment and the renewal
of Canadian life, although its most conspicuous feature was a massive financial drive in thanksgiving for the restoration of peace. The movement was
remarkably successful, at least in the financial response, although a last-
minute Baptist withdrawal deprived it of its hoped-for unanimity. This cloud
was to prove an omen. During the coming decade, centrifugal tendencies
would dominate Canadian society, and good feelings among and within the
churches would be one of the chief casualties.

## THE GAP BETWEEN THE TWO CULTURES

Canada's primordial tension, between those speaking English and those
speaking French, had already shown signs of aggravation during what was
otherwise a period of harmony. Laurier's victory in 1896 had signalled a

fading of old hostilities, although he probably owed a good deal of support in Quebec to a natural desire to vote for one of the family. During the 1900s, however, schemes of imperial federation, attempts to anglicize new Canadians and Protestant moral campaigns had combined to create the impression of an aggressive English Canada. Bourassa's cries of alarm resulted in the election in 1911 of a large bloc of Quebec nationalists who contributed to Laurier's defeat and put the Conservative Robert L. Borden in power. Even more significantly, perhaps, coteries of Catholic intellectuals were beginning to adopt the national cause and to promote it through such organizations as *l'Action catholique*. The inevitable result of mutual suspicion was to heighten tensions between the two language groups, most acutely within the Roman Catholic Church itself.

The most serious encounter was over the language of instruction in Ontario schools. Elementary education in French had always been customary in some areas, as German had once been allowed in Waterloo county. Its quality was not always good, and in 1910 a French-language congress at Ottawa demanded improvement. Any extension of French-language instruction was opposed by the Orangemen and the *Christian Guardian*, although so vociferously also by Bishop Fallon and other Irish Catholics that the issue did not become primarily a religious one. In 1912 the Conservative government of James Whitney answered the French-Canadian request by imposing further restrictions on the use of French in Ontario schools. Instruction 17 made few actual changes but was so introduced as to give the impression that French-speaking children were being offered the favour of instruction in English. Whitney genuinely seems to have had no suspicion that he would offend the sensibilities of any group, but educational officials enforced the regulation in a manner that gave colour to French-Canadian charges of brutality.[11]

The outbreak of war provided an opportunity for reconciliation, and for a short time it seemed that it would be seized. That it was not was chiefly due to the provincialism of English Canadians, who insisted on waging the war as a British enterprise. Those who spoke English deplored the lower proportion of enlistments among those who spoke French, although the difference was less striking when the comparison was limited to native-born Canadians. French Canadians in return resented the imposition of conscription in 1917, which they regarded as directed against them, and they especially resented its enforcement by English-speaking officials. Most of the lower clergy shared their feelings, and respect for the hierarchy waned as a result of its consistent support of the war and its apparent willingness to sacrifice French-Canadian interests for the sake of national unity.

The formation of *L'Action française* by Abbé Lionel Groulx in 1918 signalled the rise of a significant new force in Quebec. Consisting of thoughtful young priests and fervently Catholic laymen, the movement called upon French Canadians to become masters of their own society. The new nationalists inherited Laflèche's conception of a state that would rest on the twin foundations of the French language and the Roman Catholic religion, adding at the insistence of Esdras Minville the thesis that self-government must have a firm economic base. Their greatest merit was a sense of economic realism that had been lacking in earlier nationalists, their greatest fault a tendency to bolster their cause with appeals to anti-English and sometimes anti-Semitic prejudice. They made little immediate impression either on the hierarchy or on the bulk of the faithful. Their ideas were preserved for the future, however, by the adherence of many young people and by the impact of Groulx's clerical rewriting of Quebec history.

Meanwhile, the intensification of Quebec's isolation from the rest of Canada that followed the conscription crisis helped the church to postpone a decisive confrontation with modern urbanism. Organizations restricting their membership to Catholics multiplied during the early 1920s, notable additions being *la Confédération des Travailleurs catholiques du Canada* in 1921 and *l'Union catholique des Cultivateurs* in 1924. There was a strange ambiguity, however, in the church's attitude to outside influences. On the one hand, it deplored the moral effects of industrialization and sought to preserve its people from contamination by them. On the other, its conservative attitude to property rights fostered in Catholic unions a docility towards employers that became one of the province's chief attractions for foreign investors. It was dissatisfaction with this self-defeating policy, more than anything else, that made Groulx a hero to many young French Canadians.

### THE FAILURE OF ASSIMILATION

The war had less spectacular but equally profound effects on relations between the English-speaking majority and other ethnic groups. By 1914 churchmen were becoming sensitive to the feelings of the new Canadians, and terms like "newcomer" and "stranger" were replacing the earlier "foreigner." This trend continued among progressive leaders, but the war fostered popular prejudices first against Germans and then by extension against all others with strange accents or names. The difficulties were compounded by post-war fears of Bolshevik agitators, who were usually pictured not merely as foreigners but specifically as Slavs. Probably not many would have followed the Methodist chaplain Wellington Bridgman in attributing to all central Europeans a "morbid passion to shed blood,"[12] but the nativist and anti-Catholic Ku Klux Klan flourished in Saskatchewan in the 1920s. Non-Anglo-Saxons, in return, began to resent relegation to the status of second-class citizens and to demand a recognized place in Canadian society. Not only immigrants but native Canadians were affected. A number of Iroquois on the Ohshweken Reserve near Brantford demonstrated their disregard for the white man's ways by returning to the longhouse religion of their ancestors.

The Lutherans, on the whole, opted for assimilation.[13] Until 1930 they continued to obtain many of their ministers from Germany, but sensing the unpopularity of the German language they changed over fairly rapidly to the use of English. Having equipped themselves just before the war with educational institutions at Waterloo and Edmonton, they were beginning the climb that has made them one of Canada's major denominations. Their naturalization was delayed, however, by dependence on headquarters in the United States and by division along both ethnic and theological lines. They were rapidly becoming North American, but they would only gradually learn to think in Canadian terms.

The Orthodox churches, by contrast, took an increasing interest in European developments. Ukrainian nationalists were active even before the war, and national sentiments were further stimulated by the temporary independence of the Ukraine after the Russian revolution. Immigrants of the 1920s, chiefly from Galicia, were fervent nationalists and resisted assimilation.[14] In these circumstances Protestant propaganda lost its appeal. The Greek Catholic Church was also handicapped by being labelled "Ruthenian," and even after changing its title to "Ukrainian" it suffered from memories of forced conversions from Orthodoxy under Austrian rule. The rising force was the Ukrainian Greek Orthodox Church, founded in 1918 on the model of a similar organization in the Ukraine. It sought to provide a rallying point for group consciousness, and many of its priests were men ordained in maturity who had already been leaders in other professions. Other Orthodox bodies, notably the Russian and the Serbian, were organized on old-world national lines. Like the Ukrainians, they were affected and often divided by European political issues.

Canadians were increasingly aware after the war of some other groups that refused to become integral parts of their society. Several colonies of pacifist Hutterian Brethren, finding life in the United States made unbearable by conscription and war-time regulations, migrated in 1918 to Alberta Manitoba.[15] An ultra-conservative group with a tradition of dissent that went back to the Protestant Reformation, the Hutterites had maintained over the centuries a tightly knit communal organization in which authority rested with a group of elders. In Canada they proved to be well behaved and inoffensive. Most early reports on them were favourable, although the tendency of their multiplying colonies to bypass local merchants in favour of wholesale buying would make them increasingly unpopular with their neighbours.

A more conspicuous group were the Doukhobors, pacifist Russian sectarians who had come to Canada in 1899 on the assurance that they would be exempt from military service.[16] Professing a religion of the inner light, the Doukhobors rejected all institutionally based authority but attached great weight to group consensus and to natural leaders who were believed to embody and declare it. Under the influence of Leo Tolstoy, they had adopted vegetarianism and a doctrinaire attachment to the simple life. In 1902, some members of the community, who would later be known as Sons of Freedom, made the headlines with a nude march that was intended to lead to a promised land in the sun. Even the more orthodox had anarchical views that made adjustment to Canadian law almost impossible. Generally, however, the Doukhobors were respected for their industry, cleanliness, and inoffensiveness. Some of them soon became independent farmers. Peter Vasil'evich Verigin, the inspired leader, kept the main body out of serious trouble with the government, and after moving it to British Columbia in 1908 seemed to be establishing it on a sound economic basis. In the early 1920s, however, the appearance of the Sons of Freedom in British Columbia was followed by the withdrawal of children from school, nude parades, and acts of terrorism that culminated in Verigin's death in a bomb explosion.

A similar restlessness showed itself among the long-settled Mennonites of Manitoba, who suffered from increasing internal tensions as pressures towards assimilation mounted. Relations with the provincial government had begun to deteriorate in the 1890s with the abolition of denominational school systems, and they were further strained in 1907 by an official policy requiring flags to be flown over public schools. Wartime tensions, however, were the chief factor in convincing many conservative Mennonites that they had no secure future in Canada. In 1916 the use of English was made compulsory in public schools, and during the next few years most Mennonite private schools were condemned as substandard and closed. The federal government also abolished the automatic exemption of Mennonites from conscription, although too late for its action to have practical effect. Conservatives began to threaten emigration, and in the post-war atmosphere of suspicion it became evident that the authorities would welcome their departure. Some began to leave for Mexico in 1922, and another settlement was later established in Paraguay.[17] In the wake of emigration, the Mennonite community itself was rent with dissension between supporters and opponents of greater accommodation to Canadian ways. During the same decade, however, a new wave of refugees from Russia introduced a more liberal outlook that has greatly affected many Canadian Mennonites.

Among Catholics, who received a larger proportion of immigrants than before 1914, resistance to assimilation confirmed a trend to ethnic pluralism and compelled greater recognition of conflicting national aspirations. To Protestants it meant the collapse of what I. F. Mackinnon has called the "old home mission policy,"[18] which had sought to persuade immigrants to adopt traditional Canadian values and ultimately to comprehend them within existing Canadian churches. Church leaders began to admit their previous arrogance and added race prejudice to their catalogue of sins. Typical of the new experiments was one among Ukrainians at Insinger, Saskatchewan, where proselytism was eschewed and orientation to Canadian ways was tempered with respect for Ukrainian traditions.[19] The concept of Canada as a mosaic rather than a melting-pot of races began to emerge, and churches cooperated with schools and service clubs to promote it.

## THE ECLIPSE OF THE SOCIAL GOSPEL

The growing agreement of the churches on ambitious social goals was another casualty of the 1920s. The first signal of coming trouble appeared at Winnipeg in 1919. In May of that year a general sympathetic strike was called in support of an ironworkers' union that had been refused certification. Several graduates of Wesley College spoke publicly on behalf of the strike, and Canon F. G. Scott lent it the prestige of his fame as a wartime chaplain. The unaccustomed massiveness of the strike, however, frightened not only the well-to-do but many who had shown considerable sympathy for labour. A citizens' committee of prominent men raised the cry of Bolshevism and blamed foreign agitators for the trouble, although most of the strikers were native-born and many were war veterans. Several men associated with the strike were arrested, including J. S. Woodsworth, who had left the Methodist ministry because of his pacifism, and William Ivens, who was still a Methodist minister. Despite scare headlines the churches refused to be stampeded into a witch-hunt and church papers and officials tended to a favourable or at least moderate appraisal of the strike.[20] Nevertheless, the experience destroyed the existing impression of unanimity. Radical ministers sensed a lack of solid support within the church, and some of them withdrew from it. Conservatives were alerted to the unpleasant consequences of taking the rhetoric of the social gospel seriously, and many members of the middle class were shocked to discover how divisive it could be.

As radical ministers came to despair of the conventional churches, they began to organize independent congregations based on a socialist interpretation of the teachings of Jesus and dedicated to free discussion of current issues. These "labour churches" took their name from earlier British models, but in Canada they grew out of people's forums that had been organized by leading social gospellers. William Ivens founded the first in Winnipeg in 1918 after he had been forced out of McDougall Methodist Church by opposition within the congregation. The new church became a rallying point for labour during the Winnipeg strike, and as a result the movement spread to other cities especially in the west. For its leaders, the labour church proved to be a way station on a road leading out of the church into politics. They had already rejected the traditional dogmas of Christianity, but they found it more difficult to surrender its evangelical fervour and its sense of personal fellowship. By 1925, however, their congregations had all dispensed with religious observances and become labour forums. To the churches, the movement served as a warning of where the social gospel could lead. Methodist officials almost unanimously opposed it, and for two years T. Albert Moore of the Board of Evangelism and Social Service exchanged information on its activities with the RCMP.[21] Ecclesiastical alarm seems to have been aroused not so much by the social radicalism or theological liberalism of the labour churches as by their desertion of official Methodism.

After 1920, exponents of social Christianity rapidly began to lose their sense of common purpose. Friends of labour in the Anglican and Presbyterian churches, such as Canon Scott and Dr. C. W. Gordon, showed little inclination to identify themselves with Methodist proposals for a closely regulated society. Even within Methodism, moral reformists increasingly dissociated themselves from sweeping statements on economic and industrial issues, while progressives concentrated their energies on the achievement of church union. There were also growing signs of disaffection among those whom socially minded Christians regarded as natural allies. A printers' strike in 1921 that affected the Methodist publishing house appeared to labour a test of the church's sincerity. When S. W. Fallis, the book steward, allowed himself to be named chairman of the Employers' Defence Committee, the social gospel itself was somewhat discredited.[22] Within the Social Service Council there was a growing rift between those for whom social work was a divine vocation and those for whom it was a scientific profession. By the late 1920s, when an economic boom erased memories of depression, churchmen were less interested in social reconstruction than in the abolition of war and the cultivation of personal religion. To dedicated social gospellers the crowning blow was the abandonment of prohibition by Ontario in 1926. Prohibition had been the coping stone of their program, and its final rejection suggested that Canadians were no longer willing to accept social guidance from the church.

On the whole, the social gospel was not crushed by blows from without but collapsed under its own weight. One difficulty was that the influence of the movement had never penetrated far beyond the clergy and the service professions. It secured neither the commitment of the middle class nor the confidence of labour, and the agrarian leaders whom it did influence proved to be politically inept. Even more serious was a failure to come to grips with the realities of power. The social gospel depended on an optimistic faith in the perfectability of man and was therefore readily blighted by human failure. For many it was a substitute gospel rather than a practical social program.

## THE ATTACK ON MODERNISM

Theological controversy, which had shown signs of fading during the Laurier era, flared up with great intensity in the 1920s. The Baptists, who were most directly affected, had indeed never been entirely free from it since 1908 when criticism was first levelled against Professor I. G. Matthews of McMaster. McMaster continued to be suspect to conservatives, and Brandon College was intermittently under attack from 1912. From early days, a premillennial strain in some sections of the Canadian Baptists had resisted any form of accommodation to modern learning. Nevertheless, the resurgence of controversy in the 1920s resulted from the intrusion of a new influence. Fundamentalism, which was winning adherents among all denominations of evangelical background in the United States at the time, resembled strains of the older conservatism in its emphasis on the inerrancy of the Bible, on interpretation of the atonement in terms of Christ's death as a substitute for sinners, and on a literal second coming of Christ. To these, in reaction against the widespread acceptance within the church of Darwinism, biblical criticism, and political involvement, it added the vigour and intolerance of crusading counter-revolution. In Canada it provoked assaults on Brandon College that contributed to its secularization in 1939, split the British Columbia Convention in 1925, and gave rise to a controversy in Ontario that calls for more extended notice.

Dissension began within Jarvis Street Baptist Church, Toronto, the largest and wealthiest congregation in the Convention of Ontario and Quebec.[23] T. T. Shields, its pastor since 1910, had a continent-wide reputation among fundamentalists and at one time combined the presidency of an Iowa college with his Toronto pastorate. He sought to make Jarvis Street a centre for Canadian fundamentalism, importing many American preachers whose sensational exposés of modernism were not to the taste of most of his parishioners. In 1921, he was asked to resign but managed to hang on, and as a result many members withdrew to form Park Road Church. Thus ensured the support of a congregation of personal followers, Shields began to seek targets elsewhere. McMaster was especially vulnerable, and many of his former parishioners were on its board. In the Convention and through the *Gospel Witness*, founded in 1922, he and his associates condemned the teaching of L. H. Marshall, the proposed appointment of several governors, and the offer of an honorary degree to an alleged modernist. In these controversies, Shields never shrank from personal invective. Sessions of the Convention were thrown into such an uproar that it was difficult to transact normal business, but a majority refused to uphold his allegations.

In 1926, Shields and his followers withdrew their support from the projects of the Convention, setting up their own college and missionary organization. They continued, however, to demand a voice in its deliberations. The Convention, having no constitutional procedure for expelling congregations, now found itself in the embarrassing position of having to secure legislation from Parliament authorizing a change in its rules. In 1928 some of the dissidents founded the Union of Regular Baptist Churches, and those who joined it were promptly expelled from the Convention. The new union did not succeed in embracing all who dissented from the Convention's policies, most of the rest forming the Fellowship of Independent Baptist Churches. The Convention itself, although seriously damaged, gradually recovered much of its former strength. It remained apprehensive of renewed fundamentalist attacks, however, and caution in public utterance often seemed the easiest way to avoid them.[24]

Conflict within the Church of England between Anglo-Catholics and evangelicals, which had smouldered inconclusively for decades, flared once more into public controversy. The usual exchange of polemical pamphlets ensued, and in Toronto, aroused evangelicals demonstrated their loyalty to the principles of the Reformation by snatching vestments from St. Thomas's Church and trampling them in the mud. Although preoccupied with distinctively Anglican issues, the evangelical party owed its resurgence in large measure to fundamentalist agitation. Dyson Hague, a Toronto rector whom the militants acknowledged as their leader, was both in sympathy and in contact with prominent fundamentalists.

## THE DEBATE OVER CHURCH UNION

Consideration of church union, which had been postponed by the Presbyterians in 1912, was taken up again by the general assembly of 1916. Meanwhile, another popular vote in 1915 had revealed not the unanimity for which the unionists had hoped but a somewhat larger negative vote.[25] On the other hand, an unexpected surge of local unions served notice that if the Presbyterian Church failed to consummate the union it was in danger of losing many of its western congregations and with them its standing as a national body. The commissioners decided to proceed, but postponed action until the fighting men should have returned from Europe. In 1917 there was a further agreement to suspend controversy until a year after the war's end. Thus the final stages of the movement towards union took place during the ill-tempered twenties. There could scarcely have been a decade less conducive to such a project. Union was to have been the culmination of an era of consensus, but when it took place that consensus was in its final stages of disintegration. Paradoxically, the desire to give Christian fellowship a more adequate embodiment set off one of the most bitter controversies in the experience of the Canadian church.

The atmosphere of the 1920s cannot be held responsible for the lack of unanimity in the Presbyterian Church on the union issue. The first vote in 1912 showed that a substantial minority was unconvinced of the desirability of union. Organized opposition appeared as early as 1910 with the formation of the Presbyterian Association for the Federation of the Protestant Denominations, and it became more effective in 1916 when the Presbyterian Church Association based its appeal on the simpler propositions of maintaining the existing denominational structure. With the advantage of hindsight it can be argued that schism in the Presbyterian Church was inherent in the first steps towards union. Unionist leaders were not altogether unreasonable, however, in anticipating that growth in mutual understanding and further clarification of the issues would result in an increased majority for union. They had even more reason, in view of past Canadian experience, to hope that those who voted against union would finally acquiesce in the decision of the church as a whole. There had been vigorous and sometimes acrimonious debate in the Canada Presbyterian Church before the union of 1875, but practically the entire body had entered the Presbyterian Church in Canada. Even those who did not enter the United Church at the outset might be expected to do so later, following the example set by elements of the Kirk after 1875. It seems reasonable to regard the increasing—and increasingly determined—resistance not as an inevitable consequence of prolonged reflection but as one of the first symptoms of a polarization of opinion that would be one of the most pronounced characteristics of the church life of the decade after the war.

There were, certainly, parallels between the arguments of the non-concurrents and attitudes that were current far beyond the boundaries of Presbyterianism. The same intensification of ethnic consciousness that affected French Canadians and Ukrainians may have contributed to the prominence in the anti-unionist ranks of ministers recently out from Scotland and especially Ireland. Reaction against some of the radical manifestations of the social gospel was easily translated into suspicions of political Methodism. In 1922, S. D. Chown, the Methodist general superintendent, was said to have urged church union as a means to "religio-political" control of the nation. Although his meaning had been rather different, the alacrity with which anti-unionists seized on the issue indicated considerable drawing back from earlier visions of the church as an arbiter of Canadian life.[26] Fundamentalism also had its effects on the controversy. The orthodoxy of the Basis of Union had seldom been questioned by early opponents of union, indeed the chief complaint of such leaders as Principal D. J. Fraser of the Presbyterian College at Montreal had been that it was too restrictive. A very different position was adopted by those who in 1924 took out a writ against prominent unionists on the ground that the United Church would not be committed to all the doctrines of the Westminster Assembly and specifically cited predestination both to eternal life and to eternal damnation. The issue that aroused most bitterness was the fundamental one of the right even of church courts to merge the Presbyterian Church into a larger body. It had been raised almost at the outset of the union movement, but insistence on the immutability of ecclesiastical as well as ethnic and theological identity was particularly congenial to the mentality of the 1920s.

In 1921, the general assembly ended an uneasy truce by resolving to unite "as expeditiously as possible."[27] The commissioners realized by this time that all hope of unanimity was gone, but meanwhile the continuance of local unions with the consent and even the backing of the non-concurrents had made turning back more difficult than ever. The two sides prepared for action. The Presbyterian union committee was chaired by George C. Pidgeon of Bloor Street Church, Toronto, while Methodist and Congregational committees offered moral but not too conspicuous support. The Presbyterian Church Association, which had disbanded during the truce, reorganized in 1922 and enlisted an active women's auxiliary.

Even at this late stage there were attempts to produce a result other than the one that seemed to be shaping up. In 1920 the Lambeth conference had reissued its famous quadrilateral with revisions designed to facilitate union with non-episcopal churches and had urged member churches to take the initiative in seeking such union. Archbishop S. P. Matheson, the primate of the Church of England in Canada, was accordingly instructed by the House of Bishops to send copies to the presiding officers of other leading communions.[28] Shortly thereafter a group of prominent ministers in Montreal, including Anglicans as well as Presbyterians of both parties, expressed their willingness to accept some form of mutual commissioning in order to facilitate union. These initiatives provoked fears that current prospects of union would be jeopardized, and indeed Matheson had hinted in his approach that he did not really expect immediate action. He was politely thanked and promised a future reopening of the question that would take place only many years later. A similar initiative from the Disciples of Christ in 1923 was referred to the first general council of the United Church without any greater result.

In 1923, D. R. Drummond, secretary of the general board of the Presbyterian Church and hitherto a supporter of union, suggested that controversy had become so disruptive that a solution other than organic union had to be sought. In a pamphlet, *Is There Not a Way Out?*[29] he revived the alternative of federation that had been rejected in 1906. He received a warm initial response, but at the assembly in 1923 at Port Arthur his proposal attracted fewer votes than outright rejection of union. After a classic debate the assembly determined to unite "forthwith,"[30] and the two factions summoned their clans to what can only be described as battle.

The contest resolved itself into two rather distinct actions, one directed towards legislators, the other towards the people. Theoretically the churches could simply have united and then allowed the courts to settle the property questions that would inevitably arise. Such a course would have been full of uncertainties, for the courts might have awarded all the property to either group or divided it arbitrarily between them. It would also have delayed a final settlement for several years and thus prolonged controversy and mutual suspicion. The churches therefore determined to seek enabling legislation, while the nonconcurrents opposed it as an invasion by the state of the rights of the church. The two sides confronted one another both in the federal parliament and in the provincial legislatures, which had authority over property and civil rights. Whatever their preference might have been, the church authorities were plainly told by their legal advisers that legislation would be granted only on the basis of an equitable division of property.[31] They also recognized that individual Presbyterian congregations would have to be given the right to decide whether they would enter the United Church. This precedent had been set in 1875 and even in earlier Presbyterian unions, and courts throughout North America had always tended to give priority to congregational rights. It was thus important for each side to enlist popular support, especially in strategic congregations.

The legislative struggle was marked by dramatic incidents, cloak-and-dagger intrigues, and sudden reversals of fortune. It was embittered less by disputes over details than by the last-ditch determination of the opposition to prevent a union whose validity they refused to recognize. The position of the unionists was made more difficult by the inclination of many Anglicans and Roman Catholics to regard the project as a threat to their position rather than as a step towards wider union, somewhat eased by the reluctance of many French-Canadian members to take any part in the proceedings. At Ottawa the Private Bills Committee accepted an amendment that would have referred the whole matter to the courts,[32] but after prolonged debate Parliament took the unusual step of refusing its advice and passed the original bill almost unchanged. Although the vote did not follow party lines, the drama of the debate was heightened by the position on opposite sides of Prime Minister Mackenzie King and Opposition Leader Arthur Meighen. Meighen was the abler debater, and unionists gave him considerable credit for helping to turn the tide. In 1924, the Ontario union bill was altered in committee, not only to award the identity of the Presbyterian Church in Canada to the nonconcurrents, but to do a like favour for non-existent continuing Methodist and Congregational groups.[33] The bill was withdrawn, and passed in the following year only when opponents waived their objections on the understanding that Knox College would be awarded to the nonconcurrents. Similar negotiations took place not only in all other provinces but in Newfoundland and Bermuda.

Attempts by both parties to sway opinion within the church resulted in a deluge of paper. In general, however, the unionists placed greater reliance on literature, and the nonconcurrents on personal canvassing. Since congregations would go into the United Church unless they requested otherwise, unionists usually allowed their opponents to raise the issue and thus often lost the initiative. In the end an approximately equal number of votes were cast on both sides, although especially in the west and in rural areas many congregations entered union without a vote. About two-thirds of the Presbyterian membership entered The United Church of Canada, including a larger proportion of elders and an overwhelming majority of ministers. The remainder insisted that they represented those who had been faithful to the Presbyterian Church in Canada.

Conflicting claims to identity aside, what were in some respects two new churches came into being on June 10, 1925. Both were launched with great fervour and with some disappointment. Both performed impressively. The United Church of Canada had remarkable success in uniting its diverse traditions and became, in a measure, the church of national consensus it had hoped to be. The Presbyterian Church in Canada, bereft of ministers and organization although not of wealth, became a functioning denomination more quickly than it had dared to hope. For neither, however, was the time an easy one. The United Church came into existence when the vision that had inspired it was fading, and its leaders waited in vain for an expected revival of religion. The Presbyterians had great difficulty in establishing a consensus of their own among those who for one reason or another had voted against consensus, and many were attracted to forms of biblical and credal fundamentalism that had not previously been typical of Canadian Presbyterianism.

## THE EMERGENCE OF NEW DENOMINATIONS

The most startling reversal of the ecumenical tendency so evident in the early years of the century took place in western Canada. Hitherto a hotbed of unionist sentiment, it had become by 1930 the recognized breeding ground of sectarian movements. Most of the new denominations that would effect this transformation had actually appeared before the first world war, but with followings so small that they were scarcely noticed. In 1890 a Canadian, A. B. Simpson, founded the Christian and Missionary Alliance. The Church of the Nazarene appeared in Canada in 1908. In 1906 R. E. McAlister was reputed to be the first Canadian to receive the Pentecostal experience of speaking with tongues, and in 1919 the movement had taken definitive form in the Pentecostal Assemblies of Canada.[34] In 1922 the Prairie Bible Institute at Three Hills, Alberta, undenominational but fundamentalist, began its work of training emissaries for a great variety of conservative denominations. In 1927 William Aberhart broke with the Baptists to found the Prophetic Bible Institute at Calgary. Almost without exception, sects of any magnitude took advantage of the new medium of radio to extend their range far beyond what any number of travelling evangelists would have been able to accomplish.

Despite the popularity of church union in many circles, these movements found opportunities already prepared for them in western Canada. Many westerners had come from parts of the United States where populist movements had been impregnated with the fundamentalism of William Jennings Bryan and were thus prepared to welcome religious enthusiasts. Rural areas untouched by the churches, served only in the summer by student ministers, or left vacant during wartime provided plentiful openings where new denominations could establish causes. The abandonment of traditional evangelistic techniques by the Methodists and later by the United Church left a residue of unmet religious needs. The unsatisfied scarcely counted in terms of the support of national churches, but there were enough of them to provide atractive openings for untrained and often part-time evangelists.

The newer groups would not have made such rapid progress, however, apart from the general religious atmosphere of the 1920s. The varied elements of their appeal corresponded precisely with moods current in that decade. Their rise coincided with the stiffening of resistance among immigrants to acculturation into the standard Canadian pattern. W. E. Mann estimated in 1955 that 60 per cent of the sectarians of Alberta were of non-Anglo-Saxon origin and that more than half of these were of German background.[35] English-speaking newcomers, he noted, gravitated rather to a heterodox cultic world of greater intellectual pretensions.[36] Socially, sectarianism represented a reaction both against the old individualistic Canadian ideal and the new collectivist one. It appealed to country-dwellers and to those on the margin of urban life, people who resisted identification with labour and felt equally estranged from business and from cooperative farm organizations. Such outsiders naturally gravitated to charismatic denominations where they could find in ecstasy the fulfilment that was denied them in daily life. Theologically, almost all successful sects fitted within the spectrum of fundamentalism. Ecclesiastically, they shared with continuing Presbyterians a profound distaste for the United Church, which became and remained for them a sort of Canadian antichrist. So great was the antipathy that some have explained the rise of sectarianism as a response of Methodists who did not feel at home in the United Church. It might be more accurate to describe it as a reaction against the consensus out of which the United Church was born and against the middle class that formulated it.

## THE END OF CONSENSUS

Sectarianism, fundamentalism, opposition to church union, and resistance to cultural assimilation were all, in their varied ways, expressions of a lack of confidence in the clerical leadership that had been seeking since confederation to give a religious shape to Canadian life. All of them were marked by hostility to official or unofficial establishments and by resentment against ecclesiastical involvement in secular affairs. The real purpose of T. T. Shields' witch-hunts was not to discredit a few theological professors but to dislodge from positions of influence the prominent men to whom the Baptist Convention was accustomed to look with respect. Few leaders of the nonconcurrent Presbyterians had been particularly influential before the union issue was raised, and the party consistently claimed to represent "the people" over against the legislative courts of the church. This hostility to the standing order was equally obvious in ethnic and sectarian movements.

Although the loudest protests against the conventional churches came from the right, there was also much dissatisfaction on the part of Canadians who thought that the churches were not liberal enough. This group was usually less articulate, but probably represented more accurately the direction in which Canada as a whole was moving. Its point of view was expressed most explicitly by the Student Christian Movement of Canada, which was founded in 1920 as an outgrowth of student YMCAs and YWCAs. Many students of the post-war generation were disillusioned with Christian leaders who had blessed the conflict and with the general lack of a spirit of adventure within the church. The SCM translated this mood into trenchant criticism, and politically active leaders found a ready vehicle in the newly founded *Canadian Forum*.[37] During the late 1920s the SCM wearied temporarily of social involvement and turned to the cultivation of a form of introspective religion that largely ignored the supernatural and concentrated on personal fulfilment.[38] Its anti-ecclesiastical bent remained, however, and many of its early leaders would carry into secular affairs a personal Christian commitment that would in an earlier period have been channelled through the church. Other churchmen, including many participants in the Alberta School of Religion (founded 1925), moved from a theology of affirmation to one of search. Many Canadians of the decade, less responsive to liberal Christianity, silently left the church or withdrew to its fringes. They included a substantial proportion of the working class.

The changed atmosphere of the 1920s was a reflection in Canada of a process of secularization that had been affecting western civilization for centuries but was speeded up by the first world war. Canadians had been somewhat sheltered from its effects by their lack of sophistication and by their consequent reliance on the clergy for moral direction. Among Protestants, at least, the generation after the war was different. It was probably the first for which the evangelical experience of conversion was no longer an almost universal norm and to which, therefore, the evangelical vocabulary was ceasing to communicate. It was also the first to deny almost automatic respect to evangelical taboos, although scarcely the first to break them on occasion.

## THE BRIGHT SIDE OF THE TWENTIES

A. R. M. Lower has painted a rather lurid picture of post-war rebellion:

> During the generation between the two wars, Canadians, like Americans, seemed to be determined to kick their institutions to pieces. They made fun of their politicians; they jeered at their preachers and the faithful who followed them, and mocked their parents' decorous youth. In a hundred ways they attempted to cast off the puritanism in which they and their forebears had been steeped. There was no sophistication about Canadian sin; it was just ugly.[39]

If the 1920s were quite that bad, however, the churches were apparently unaware of it. Lower's remarks were scarcely intended to apply to French Canada, and even vigilant Protestant officials found few occasions to complain of the promotion of sweepstakes or of threats to the sanctity of the sabbath or the permanence of marriage. Despite protests from the right and desertions on the left, the churches retained their customary place in the centre of Canadian community life. In some respects, indeed, the years during and after the first world war were a very constructive period for them.

Although the churches had begun to provide midweek activities for various age groups before the end of the nineteenth century, these were reaching professional standards only in the war and post-war years. As in the United States, facilities that had originally been developed for service to under-privileged neighbourhoods gradually became standard equipment in well-to-do urban parishes. During the 1920s there was a proliferation of church gymnasia, including swimming pools, basketball courts, and dressing rooms. Campsites in resort areas supplemented these in summer. Many of these items later became obsolete as communities developed their own facilities, but at the time they both provided needed services and gave many young people at least a marginal attachment to the church.

Young people's work was, indeed, at its zenith. Just before the war the Canadian YMCA, under the leadership of Taylor Statten, had developed the Canadian Standard Efficiency Tests for teen-aged boys.[40] The emphasis of these tests, in harmony with the liberal thinking of the time, was on gradual growth rather than sudden conversion. Programs for Tuxis Boys and Trail Rangers, which featured them, would be regular features of urban Protestantism for several decades, and the parallel Canadian Girls in Training are still flourishing. These programs, although adapted from American models, were provided with Canadian content in line with the nationalistic sentiments of the period. Anglicans, who had lagged somewhat in providing for young people, entered the field seriously with the formation of the General Board of Religious Education in 1918. They and some others preferred the British-based Boy Scouts and Girl Guides, although these were sometimes criticized because their programs were not specifically designed for use by churches. By the 1920s a number of larger congregations were employing full-time directors of Christian education. Candidates for the ministry, who had previously been stimulated by preaching or by service as altar boys, now more often obtained their apprenticeship in youth programs and carried their enthusiasm for group work into their ministries.

Interest in new techniques of communication was stimulated by the invention of radio. On the whole, the churches failed to take advantage of the subtle possibilities of the new medium. The conventional churches confined themselves largely to the broadcasting of church services, which pleased shut-ins but were not very effective in attracting casual listeners. The sects, often more effective although seldom more imaginative, used radio talks as a means of attracting followers and raising money. Whatever their limitations in technique, the churches were at least quick to use the medium and soon had a fair amount of time at their disposal.

The missionary enterprise for which the churches had constantly pressed back the frontiers of Canada was now achieving its most impressive results in the last frontier of the north. In 1913 Bishop Lucas of Mackenzie River began to infuse new energy into Anglican work among the Eskimos of the western Arctic. Missions were established at Coronation Gulf and Victoria Island, and in 1919 Aklavik was founded as a centre of work among the Eskimos. Work also went forward in the eastern Arctic. The enterprise was consolidated in 1927 under Archibald Fleming as Archdeacon of the Arctic, and in 1933 as bishop he instituted the colourful signature of "Archibald the Arctic."[41] Meanwhile in 1912 the Roman Catholics had established their first permanent mission among the Canadian Eskimos, and in 1924 their Eskimo missions were erected into a prefecture apostolic.

If the churches were less uniformly successful in shaping Canadian society during the 1920s than they had been in previous decades, they nevertheless showed increased signs of maturity. There were many indications at the time that Canada itself was coming of age after its innocent Victorian childhood. Pride in the nation flourished as a result of Canada's performance in battle and her attainment of equal status at the peace table and in the League of Nations. With even more reason, Canadians could have been proud that the Group of Seven in painting and E. J. Pratt in poetry had given Canada at last a distinctive if not yet compelling presence in the realm of arts and letters. The churches shared in this development, although they did not always keep pace with it.

The churches responded to the new national consciousness by seeking to become more self-sufficient at home and more significantly involved in decisions abroad. In 1920 the Church of England in Canada inaugurated a policy of gradually dispensing with British aid, in the following year the Methodists decided to seek no further ministerial recruits in Britain, and meanwhile St.

Augustine's Seminary in Scarborough was helping to relieve a chronic undersupply of English-speaking priests in the Roman Catholic Church. Catholic participation in missionary efforts abroad became more direct with the assignment of special areas to Canadian religious orders, and newly founded societies for foreign missions at Quebec and Scarborough directed the efforts of secular priests overseas. Protestant and Orthodox churches were beginning to take part in the developing ecumenical movement.

Originality in literary and artistic expression was less conspicuous, although the foundation of the *Canadian Journal of Religious Thought* in 1924 provided a forum for theological exploration. From 1920, too, Lorne Pierce at The Ryerson Press made the Methodist and later the United Church a sometimes unwitting patron of new trends in poetry and fiction. More typical of the period, however, was an attempt to gather up the riches of the Christian tradition and naturalize them in Canada. At St. Michael's College, Toronto, an Institute of Mediaeval Studies was founded in 1929 with Etienne Gilson of Paris as its director of studies. Combining fidelity to the philosophical heritage of St. Thomas Aquinas with contemporary methods of scholarly research, it would speedily gain an international reputation and in 1939 obtain a pontifical charter.[42] A flowering of liturgical expression, surprising in a country as young as Canada, was especially marked in service and hymn books of the Presbyterian Church just before union and of the United Church just afterwards. Composers for the organ, most notably Healey Willan, drew heavily on the English tradition of church music. In architecture there was a belated Gothic revival. Liturgical scholars and artists of the period were more derivative than original, but the catholicity of their taste and the quality of their work earned them respect and imitation in other countries.

In taking these steps towards a more distinctive expression of Canadian Christianity and towards fuller participation in worldwide Christianity, unfortunately, the churches only widened the gulf that separated them from their dissatisfied members. To some Canadians these gestures were but additional evidence of the hidebound traditionalism of the churches, to others further symptoms of retreat from the less complex spirituality of earlier days. The earthquake shocks of controversy that marked the 1920s would soon subside. The new lines of fissure they revealed would only widen in succeeding years.

### NOTES TO CHAPTER SIX

1. Quoted in Kenneth McNaught, *A Prophet in Politics: A Biography of J. S. Woodsworth* (Toronto: University of Toronto Press, 1959), p. 70.
2. J. M. Bliss, "The Methodist Church and World War I," *Canadian Historical Review*, Vol. XLIX, No. 3 (September 1968), p. 231.
3. Ruth E. Spence, *Prohibition in Canada*, p. 378.

4. *Ibid.*, pp. 444-445.

5. Journal of Proceedings of the General Conference of the Methodist Church, 1918, pp. 341-342; Acts and Proceedings of the 45th General Assembly of the Presbyterian Church in Canada, 1919, p. 79; Journal of Proceedings of the General Synod of the Church of England in Canada, 1918, pp. 320-324.

6. George E. Levy, *The Baptists of the Maritime Provinces, 1753-1946*, p. 299.

7. Richard Allen, *The Social Passion*, pp. 75-78.

8. T. C. B. Boon, *The Anglican Church from the Bay to the Rockies*, p. 319; C. C. McLaurin, *Pioneering in Western Canada*, p. 197.

9. McNaught, *op. cit.*, p. 12.

10. W. A. Visser 't Hooft, *The Background of the Social Gospel in America* (St. Louis: Bethany, n.d.), p. 29.

11. Franklin A. Walker, *Catholic Education and Politics in Ontario*, p. 271.

12. Wellington Bridgman, *Breaking Prairie Sod*, p. 163.

13. See Welf H. Heick, "Becoming an Indigenous Church: the Lutheran Church in Waterloo County, Ontario," *Ontario History*, Vol. LVI, No. 4 (December 1964), pp. 249-260.

14. Paul Yuzyk, *The Ukrainians in Manitoba*, p. 170.

15. Victor Peters, *All Things Common: The Hutterian Way of Life* (Minneapolis: University of Minnesota Press, 1965), pp. 45-48.

16. The fullest and most reliable account of the Doukhobors in Canada is George Woodcock and Ivan Avakumovic, *The Doukhobors* (Toronto: Oxford University Press, 1968).

17. For this account of Mennonite movements of emigration and their effects I am indebted to Abraham Friesen, "Emigration in Mennonite History with Special Reference to the Conservative Mennonite Emigration from Canada to Mexico and South America after World War One," M.A. thesis, University of Manitoba, 1960.

18. I. F. Mackinnon, *Canada and the Minority Churches of Eastern Europe, 1945-1950*, p. 27.

19. Michael Zuk, "The Ukrainian Protestant Missions in Canada," pp. 65-68.

20. A. R. Allen, "The Social Gospel and the Reform Tradition in Canada, 1890-1928," *Canadian Historical Review*, Vol. XLIX, No. 4 (December 1968), p. 394.

21. Correspondence, Methodist Industrial Relations, 1920-22, Archives of Victoria University and The United Church of Canada.

22. Allen, *The Social Passion*, p. 177.

23. For a careful account of the controversy from a point of view sympathetic to the Baptist Convention, see W. Gordon Carder, "Controversy in the Baptist Convention of Ontario and Quebec 1908-1928," *The Canadian Society of Church History Papers*, 1968, pp. 63-90.

24. Stuart Ivison, "Is There a Canadian Baptist Tradition?" in J. W. Grant, ed., *The Churches and the Canadian Experience*, p. 64.

25. For a detailed account of the vote, see C. E. Silcox, *Church Union in Canada*, p. 173.

26. Chown's actual words were as follows: "One does not like to stir up religious controversy, and I will not trade with religious bigotry, but if I may venture to prophesy, I would say with all conviction that if the major churches of Protestantism cannot unite, the battle which is going on now so definitely for the religious control of the country will be lost within the next few years. I do not refer to the school question alone, but to the whole movement within Canada in the religio-political realm." Quoted in *ibid.*, p. 207n.

27. Acts and Proceedings of the 47th General Assembly of the Presbyterian Church in Canada, 1921, pp. 30, 46.

28. Church union file in the Archives of Victoria University and The United Church of Canada.

29. Memorandum published by St. Paul's Church, Hamilton, Ontario.

30. Acts and Proceedings of the 49th General Assembly of the Presbyterian Church in Canada, 1923, pp. 28, 82.

31. Silcox, *op. cit.*, p. 254.

32. Gershom W. Mason, *The Legislative Struggle for Church Union* (Toronto: Ryerson, 1956), p. 96.

33. *Ibid.*, p. 41.

34. E. N. O. Culbeck, "A Brief History of the Pentecostal Assemblies of Canada," in *Canada's Centennial* (Pentecostal Assemblies of Canada, 1967), p. 20.

35. W. E. Mann, *Sect, Cult and Church in Alberta* (Toronto: University of Toronto Press, 1955), p. 35.

36. *Ibid.*, p. 39.

37. Allen, *op. cit.*, p. 302.

38. *Ibid.*, p. 310.

39. A. R. M. Lower, "Religion and Religious Institutions," in George W. Brown, ed., *Canada* (Toronto: University of Toronto Press, 1950), p. 481.

40. C. A. M. Edwards, *Taylor Statten* (Toronto: Ryerson, 1960), pp. 46-47.

41. See his autobiography, *Archibald the Arctic* (Toronto: Saunders, 1965).

42. Lawrence K. Shook, csb, "The Pontifical Institute of Mediaeval Studies: An Historical Survey," in Gerard Mulligan, *Were the Dean's Windows Dusty?* (Montreal: the author, 1966), pp. T1-T31.

# SEVEN

# Years of Crisis

The stock market crash of October 1929 ushered in a worldwide economic depression that would engage the almost obsessive attention of leaders and common people alike until its problems were in turn overshadowed by the threat of war. Canada felt its effects with unusual severity, for dependence on the export of a few staple commodities made its economy especially vulnerable to fluctuations in international trade. Even within the nation some classes and regions were affected much more seriously than others. Dividends and salaries declined by only 14 per cent between 1929 and 1932, although some business and professional men were ruined. Wages fell during the same period by 41.7 per cent, and by 1933 more than a quarter of the labour force was unemployed. Incomes held up better in central Canada, which produced for a protected home market, than in the extremities of the country where exports were all-important. Hardest hit of all were the prairie provinces, where the loss of markets was aggravated by the necessity of paying high interest on debts that had been incurred for earlier expansion and by a prolonged drought that reduced wheat production from 321 million bushels in 1928 to 37 million in 1937. Such inequalities inevitably heightened existing tensions among segments of the Canadian people.

## THE IMPACT OF THE DEPRESSION

Depressions are never opportune, but that of 1929 came at a particularly awkward time for several denominations. The new United Church of Canada, its running-in period scarcely completed, had not seriously begun to think out its place in Canadian society. The Presbyterians were recovering from the wounds of church union, the Baptists from those inflicted by T. T. Shields. The Anglicans were attempting, painfully and as yet not very successfully, to operate with reduced subsidies from England. The Roman Catholics were in some ways the least vulnerable, but in English Canada their resources were already strained by the rising cost of separate schools and in French Canada their religiously oriented trade unions had never been tested by serious economic crisis.

The churches, like all organized communities, had to learn to operate within smaller budgets. All denominations shared in the prevailing scarcity of funds, but the Anglicans came closest to catastrophe. In 1932 the authorities of the ecclesiastical province of Rupert's Land, along with those of the University of Manitoba, learned that J. A. Machray, the respected business man to whom they had entrusted the investment of their capital funds, had frittered them away on the stock market. Each lost an estimated eight hundred thousand dollars, which during the trough of the depression seemed almost impossible to replace. The endowments of the diocese of Rupert's Land, its cathedral, and St. John's College had practically disappeared, while other dioceses of the province suffered substantial losses. To make matters worse, the affected areas had never been financially self-sufficient even in good times and were among the hardest hit by the depression. The church immediately launched a restoration fund, and in narthexes throughout Canada parishioners were confronted with maps on which the stricken dioceses were crisscrossed by black lines of varying thickness. In adversity the Church of England in Canada achieved greater unity and determination than it had ever shown before. The fund was eventually oversubscribed, although T. C. B. Boon has pointed out that at the deflated interest rates of the time it could not replace the revenues that had been lost.[1]

The clergy of the various churches absorbed much of the financial deficiency by accepting cuts in their salaries, in some cases following an example voluntarily set by headquarters staffs. United Church salaries fell by one third,[2] while those of many western Baptists were halved.[3] Buying gasoline to keep outside preaching appointments was a serious problem for many rural ministers. The United Church incurred a debt of $1,700,000 to keep its work going, and Roman Catholics overspent so greatly that the archbishop of Regina found it necessary in 1931 to announce that the church would pay its debts in full.[4] Despite these measures the churches were compelled to cut back on their operations. Ministers were asked to enlarge their territories, college and headquarters staffs were reduced, and some educational and welfare operations were turned over to secular agencies.

The most drastic reductions were in aid to overseas missions, which before the depression had been steadily increasing. The Presbyterians, with relatively few overseas responsibilities and with money invested in bonds that showed "splendid stability,"[5] were not too greatly affected. The Baptists organized a "keeping faith" campaign that made possible the continuing support of missionaries already in the field.[6] At the other end of the scale, however, United Church appropriations to foreign missions fell by more than one half from 1928 to 1935. Some missionaries had to be brought back, and it has been said that only active lobbying behind the scenes forestalled a decision to withdraw from several fields altogether. If support from the Women's Missionary Society had not held up fairly well, even greater retrenchment would have been necessary.

The special difficulties of the United Church arose largely from the extent of its commitments on the prairies, where many hitherto self-supporting congregations had to be subsidized even to pay diminished salaries. In all Protestant churches, however, questions were being raised about the value of overseas missions. Old-style zeal for saving the souls of the heathen from hell fire was on the wane, and in 1932 a group of prominent American laymen promulgated a philosophy of cooperation with other religious communities.[7] Many concluded that in a time of financial strain the foreign missionary enterprise was expendable, although recognition that Christians live in what Wendell Willkie called "one world" brought some revival of interest by the end of the decade.

Some measure of retrenchment was probably good for the church in the long run. The Presbyterians abandoned some marginal causes. The United Church was able to effect local amalgamations that were part of the unfinished business of union. A few enterprises that had served their day were closed out. Some work overseas that had been reserved to missionaries only through institutional inertia was turned over to nationals. Unfortunately, however, the continuance of services had to depend to a considerable extent on ability to pay for them. Cuts were felt most keenly on the frontiers, in overseas or Indian work. Recruiting for the ministry was discouraged, thus preparing the way for a future shortage. Worse still, depression financing put a brake on experimentation in such fields as communication and social involvement. There was enough money to keep the existing machinery from breaking down, but seldom enough to permit bold innovation.

## MUTUAL AID AND SELF-HELP

The first concern of the churches, despite their own financial reverses, was to meet the immediate needs of people who were suffering economically and sometimes physically. The most urgent calls came from the prairies, where agricultural disaster interrupted decades of almost continuous prosperity and expansion. A poor harvest in southwestern Saskatchewan in 1929 was a prelude to eight years of complete or partial crop failure over large sections of the southern prairies. Drought combined with plummeting wheat prices to wreck the economic base of the region, and failure to use methods that would have provided reserves of moisture ruined even vegetable gardens and sent great clouds of dust over the prairies. Many migrated further north, abandoning once-lucrative farms that had become temporarily worthless.

The churches responded by sending carloads of clothing and food to the stricken areas. Their effort was an ecumenical one in which Protestants and

Catholics collaborated not only with each other but with the YMCA, the federal government, and the railways. The needs of the prairies presented a special challenge to The United Church of Canada, which was strongly represented in the drought area and which had as its moderator during the crucial years from 1930 to 1932 the church historian Edmund H. Oliver of Saskatchewan. In 1931 this church set up a National Emergency Relief Commission, but missionary superintendent George Dorey had already made himself a one-man lobby to enlist all possible supporters in a program of instant rescue. This was the first occasion on which the young church was dramatically called upon to give leadership in a national effort, and in proving itself capable it consolidated the emotional loyalties of many of its members.

Other aspects of the depression called for more sustained and diversified efforts. Institutional missions in the cities took on a renewed importance, and some of them began to experiment with more sophisticated community programs. All Peoples' Missions temporarily became popular again by providing resources that immigrant churches could not match,[8] while a number of Anglican hostels for immigrants became shelters for transients.[9] In the drought belt of Saskatchewan, Father Athol Murray opened a college to make available to farm boys an education they could not otherwise have afforded. In Quebec, where a mounting surplus of labour was aggravated by American restrictions on immigration, the church revived its flagging interest in colonization. Most settlers were jobless workers from the cities who adopted out of necessity a manner of life for which they had neither aptitude nor taste, and most of them failed. Enough succeeded, however, to add Abitibi to the list of Canada's important agricultural areas.

In eastern Nova Scotia, where the depression merely aggravated chronic hard times, the local Roman Catholic university sponsored a remarkable enterprise of self-help. As in Quebec, cooperatives had existed long before the depression. The first was organized among farmers about 1914 by Hugh Macpherson, president of St. Francis Xavier University in Antigonish. He was assisted by James Tompkins, the vice-president, who in 1922 was discreetly sent to the outport of Canso as parish priest after taking a position on university federation in Nova Scotia that displeased some Catholics. In 1924 the university began to sponsor an annual conference on social and economic problems, and in 1928 it set up an extension department to promote adult education. These efforts, although persistent, were on a relatively small scale.

Bigger things became possible in 1930, when as the result of a royal commission on the economy of the region the government urged the extension department to undertake a program of community development among fishermen. With financial aid from the Carnegie Corporation, the university set out to educate and organize the common people. Father Tompkins gave the movement its basic philosophy, along with an enthusiasm that never flagged. M. M. Coady, director of the extension department, was the chief planner and interpreter of the program. J. D. N. MacDonald, a rural minister of the United Church, represented an important ecumenical dimension. Credit unions and cooperatives for buying and selling sprang up throughout eastern Nova Scotia and Cape Breton Island, especially in Catholic communities, and Tompkins' appointment to the coal-mining village of Reserve in 1935 led to the addition of cooperative housing. Leaders of the movement emphasized practical education, and many fishermen, farmers, and miners were challenged to devise solutions to their own economic problems.

The cooperative movement found theological support in Pius XI's encyclical *Quadragesimo Anno* of 1931, which contained strictures against grasping middlemen even stronger than those of *Rerum Novarum*[10] and lauded voluntary associations for mutual help.[11] It was promoted, on occasion, as a counterweight to the current popularity of Communism among Cape Breton miners. Basically, however, cooperation was an indigenous response to the inequities of a regional pattern of business known as the "truck" system. Company stores kept their customers supplied with goods and in return accepted produce on account. Many villagers were under perpetual obligation to merchants, who thus had unusual opportunities to fix both the prices they paid and the prices they charged. Clergymen were naturally concerned with the welfare of their people, and as early as 1882 Neil McNeil's magazine *The Aurora* had noted the attempt of one parish priest to secure alternative markets for fish.[12] The cooperative movement of the 1930s was essentially an attempt to rescue producers of primary products from virtual peonage. At first there was considerable opposition from the powerful, but the commendation of Pius XI in 1938 made the movement thoroughly respectable. Its economic results were not spectacular, but by teaching people how to improve their own circumstances it helped to dispel an ingrained sense of helplessness. Towards the end of the depression its influence spread to Prince Edward Island and then to Quebec.

PROTESTANT MOVEMENTS OF SOCIAL REFORM

Coming after several decades of prosperity and spectacular national growth, the depression seemed to most Canadians not only unfortunate but unnatural. It seemed doubly so to churchmen who had become accustomed to expect the imminent coming of the Kingdom of God on earth and who associated its coming, however vaguely, with major changes in the structure of society. In some circles the conviction took hold that programs of short-term relief and small-scale voluntary cooperation, however commendable in themselves, did nothing to remove the inherent defects of the current economic system. Pity for ruined farmers and unemployed workers was readily translated into indignation against the capitalists and financiers whose manipulations had apparently caused the slump. In the case of underpaid clergy, sympathy for the unfortunate was reinforced by resentment against ministers of wealthy congregations who continued to receive comparatively large salaries. The United Church established a series of emergency funds and in 1938 invited ministers to contribute on a sliding scale, but there was no compulsion and little effective equalization resulted.[13]

Resentments and suspicions of injustice gradually crystallized into specific movements of reform that originated within the church and claimed to embody Christian principles. These revived many of the emphases of the social gospel, but their motivation was in some respects quite different. Whereas the social gospel had been patronized and to a large extent formulated by the established leadership of the churches, the radicalism of the depression era developed in conscious opposition to it. Movements of the period tended either to the left or to the right, and despite some common features there was little traffic between the two. Those of the left, which originated chiefly within the more conventional Protestant churches, blamed most of the ills of society on private control of the means of production and desired to replace capitalism with some form of socialism. Those of the right, which were most often products of a sectarian environment, blamed most of the ills of society on the improper regulation of money and credit and sought financial remedies within the capitalistic system. The radical left was especially concerned with the plight of the underpaid or unemployed worker, the radical right with that of the hard-pressed debtor.

Radicals of the left were most conspicuous in the United Church, where the social gospel's promise of a better society had by no means been forgotten. In April 1931 a group of socially concerned members met at Carlton Street United Church, Toronto, to formulate a program of action. They organized themselves as a "Movement for a Christian Social Order," condemned the existing economic system, and declared as one of their convictions "that the achieving of a Christian social order would entail the socializing of the organized agencies of production."[14] In 1934 this movement took more formal shape as the Fellowship for a Christian Social Order, which became an unofficial ginger group within the United Church and later opened its membership to other denominations. The Fellowship organized branches in United Church conferences, of which some soon became moribund but others remained active for years. It contributed regular columns to the church-sponsored *New Outlook* and to *The United Churchman* of Sackville, New Brunswick. Its most ambitious project was the publication in 1936 of a substantial symposium entitled *Towards the Christian Revolution*.[15]

Similar demands for extensive changes in the economic system were heard in other denominations. M. J. Coldwell, who was to become the second leader of the CCF, owed many of his economic ideas to a tradition of Christian socialism within the Church of England. Robert Connell of British Columbia, under whose leadership the CCF first became the official opposition in a provincial legislature, was an Anglican clergyman. Most eastern Baptists were conservative, but there was a strong strain of social radicalism on the prairies. Prospective ministers from this region usually studied theology in the United States rather than at McMaster, and many of them attended Rochester Seminary where Walter Rauschenbusch had established a tradition of social Christianity. T. C. Douglas and John G. Diefenbaker represent widely varying types of western radicalism that emerged within the Baptist denomination. Presbyterians were for the most part suspicious of the social gospel, which was actually what some of them voted against in 1925. W. G. Brown promoted a vigorous Tory radicalism on the prairies, however, and a few Presbyterian members would help to push the Fellowship for a Christian Social Order further to the left in its later days.

Many of the ideas of these movements were, inevitably, borrowed from earlier years. Anglicans looked to the Christian socialism of F. D. Maurice or of high church fellowships for social action, Presbyterians to the involvement of Thomas Chalmers in urban renewal, United Churchmen and Baptists to the American social gospel or to a radical strain within English dissent. The very name of the Fellowship for a Christian Social Order recalled the optimism and perfectionism that had flourished around the turn of the twentieth century. There was now, however, a much more general readiness to promote social change through direct political action than before. When the CCF was formed in 1932 most radicals within the churches rallied to its support, taking encouragement from the presence within its ranks of such alumni of the social gospel as Woodsworth, Douglas, and S. H. Knowles. They contributed several leading members to the League for Social Reconstruction, which functioned in the early years as an intellectual arm of the CCF. Many ministers became candidates for public office, either for the CCF or for H. H. Stevens' abortive Reconstruction party in 1935. The paternalistic aspect of the older social gospel held much less attraction for reformers of the new breed. They had no inclination to save workers from themselves and therefore quietly dropped prohibition and other moral issues from their agenda of urgent concerns. Committees of evangelism and social service became uneasy coalitions of old-style moralists and new-style radicals, each willing to sponsor the others' resolutions for the sake of having their own brought forward.

Another kind of protest had begun to be heard in 1932 when William Aberhart, pastor of the Calgary Prophetic Bible Institute, introduced the Social Credit theories of C. H. Douglas into his weekly program of religious radio.[16] Fundamentalist Albertans readily extended to Aberhart's economic theories the authority they were accustomed to accord to his expositions of the Book of Revelation, and the force of his charismatic personality swept up many others who were prepared to welcome any remedy for depression. In the provincial election of 1935 a motley aggregation of candidates unseated the venerable but scandal-racked administration of the United Farmers of Alberta by offering a program of monetary reform that included a monthly dividend of twenty-five dollars, backed only by the province's resources, to each man, woman, and child. Aberhart became premier in a government that always retained some of the aspects of a religious movement and on his retirement in 1943 handed over power to E. C. Manning, who had already succeeded him as pastor of the Prophetic Bible Institute. When the new administration sought to implement measures of Social Credit and to bring the banks under its control, however, the federal government made use of powers of disallowance that had almost been allowed to lapse. Since that time Social Credit has been content to encourage the conservative virtues of enterprise and thrift.

The ideological background of Social Credit contrasted sharply with that of the various types of Christian socialism. It took shape in a milieu of sectarian Protestantism where the worldliness of the social gospel had always been suspect, although it absorbed many social gospel ideas that had been popularized by the United Farmers. It came to public notice not through the medium of organizations dedicated to social change but in direct association with the preaching of an otherworldly message. It represented an approach to social change that was never, then or later, taken seriously in the courts of conventional churches. It resulted, despite the hostility of its promoters to political Christianity, in the formation of a political party that until recently always opened its rallies with the singing of a hymn.

Like the United Farmers whom they overthrew, however, spokesmen for Social Credit thought of their movement not as a new political party but rather as an alternative to politics. "Progress, not politics" was the slogan on which W. A. C. Bennett of British Columbia won one of his numerous elections. Social Credit was essentially a people's movement that drew most of its early support, like the religious sects with which it had an obvious affinity, from classes that felt themselves cut off from access to power. It found its typical candidates, not like the old parties in the business establishment, not like the CCF among leaders of farm and labour organizations, but in vocations that had seldom been represented in legislatures, such as farming, small-town business, and the Christian ministry. Despite its pretentious ideological base it leaned to homemade remedies. Its object was not to change the economic system but to rid the system of parasites and manipulators. Some early spokesmen had an unfortunate tendency to imagine an international conspiracy of Jewish financiers and Communists, but the leaders soon disclaimed them.

## CATHOLIC MOVEMENTS OF SOCIAL REFORM

Protestant critics of the prevailing economic system had their counter-parts in Roman Catholic Quebec. Priests who worked in urban parishes or served as chaplains to Catholic unions sometimes imbibed a militancy that set them in sharp opposition to employers and led them to demand national-ization of such vital industries as electricity. Others, more responsive to the complaints of farmers or retail merchants, inclined to the Quebec version of Social Credit. As in Alberta these liked to think of Social Credit as a religious movement rather than as a political program, to the point where Cardinal Villeneuve of Quebec had to repudiate their claim to be the only true inter-preters of papal social doctrine.[17]

Differences in mental climate between Quebec and the rest of Canada were so great, however, that such parallels are likely to be more misleading than helpful. Among English-speaking Canadians liberal democracy enjoyed a prestige, and socialism a measure of respectability, that neither had achieved in Quebec even among socially engaged Catholics. Through fear of Communism, respect for public order, and preference for an organic view of society, on the other hand, many French-Canadian Catholics had a sympathy for authoritarian governments of the right that never failed to shock Protestants. Most of them outspokenly supported Franco's nationalists in the Spanish civil war and later covertly sympathized with Pétain's regime at Vichy, although in 1938 the local fascist *Parti National Social Chrétien* was officially condemned by the coadjutor archbishop of Montreal.[18] Thus neither set of earnest reformers recognized much affinity with the other, and the distance was further increased by the near-identification in Quebec of the search for social justice with the defence of ethnic identity.

The most influential social reformers in Quebec during the depression were neither Social Crediters nor socialists. Following no precise party line, they nevertheless had enough in common to constitute a movement. They opposed political corruption and economic monopoly (especially in foreign hands), and favoured economic planning through the voluntary collabora-tion of segments of the community. So far they could count on ready sym-pathy from many radical Protestants, but nothing could have been more calculated to repel the latter than the xenophobia and occasional anti-Semitism of organizations such as *la Jeunesse ouvrière catholique* and *la Jeunesse étudiante catholique* through which they made their impact upon the youth of the province. They were, indeed, direct heirs of the clerical nationalism of the 1920s and through it of the crusading ultramontanism of the late nineteenth century. Increasingly, however, leaders turned their attention from the cultural to the economic bases of ethnic and religious survival.

The theological base of reform was strengthened by the research of the

Jesuit-sponsored *Ecole Sociale Populaire*, which first systematically sought to apply the teaching of the papal encyclicals to the realities of industrial Quebec. Enlisting a number of lay intellectuals, the school published in 1933 a program of social restoration that would be immensely influential in shaping the future. The movement found a political arm in *l'Action Liberale Nationale*, which under the leadership of Paul Gouin helped to unseat the Liberals in the provincial election of 1936. In the coalition that resulted, however, the Conservative leader Maurice Duplessis emerged as the holder of real power. Those who had hoped for social restoration were temporarily disappointed, but the seeds of radical change had taken firm root.

The social ideal of almost all Catholic reformers in Quebec was corporatism, a system in which conflict would be minimized by the cooperation of associations representing different elements of society. The formation of such professional groups, which were to be motivated by Christian concern and instructed in Catholic social doctrine, had been urged in several encyclicals as an alternative to outright individualism or collectivism. Corporatists desired to reconstitute society as an organism rather than as a mass of atomic individuals, in a manner comparable to St. Paul's metaphor of the church as a body consisting of interdependent members.[19] To Protestants the word "corporatism" suggested a fascist orientation, for professional corporations were favoured both in Mussolini's Italy and in Franco's Spain. In fact the concept was broad enough to allow development along either authoritarian or popular lines. Corporatists of the right desired an isolationist, tightly organized clerical state. Corporatists of the left anticipated current demands for participatory democracy and for the decentralization of decision-making. They drew on the tradition of Henri Bourassa, whose desire for a cooperative society to be achieved by democratic means made him at times an informal ally of J. S. Woodsworth,[20] and in the 1930s looked chiefly to the leadership of Georges-Henri Lévesque of Laval University.

## FORMULATING SOCIAL POLICIES

Amid this welter of movements and ideologies the churches had to decide how much and what to say officially about social and economic issues. The resources with which Protestants and Roman Catholics entered the period contrasted sharply. Protestants were left with tattered remnants of the social gospel, which predisposed them to a somewhat progressive stance but gave them little guidance on specific questions. Catholics had the social doctrine of *Rerum Novarum*, developed somewhat in later encyclicals but hitherto usually interpreted in Canada in a fairly conservative sense. The problem of Protestants was to transform a general bias into a policy, that of Catholics to adapt a fairly rigid line to new and unprecedented circumstances.

Some communions were much readier to express opinions about social issues than others. The Presbyterians were more interested in their own internal reconstruction, having retained few social activists in 1925. Until 1933 they did not even have a national committee responsible for initiating social policy, and the committee then formed bore the noncommital title of "Evangelism and Church Life and Work." Public statements were largely restricted to such moral questions as the sanctity of the sabbath. The Baptists, always reticent about giving advice to the state and not yet recovered from the effects of controversy in the 1920s, had little to say on social questions during the early years of the depression. In 1937, however, the Convention of Ontario and Quebec endorsed collective bargaining and unemployment insurance.[21] The Anglicans had no such inhibitions against secular involvement. The scars of earlier party conflicts had made them wary of controversial public pronouncements, however, and evangelical insistence on the primacy of individual conversion confirmed them in their caution. In 1931 their triennial general synod called for emergency measures to meet the depression, largely at the prompting of Canon C. W. Vernon, the energetic secretary of their Council for Social Service. Vernon died in early 1934, and the general synods of 1934 and 1937 suggested few radical reforms. The most articulate non-Roman communion was the United Church of Canada, which inherited concern for social expression from all of its components and which was compelled by events to resolve divergent points of view in a hurry. A rash of resolutions and debates attracted public notice and gave the church a reputation for social radicalism. The truth was somewhat more complex.

During the depression there was, undoubtedly, a sustained attempt to commit the United Church to a socialist program. Activists were prominent in evangelism and social service committees at all levels, and they had considerable success in piloting resolutions through presbyteries and conferences. They reached the peak of their success at the Toronto Conference of 1933, which at the prompting of Professor John Line of Emmanuel College passed a series of resolutions which declared, among other things, "that the application of the principle of Jesus to economic conditions would mean the end of the capitalistic system."[22] The report specified the socialization of banks, natural resources, transportation, and other key services and industries as legitimate goals for a Christian society. Similar demands for radical social changes were made by the Toronto, Saskatchewan, and British Columbia conferences in 1935.

There were limits, however, beyond which the United Church as a whole could not be persuaded to go. A commission on the church and industry suggested in 1932 that the church should be an active agent of social change, but it disclaimed any intention of speaking for the church as such.[23] A commission on the social order under the chairmanship of Sir Robert Falconer presented an even more ambitious report in 1934. The commission urged the church to commit itself to the search for a society "approximating the Kingdom of God on earth" and listed various criteria of such a society.[24] It declined to specify the means by which it might be attained, however, although a minority report asked for communal ownership and control of important means of production.[25] Later general councils were even more cautious. Every radical resolution was carefully scrutinized, and demands for a closed shop at the United Church Publishing House were refused in 1936 and again in 1938.

Despite their refusal to commit themselves to revolutionary social programs, the major Protestant churches were sympathetic to evolutionary changes. They had always regarded social welfare as an area of direct concern, and although other agencies were now taking over major responsibility for it they continued to press governments for action to meet pressing needs and to bring about a measure of economic equalization. The United Church spoke regularly in favour of penal reform, civil liberties, and birth control. Vernon persuaded the Council for Social Service and eventually the Anglican Church as a whole that the state was responsible for the social security of its citizens. In Nova Scotia Dr. S. H. Prince, an Anglican clergyman and university professor, formulated most of the province's social legislation. Such pressures would ultimately prove more significant than they seemed to zealots at the time.

The Roman Catholic hierarchy, following a long tradition of concern for the social welfare of their people, did not hesitate to issue declarations on social and economic matters. More often than not, these reasserted positions that were already well known. The bishops continued to condemn Communism, all the more strongly after the promulgation of Pius XI's encyclical *Divini Redemptoris* in 1937. After 1932 their strictures regularly included the CCF, and in 1934 Archbishop Gauthier of Montreal warned the faithful of his diocese to have no part in it.[26] In Quebec, where the Trades and Labour Congress launched in 1929 a campaign to extend its membership, the bishops continued their support of specifically Catholic unions. In general, the hierarchy maintained its policy of stressing the limits of state aid while calling attention to "abuses" of capitalism.

Although the content of episcopal pronouncements was fairly predictable, their tone gradually changed. Especially after *Quadragesimo Anno*, which practically equated economic liberalism with the political liberalism so often condemned by the church, they were marked by an increased emphasis on the abuses of capitalism, more frequent denunciations of *laissez faire* economics, and occasional attacks on the methods of international finance. In Quebec the bishops had steadily less to say about the virtues of the agricultural life, more about the problems of urban workers. Chaplains of Catholic unions became aware of the realities of industrial conflict, discovered the need for effective techniques of collective bargaining, and even acknowledged the necessity of the strike as an ultimate weapon. Monseigneur Decelles of St. Hyacinthe, in 1933, was the first Canadian bishop to mention the closed shop without condemning it.[27] A sign of increased readiness to evaluate the Canadian industrial situation in its own terms was the assertion of Archbishop McGuigan of Toronto in 1939 that the church must turn "from talk against Communism to work for social justice."[28]

## SPIRITUAL LIFE IN THE THIRTIES

Despite the calamities it brought to many Canadians, the depression was not an unrelieved misfortune. Its most blighting effects were on community life. In many localities the lack of job opportunities and of money to provide adequate facilities for recreation led to a feeling that nothing was going on. Even the roads and the rods, to which many young people took in the hope of discovering scenes of greater activity, usually led only to shack colonies where enforced idleness was unrelieved by the presence of any organized pattern of communal living. Hard times brought neighbours together in a new camaraderie, however, and economic necessity stimulated both individual study and group discussion. Many who survived the thirties would remember them with some affection as an era of narrowed opportunities but also of broadened perspectives. Canada owes to them the inauguration of Air Canada and of the Canadian Broadcasting Corporation.

In the inner life of the church there was the same combination of loss and gain. Congregations that grew steadily smaller as young people drifted away in search of jobs met in increasingly dingy buildings for which there was no immediate prospect of repair. Sunday schools began to show the effects of a declining birth rate. Many ministers broke physically under the strain of providing spiritual comfort and material relief, often over greatly enlarged territories.[29] Preoccupation with economic problems diverted attention from theological reflection and devotional practice. During the 1930s there were no notable spiritual movements, no major attempts to restructure ecclesiastical institutions, few bold experiments in communication or in pastoral style. The churches had comparatively little to say even on the moral issues that had concerned them so much in the past.

On the other hand, adversity brought about a renewed seriousness that led many Canadians to explore their faith more deeply. Candidates for the ministry and priesthood came forward in satisfactory numbers. Torontonians flocked to Denton Massey's York Bible Class in the Maple Leaf Gardens, where the mood was one of earnest examination rather than of flamboyant proclamation. Newer denominations continued to attract members on the prairies and increasingly made their presence felt elsewhere. Radio preachers reached their widest audiences, partly because they provided the only form of entertainment that many people could afford.

The nearest approach to an old-time revival followed the sudden appearance in 1932 of Frank Buchman's Oxford Group, which was soon familiar to members of all denominations from coast to coast. The Group's practice of sharing or mutual confession was reminiscent of the Methodist class meeting. Its four moral absolutes of honesty, purity, unselfishness, and love recalled Methodist perfectionism. Its gracious house parties, by contrast, gave the movement access to a social class that had been little affected by early Methodist preaching. After a few years the Group vanished almost as suddenly as it had appeared, leaving behind cells of concerned Christians who prepared the way for vigorous lay movements in later years. An official Inter-Church Campaign for the Christianization of Canadian Life evoked less response. Its traditional combination of evangelism and Christian patriotism had become old-fashioned, and neither pietists nor social radicals were greatly moved by it.

The depression helped the churches to rethink their priorities and to rid themselves of some persistent illusions. It delivered French-Canadian Catholic intellectuals from their obsession with the family farm. It helped to take the minds of Presbyterians and Baptists off divisive controversies of the 1920s. It encouraged Anglicans in habits of self-reliance and gave them the satisfaction of repairing the damage of the Machray defalcations by their own efforts. It knit the strands of The United Church of Canada as no equivalent period of prosperity could have done. Canadians, meanwhile, discovered that the presence of the church meant more to them than they had realized. One western layman told his home mission secretary, "The bootleggers have gone, the movies have gone, credit is gone, social life is gone, but thank God the Church remains."[30] It was a noteworthy sign of the time that in the drought-stricken Anglican diocese of Qu'Appelle, where revenues shrank by more than a half in the decade, the number of communicant members increased.[31]

## THE SECOND WORLD WAR

The 1930s were overshadowed not only by economic depression but by the growing threat of war. The possibility of a renewal of conflict had been foreseen soon after the end of the first war, and churchmen were among the first to sound the warning. During the 1920s, pacifism became the typical attitude of concerned young Christians with questioning minds. The veteran social gospeller W. B. Creighton, for thirty-two years editor of the *Christian Guardian* and its successor the *New Outlook*, announced his conversion to it. Heirs of the venerable tradition of moral reform, including S. D. Chown

and George C. Pidgeon, turned against war some of the old fervour of
the temperance crusade without necessarily becoming outright pacifists.
Public men of the stature of N. W. Rowell and Canon H. J. Cody concentrated on the search for means to prevent war. During the 1930s almost
every general council of the United Church recorded its conviction that
"war is contrary to the mind of Christ." The anti-war movement enlisted
both conservatives and social radicals. A disarmament rally of 1931 under
the chairmanship of W. L. Grant, headmaster of Upper Canada College,
would have to be classified as conservative despite close surveillance by the
police. A more controversial type of protest was represented by R. Edis Fair-
bairn, who in a series of articles in the *New Outlook* in 1929 described war
as a product of capitalism and demanded that the church should take an
uncompromising stand against both.

War ceased to be a merely theoretical possibility when Adolf Hitler came
to power in Germany in 1933. The first of heightened international tension
was to spur pacifists to greater activity than ever. In 1934 J. Lavell Smith
led a campaign for pledges of nonparticipation in future wars, and in 1935
almost every conference of the United Church reiterated its objections to
war.[32] As the world began to polarize into two camps, however, the anti-
war consensus within the church gradually crumbled. Those whose pacifism had never been absolute desisted from protests that would, they
believed, only encourage Hitler in plans of world conquest. Social radicals
had second thoughts about pacifism when the extreme right emerged as
a potential enemy, and those who had denounced all war as imperialistic
were unable to apply their thesis to the defence of China, Ethiopia, or
republican Spain. Those who stuck to their pacifist convictions were compelled to shift their attention from the prevention of war to the refusal of
military service as a religious witness. No section of the church manifested
any enthusiasm for war, which most Canadians continued to regard with
horror, but many began to ask what the church should do when war came.
In 1938 the United Church declared that rights of conscience should be safe-
guarded in a conflict, while adding to its usual condemnation of war an
acknowledgment that Christians disagreed on the legitimacy of participat-
ing in war in some circumstances.[33]

When war finally broke out in 1939, most Canadians were shocked but
also relieved that what had come to seem an inevitable showdown would
no longer be delayed. They were convinced that Hitler was a tyrant who
had to be resisted, and most ministers and the great bulk of church members
were in accord with the national commitment. The churches adapted themselves to the peculiar requirements of a state of war. They cooperated in
the appointment of service chaplains, of whom one was awarded the Victoria Cross and almost all won the respect of the men and women whom they
served. Priests and ministers at home brought comfort to survivors and to

those who anxiously awaited word of friends and relatives in Britain or occupied Europe. Lay groups provided entertainment for troops in Canada, and many church families opened their homes.

So far the role of the church was much what it had been in the first world war, but there the resemblance ended. Emotional appeals to come to the aid of the motherland, along with extravagant hopes of a millennial victory, were replaced by sober determination to finish a messy but necessary job. Supporters of the war, remembering the aftermath of the previous one and in many cases their own earlier pacifism, sought to maintain an atmosphere of freedom. Opponents, although firm in their pacifist convictions, were not inclined to take the Nazi menace lightly. Hot arguments abounded, especially among theological students, but they seldom destroyed mutual respect. Quebec saw the war differently from other provinces, but there was a general determination not to force a confrontation. Churches were thus able to avoid many of the mistakes of the Kaiser's war. They moderated their protestations of loyalty, refrained from overt participation in the war effort, and sometimes prayed for national enemies. In 1940, even while assuring the minister of national defence of willingness "to render its essential service at this time of national need," the general council of the United Church insisted that "the paramount authority of conscience" should be maintained in wartime.[34] In 1942 it resisted pressure to commit it to support for conscription. The Presbyterians, meanwhile, undertook a study of problems arising out of relations between church and state.[35]

War inevitably brings emotional strains, however, and despite the changed national mood the churches were faced with problems of conscience to which they did not always find clear-cut or convincing solutions. Soon after the outbreak of war, when seventy-five United Church ministers issued a pacifist declaration,[36] the sub-executive of the general council disavowed it so zealously as to give rise to apprehensions of a repetition of the 1914 experience.[37] This did not happen, but there were many grey areas of compromise. Churches that declared themselves in favour of freedom of conscience did not always stand behind the conscientious objectors in their ranks. Pacifist ministers were heard with respect in church assemblies, but lay opposition sometimes drove them from their pulpits. The United Church retired a debt contracted in the depression by soliciting subscriptions to a war loan, and its members showed a distinct edginess when the transaction was criticized by C. C. Morrison of the *Christian Century* as an identification of the church "as a church" with the war effort.[38] On the other hand, the quiet determination of most churchmen to resist wartime hysteria served throughout the conflict as a brake on precipitous action. Few of them spoke out against restrictions on freedom, which most regarded as necessary in the circumstances, but few were happy about them either.

Despite their commitment to freedom of conscience, the churches exercised little vigilance for the rights of unpopular minorities. When the authorities banned the Jehovah's Witnesses as a subversive organization, other denominations seemed more relieved by the elimination of a troublesome competitor than disturbed by possible implications for religious liberty. In Alberta, where the Hutterites had been regarded as an eccentric but generally admirable group, wartime suspicion culminated in 1947 in an act of the legislature restricting the expansion of their colonies. Again the churches did not protest. Most scandalous of all was the treatment of Japanese-Canadians, who were removed from the coast of British Columbia to internment camps in the interior shortly after the attack on Pearl Harbor. No justification could be cited beyond suspicions based on colour, for other enemy aliens had not been so treated and indeed many of those interned were Canadian-born. The churches were well disposed towards the Japanese, many of whom were zealous Christians, and they were foremost in efforts to relieve suffering in the camps. On the other hand, they were not prepared to express doubts in public about the propriety of government measures in wartime.[39] Even the forced sale of Japanese-Canadian properties at confiscatory prices called forth protests from the churches only after a lapse of time that rendered them almost useless, although some officials had made private representations to the government. From the outset, however, there were individual Christians who condemned the government's measures and who persisted in their advocacy of an unpopular cause until they succeeded in arousing the conscience of the churches.

## THE CHURCH IN WARTIME

Canadians did not respond to the Second World War with a burst of churchgoing, but many of them began to study theology with unaccustomed seriousness. The works of the Swiss theologian Karl Barth, which had first been drawn to the attention of Canadians through the enthusiastic sponsorship of Dr. W. W. Bryden of Knox College, gradually affected the curricula of other seminaries.[40] Ministers read Reinhold Niebuhr's *The Nature and Destiny of Man*,[41] while laymen were fascinated by the racy orthodoxy of C. S. Lewis' *Screwtape Letters*.[42] Even the universities, which had moved far from their earlier ecclesiastical orientation, had to take seriously the theologizing of T. S. Eliot and W. H. Auden. The United Church of Canada, which had gained a reputation for theological vagueness, issued a statement of faith in 1940[43] and a catechism in 1944.[44] Both reflected a return to the central themes of the Bible, although not to any form of scriptural fundamentalism. In the Roman Catholic Church, where it had never lost its prestige, theology was given a new impetus when Jacques Maritain and other eminent refugees made the Pontifical Institute of Mediaeval Studies at Toronto a leading centre of contemporary Thomism.

Despite their great diversity, several common themes distinguished the theologies that came into prominence at this time from those of the earlier part of the century. "Orthodoxy" became a respectable word again, and although not all current theologies fitted the term they nearly all had as their starting point the classical content of the Christian faith rather than the contemporary human search for God. Niebuhr rehabilitated the concept of original sin and pointed out the ambiguities inherent in all human action. Barth insisted on the active role of God in history and on the necessity of apprehending him not in terms of what we should like to believe but of what he has said and done in Jesus Christ. This whole development represented a revival of interest in St. Augustine's concepts of sin and grace, a revival of which one of the major landmarks was the publication in 1939 of *Christianity and Classical Culture* by the Canadian scholar C. N. Cochrane.[45]

Old-time liberals were scandalized by what they commonly interpreted as a theological failure of nerve, but there was more to the return to orthodoxy than that. Implicit in the church's program of missionary expansion and social involvement over the greater part of a century had been the assumption that the world, if not perfectible, is at least amenable to almost indefinite improvement. Failure to solve the problems of depression and war now made this assumption seem illusory and demanded a reappraisal of human possibilities. Under these circumstances the need for superhuman aid seemed self-evident, and even the recognition of original sin brought a sense of release from exaggerated pretensions. In learning once more to identify pride as the primal sin Christians were preparing, among other things, to divest themselves of the paternalism that had infected their relations with other races and cultures and even with secular society as a whole.

Pressure groups for social change continued their activities during wartime, generating less excitement than during the depression but perhaps gaining more adherents. Among Anglicans, indeed, social Christianity flourished as it never had before. Their enthusiasm was largely derived from Britain, where during wartime social reconstruction was very much in the air. Responsiveness to British ideas has always been a characteristic of Canadian Anglicanism, and it was made even more natural in this case by the Anglican inspiration of many elements of the British program. In January 1941 a number of socially minded Anglicans, gathered at Malvern on the initiative of Archbishop William Temple of York, recommended that production be replaced by consumption as the governing principle of economic life. In 1942 the Beveridge Report, whose recommendations were to make Britain a welfare state, reflected many of the ideas of the Malvern Conference. In the same year Temple's appointment as Archbishop of Canterbury heightened the prestige of his opinions on economics. Many of his ideas were introduced to Canada in the columns of *Canada and Christendom*, a mimeographed newsletter edited by Charles R. Feilding. In Montreal the first of a series of Arundel conferences began to popularize them in 1943, and in 1945 they received more formal backing from the Anglican Fellowship for Social Action. Late in that year two young priests founded the *Anglican Outlook*, a magazine that was intended to rouse the church from its apparent lethargy on social issues. After official bodies had declined to sponsor the venture, the Fellowship took it over in 1949 and installed H. H. Walsh into what would be a long tenure as editor.[46]

Under the threat and then the reality of war, however, the tone of social protest within the church changed considerably. On the one hand, the traditional alignment with the CCF was strongly challenged from the left. Harry F. Ward, perhaps the most prominent clerical advocate in the United States of close collaboration with Communists, was already a popular speaker at conferences of the Alberta School of Religion and elsewhere during the late 1930s. After the entry of the Soviet Union into the war more direct support of Communism through the renamed Labour-Progressive party became possible, and conflict between CCF supporters and advocates of wider left-wing collaboration resulted in the demise of the FCSO in 1945. On the other hand, many social activists responded positively to the theological trends of the period. Some of them had already been affected by the publication in 1932 of Niebuhr's *Moral Man and Immoral Society*, which stressed the ambiguities inherent in efforts towards the betterment of society.[47] Emphasis shifted from the attainment of a Christian order to participation in a struggle against oppression that promised no quick or decisive results.

These two trends were in many ways incompatible, but they were not unrelated. They both reflected disillusionment with an optimistic liberalism that had failed to reckon with such apparently demonic phenomena as the rise of Hitler. Those who conceived of social change in terms not of gradual improvement but of apocalyptic conflict found it easier than their predecessors to commit themselves to wholehearted involvement in the class struggle, and in the latter years of the war some of those who saw history as a theatre of God's activity found it possible to see his hand in the victories of the Red Army.

The direction in which the churches as a whole were moving proved to be somewhat different. They showed increasing impatience with the activities of social radicals within their ranks, and resolutions calling for the reconstitution of society almost vanished from conference agendas. On the other hand, churches were suddenly willing to accept far-reaching measures that had been bitterly resisted throughout the depression. In 1943 the Anglican general synod called for a national program of social security,[48] and in 1944 the United Church finally instructed its publishing house to institute a closed shop.[49] In an even more significant reversal, the Roman Catholic bishops issued in 1943 a statement that was clearly intended, despite some ambiguities of phrasing, to exempt the CCF from papal condemnations of socialism.[50]

During these years the churches were moving from social perfectionism to social pragmatism, from conflict over absolute principles to the acceptance of a mixed economy, from concern for abstract justice to concern for practical welfare. So were Canadians as a whole. In an astonishing number of cases, proposals that seemed bold and controversial when approved by church councils were adopted within a year or two by the state.

Although Anglicans became independent of British subsidies only in 1940, Canada emerged during the war years as one of the most important suppliers of aid to churches elsewhere. Many overseas missions were sponsored by societies in continental Europe, and when war interrupted their lines of supply they soon faced acute shortages of money and personnel. The International Missionary Council organized a program of emergency aid, and several Canadian churches participated in it. Lutherans became actively involved both in the support of orphaned missions and in post-war relief to churches in devastated areas of Europe.[51] Roman Catholic missions entered a period of remarkable expansion. French Canadians were acceptable in many areas of the world where others were politically suspect, and they speedily became an important factor in world Catholicism.[52] This extension of activity, coming when colonialism was being discredited in both east and west, would enhance the role of Canadians in working out a new conception of international Christian partnership.

## ECUMENICAL DEVELOPMENTS

The concern to bring churches together languished for some years after its peak of achievement in 1925. Although The United Church of Canada described itself officially as "united and uniting," it seems to have made no attempt to follow up earlier suggestions of wider union by Anglicans and by representatives of the Disciples of Christ. Canadians attended world Christian conferences in 1926 and 1927, but only in 1936 were these followed by conversations on "the recovery of fellowship" among Anglican, Presbyterian, and United churches in Canada. In 1936 the Baptists adopted the *Hymnary* of the United Church with minor revisions, and in 1937 they appointed a representative at the United Church Publishing House to collaborate in the editing of Christian education materials. In 1938 the United and Presbyterian churches established cordial relations, the former agreeing not to object to the latter's use of the name of the original church without prejudice to its own claim to continuing identity.[53] Even in the depths of the depression, however, there were no serious attempts to eliminate redundant effort.

Interest in unity was greatly stimulated in 1937 when ecumenical conferences at Oxford and Edinburgh proposed the formation of a World Council of Churches and set up committees to draft its constitution. The outbreak of war delayed the formal inauguration of the council until 1948, but by 1939 church leaders had set a pattern of international consultation that assumed unusual importance when political lines of communication were broken. Churches maintained a constant flow of information to and from a provisional headquarters at Geneva. Christians became aware of their interdependence as never before and organized councils of churches in many countries. The Canadian Council of Churches was formed in 1944, six years before its counterpart in the United States. Although without power to bind churches to its decisions, the council has furnished a valuable means of consultation to twelve constituent bodies ranging from two Orthodox groups to the Salvation Army as well as to three affiliated interdenominational movements. From the outset, however, it suffered from a certain ambiguity of origin. It represented on the one hand the local manifestation of an international Christian impulse, on the other the merger of several existing co-operative agencies. Denominations looked to it for services traditionally performed jointly but proved reluctant to define its functions more broadly.

Although the ecumenical movement set itself no official goals beyond the extension of conversation and cooperation among Christians, its existence inspired proposals for formal church unions in various parts of the world. Many sections of the Anglican communion were involved in such discussions, and indeed unity had been a major Anglican concern since the Lambeth conference of 1888. In 1943, therefore, the general synod of the Church of England in Canada marked its jubilee by inviting other communions to participate in conversations that might lead to greater unity.[54] The Presbyterians responded by appointing a committee to clarify areas of misunderstanding, while instructing it not to include organic union on its agenda. The United Church went further, declaring itself willing to consider major steps towards union. Anglican and United committees were soon conferring. They concentrated at first on the problem of providing a joint ministry to needy areas, a problem that was made more urgent at the time by the absence of ministers in the chaplaincy and by the burgeoning of areas of temporary wartime housing at new industrial sites. For a time hopes ran high, and important steps towards union seemed imminent.

The same ecumenical tide enabled the Baptists to fulfil at last their dream of forming a national organization to link their independent conventions. Watson Kirkconnell, a layman who later became president of Acadia University, guided negotiations that led to the birth in 1944 of the Baptist Federation of Canada. This was and has remained a purely advisory body, however, and the chief strength of the denomination has continued to be in its local churches and area associations.

The Roman Catholic communion was conspicuously absent from any of these conversations or cooperative ventures. It had always looked for unity through the return of others to its fold, and Pope Pius XI went out of his way to warn the faithful against participation in the ecumenical movement.

Relations between Canada's two major religious groups, which had never been easy, were further strained during the 1930s by controversy over state support for Catholic schools in Ontario.[55] Catholics complained of two serious disabilities. One was the failure of the law to ensure that Catholic-owned shares in corporations would be assessed for the support of separate schools. The other was the government's refusal to extend the separate school system into high school grades. Irked by what they regarded as injustice, and pressed by financial stringency, Catholics decided to organize for a better deal. Martin J. Quinn, a layman, founded the Catholic Taxpayers' Association in 1932 and insisted that the clergy should have no part in its leadership. He argued his case with a tactlessness that frightened some Catholics, united Protestant churches in opposition, and alienated many politicians. Nevertheless, the Liberal leader Mitchell Hepburn seems to have committed himself privately to more favourable legislation, and his victory at the polls was followed in 1936 by the passage of new assessment act. The public furor that followed compelled its repeal in 1937, and the financial position of Catholic schools remained shaky.

Despite such setbacks to religious unity, there were signs here and there of readiness for greater accommodation. Franklin A. Walker observed that many Protestant submissions on the Ontario school question demonstrated "moderation and culture" rather than the hysteria so common in the past.[56] Then in 1940 Georges-Henri Lévesque persuaded the cooperatives of Quebec to open their membership to non-Catholics. The move was bitterly opposed by both Jesuits and Dominicans, but a trend had been set and the principle of *non-confessionalité* lent itself to other applications. Unnoticed by most Canadians, the way was being prepared for a dramatic extension of ecumenical dialogue.

NOTES TO CHAPTER SEVEN

1. T. C. B. Boon, *The Anglican Church from the Bay to the Rockies*, pp. 275-278.

2. R. W. Barker, "The United Church and the Social Question," Th.D. thesis, Victoria University, 1961, pp. 192-193.

3. C. C. McLaurin, *Pioneering in Western Canada*, p. 222.

4. Archdiocese of Regina, Archbishop McGuigan, no. 18, November 10, 1931. Quoted in Jean Hulliger, *L'Enseignement Social des Evêques Canadiens de 1891 à 1950*, p. 169.

5. Acts and Proceedings of the 63rd General Assembly of the Presbyterian Church in Canada, 1937, pp. 156-157.

6. George E. Levy, *The Baptists of the Maritime Provinces, 1753-1946*, p. 320.

7. Commission of Appraisal, Laymen's Foreign Missions Inquiry, *Re-thinking Missions: A Laymen's Inquiry After One Hundred Years* (New York: Harper, 1932).

8. Michael Zuk, "The Ukrainian Protestant Missions in Canada," p. 71.

9. W. W. Judd, "The Vision and the Dream," *Journal of the Canadian Church Historical Society*, Vol. VII, No. 4 (December 1965), p. 86.

10. Anne Fremantle, ed., *The Papal Encyclicals*, p. 230.

11. *Ibid.*, p. 232.

12. George Boyle, *Pioneer in Purple*, p. 31.

13. Record of Proceedings of the 8th General Council of The United Church of Canada, 1938, pp. 79, 99.

14. *New Outlook*, June 17, 1931, p. 577.

15. R. B. Y. Scott and Gregory Vlastos, eds., *Towards the Christian Revolution* (Chicago: Willett, Clark and Co., 1936).

16. John A. Irving, *The Social Credit Movement in Alberta* (Toronto: University of Toronto Press, 1959), p. 51.

17. Archevêché de Québec, Cardinal Villeneuve, 7 décembre 1936, no. 34; 31 décembre 1936, XXXIX; 7 novembre 1941, no. 80; C.cl. 31, 31 décembre 1941, 381. Hulliger, *op. cit.*, pp. 203-204.

18. Archevêché de Montréal, no. 82; Circulaire de Mgr l'Archevêque-Coadjuteur, 15 mars 1938, p. 1023. *Ibid.*, p. 217.

19. I Corinthians 12.12-26.

20. Joseph Levitt, "Henri Bourassa and Modern Industrial Society, 1900-1914," *Canadian Historical Review*, Vol. L, No. 1 (March 1969), pp. 49-50.

21. Stewart Crysdale, *The Industrial Struggle and Protestant Ethics in Canada* (Toronto: Ryerson, 1961).

22. Record of Proceedings of the 9th Toronto Conference, The United Church of Canada, 1933, p. 19.

23. Record of Proceedings of the 5th General Council of The United Church of Canada, 1932, pp. 287-288.

24. Annual Report of the Board of Evangelism and Social Service of The United Church of Canada, 1935, p. 61.

25. Record of Proceedings of the 6th General Council of The United Church of Canada, 1934, p. 248.

26. Murray G. Ballantyne, "The Catholic Church and the CCF," *Report*, Canadian Catholic Historical Association, 1963, p. 34.

27. Diocèse de St. Hyacinthe, Mgr Decelles, no. 63, C.cl., 2 février 1933 (147). Hulliger, *op. cit.*, p. 149.

28. Archdiocese of Toronto, Archbishop McGuigan, Circular No. 46, Ash Wednesday, 1939. *Ibid.*, p. 219.

29. R. B. Cochrane, "The Ten Years in Home Missions," in *The United Church of Canada: Ten Years of Union, 1925-1935* (Toronto: The United Church of Canada, 1935), p. 11.

30. J. I. MacKay, *The World in Canada* (Toronto: Committee on Missionary Education and Woman's Missionary Society Literature Department of The United Church of Canada, 1938), p. 109.

31. Boon, *op. cit.*, p. 202.

32. Barker, *op. cit.*, pp. 276-279.

33. Record of Proceedings of the 8th General Council of The United Church of Canada, 1938, pp. 63, 93-94.

34. Record of Proceedings of the 9th General Council of The United Church of Canada, 1940, pp. 205-206.

35. Neil G. Smith, Allan L. Farris, and H. Keith Markell, *A Short History of the Presbyterian Church in Canada* (Toronto: Presbyterian Publications, n.d.), p. 100.

36. "A Witness Against the War," *The United Church Observer*, October 15, 1939.

37. *The United Church Observer*, November 1, 1939.

38. See N. K. Clifford, "Charles Clayton Morrison and The United Church of Canada," *Canadian Journal of Theology*, Vol. XV, No. 2 (April 1969), pp. 80-92.

39. See Frank Moritsugu, "Remember When We Caged the Japanese?" *The United Church Observer*, July 4, 1967.

40. Influential works by Barth published during the 1930s in English included *The Epistle to the Romans*, tr. E. C. Hoskyns (London: Oxford, 1933); *Credo*, tr. J. Strathearn McNab (London: Hodder, 1936); and *The Knowledge of God and the Service of God*, tr. J. L. M. Haire and Ian Henderson (London: Hodder, 1938).

41. Reinhold Niebuhr, *The Nature and Destiny of Man*, 2 vols. (New York: Scribner, 1942 and 1943).

42. C. S. Lewis, *The Screwtape Letters* (London: Bles, 1942).

43. *Statement of Faith*, a statement prepared by a commission authorized by the 7th General Council (Toronto: Board of Evangelism and Social Service of The United Church of Canada, 1940).

44. *Catechism, The United Church of Canada* (Toronto: Board of Evangelism and Social Service of The United Church of Canada, 1944). During the first year 140,000 copies were sold.

45. C. N. Cochrane, *Christianity and Classical Culture* (Oxford: Clarendon, 1939).

46. "Farewell—and Hail," editorial in *The Anglican Outlook*, Vol. XVI, No. 8 (June-July 1960), p. 6.

47. Reinhold Niebuhr, *Moral Man and Immoral Society* (New York: Scribner, 1932).

48. Journal of Proceedings, General Synod of the Church of England in Canada, 1943, pp. 259ff, 276.

49. Record of Proceedings of the 11th General Council of The United Church of Canada, 1944, pp. 52, 90.

50. Ballantyne, *op. cit.*, p. 41.

51. Carl R. Cronmiller, *A History of the Lutheran Church in Canada*, p. 225.

52. Jean Bruchési, *A History of Canada*, tr. R. W. W. Robertson (Toronto: Clark, Irwin, 1950), pp. 282-283.

53. G. A. Sisco, in *The New Outlook*, October 7, 1938, p. 843.

54. For details of the ensuing conversations, see *Growth in Understanding: A Study Guide on Church Union*, issued under the auspices of the Committee on Christian Unity of The Anglican Church of Canada and the Commission on Union of The United Church of Canada (Toronto: 1961), Chapter 3.

55. For a detailed account of the controversy, see Franklin A. Walker, *Catholic Education and Politics in Ontario*, pp. 354-451.

56. *Ibid.*, p. 441.

# EIGHT

## Affluent Churches in an Affluent Society

During the years after the second world war the church was thrown on the defensive in most parts of the world. The overseas missionary enterprise, which towards the end of the nineteenth century had shown promise of making Christianity the religion of most inhabitants of the globe, ceased to exist in China after the revolution of 1948 and was held in check elsewhere by the resurgence of ancient religions. In Latin America the Roman Catholic Church saw its traditional domination of social and intellectual life challenged by secularism and by indigenous revolutionary movements. In central and eastern Europe, where the hold of the church on popular loyalties had been especially strong, new Communist governments imposed severe restrictions on its activities. Even in western Europe, where the hostility to Christianity that had been engendered by the French Revolution was ebbing, churchgoing was coming to be regarded as a harmless eccentricity.

What happened in Canada, as in North America generally, was so different that it remains to this day a source of wonder. Men and women who had shown no more than a perfunctory interest in the church before going off to war demonstrated on their return an enthusiasm that confounded all prognosticators. From soon after 1945 until about 1960 there was a general boom in things religious. Statistics of membership, attendance and financial support resumed their upward trend after the slump of the 1930s. Religious periodicals built up their subscription lists, publishers readily sold books ranging from Norman Vincent Peale's prescriptions for success to Thomas Merton's reflections on the monastic life, and several provincial universities broke with precedent by setting up departments of religion. An increasing number of vocations for the ministry gradually alleviated a serious shortage.

### THE BOOM IN RELIGION

The first signs of an upswing appeared in the Sunday schools, where enrollment doubled and quadrupled as war veterans sought to ensure that their children would inherit the Christian values they had fought to preserve.

Then, when ministers suggested that children were likely to take Christianity seriously only if they saw evidence of their parents' interest, young couples took the hint and began to attend church with unaccustomed regularity. They sometimes found sermons difficult to understand, and the next step was enrollment in study groups. Indeed, the range of possible activities seemed to be almost limitless. Women's organizations flourished, men's clubs came alive, and service projects abounded. Many church buildings were rarely out of use during waking hours.

Existing facilities could not begin to accommodate these busy programs. Church properties had been allowed to deteriorate during the depression, and in most new subdivisions they did not even exist. Inevitably much of the energy of the church during post-war years was applied to ambitious projects of extension. Parish committees worked overtime securing sites, engaging architects, discussing endless details, and—most important of all—raising money. Denominational officials refurbished their organizations in order to coordinate congregational efforts and, where necessary, assist them with grants or loans. Professional fund-raisers, well versed in American techniques of salesmanship and social pressure, became for a time inevitable adjuncts to building programs. Most of the money would have to come from the veterans and their families, however, and despite heavy mortgages on their own homes they pitched in and raised it. Between 1945 and 1966 the United Church alone built fifteen hundred churches and church halls, as well as six hundred manses.[1] The key to financial success was systematic and proportionate giving, which had been encouraged by the churches since the 1870s but which came into its own in the 1950s through the commercial enterprise of the American-based Wells organization.

Some communions were able to take advantage of the religious boom more readily than others. Denominations whose structures enabled them to deploy their resources flexibly were better situated than ones that depended heavily on local initiative. Those whose programs helped communities to find a basis of cohesion had an advantage over those whose appeal was limited to particular segments of it. The Lutherans, who were able to draw upon American money and experience, used specialized "mission developers" to promote an unusually effective program of church extension. The Convention Baptists, by contrast, found the period somewhat inhospitable to their traditional emphasis on individual decision and congregational autonomy. Even among conservative groups, which were more exclusive on principle, "people's" or "undenominational" churches grew more rapidly than intimate fellowships of the "gospel hall" type.

The response also varied in terms of locality and class. The religious boom was largely a phenomenon of suburbia, where families with small children were most heavily concentrated and where the effects of increased affluence were most widely felt. The church merely inched ahead in small towns of static population, was unable to arrest decline in the inner city, and lost ground rapidly in rural areas. It consolidated its position among hitherto careless members of the middle class, but failed to halt the steady erosion of its appeal to organized labour and to the dispossessed. The appearance of a massive return to religion was somewhat deceptive. New churches were filled in part by emptying old ones, and Sunday schools owed much of their popularity to a rise in the birth rate that had begun in 1937. Unquestionably, however, Canadians were proving more responsive to the church's appeal than they had for a long time. The suburbs in which so many new churches were springing up accounted for most of Canada's population growth during the postwar period, and many of those who moved into them had not been near a church for years.

Such a return to religious practice had not been foreseen even by the most optimistic. The war, despite its ideological motivation, had been fought more as a technical problem than as a moral crusade. It evoked few signs of spiritual awakening among civilians, and chaplains had noted no tremendous enthusiasm for their compulsory church parades or even for their informal padre's hours. Self-appointed experts were taken as much by surprise as others, many of them having anticipated a wave of disillusionment and revolt similar to that which had followed the first world war. Neither can the sudden popularity of the church be ascribed to the influence of a few charismatic individuals, for the success of evangelistic campaigns by Billy Graham and Charles Templeton was as much a symptom as a cause of a climate favourable to religion.

One important factor was nostalgia. Men and women of the armed forces saw in their generous demobilization benefits an opportunity to rejoin the mainstream of Canadian life, and they were prepared to work hard to make up for lost years. They wanted to forget the interruption of their careers, not to talk about it incessantly like some of those who had fought in the first war. They coveted recognition as citizens, not as members of a distinct class of veterans. They were naturally favourable to the known components of Canadian life, and even more conspicuously eager that their children should enter into the heritage they had known. Church and Sunday school were parts of normalcy, and the vogue for them was related to an atmosphere of social conformism that was typical of the period.

Mere receptivity to the familiar was too passive a motive, however, to account for the seriousness with which many Canadians began to take their religion. They were also driven by a sense of anxiety that has been recognized as one of the most pervasive characteristics of the time. This anxiety was doubtless fed by the cold war and the threat of atomic destruction, compounded in the case of veterans by a sense of guilt for their participation in the unnatural activities of wartime. When Canadians talked to their priests and ministers, however, it was usually about matters of more immediate concern. Couples who had been separated during wartime worried about saving their marriages. Men who had grown up during the depression worried about holding their jobs. A near-obsession with material security developed, and many stories were told of applicants who showed more interest in minute details of pension plans than in possibilities of future advancement. Anxious people looked to the church for help in achieving personal stability and consolidating their position in the community. Undoubtedly many of them also sought spiritual security, although they were seldom very articulate about it.

Greatly as it took Canadians by surprise, the return to the church was not the result of a sudden mass impulse. In retrospect it seems obvious that the sobering experiences of the depression and war years had raised questions for which many Canadians would ultimately seek answers from the churches. Although wartime discussions of theology had little immediate effect on church attendance, their ultimate effect was to persuade many uncommitted people that Christianity deserved to be taken seriously. The work of the service chaplains, too, was clearly to bear more fruit than even they realized at the time. They had opportunities for intimate discussions with men that are almost never open to civilian pastors, and the men evidently responded. A significant indicator of a turning tide appeared as early as 1944, when the administration of George Drew introduced formal courses in religion into the public schools of Ontario.

## THE RETURN TO NORMALCY

The circumstances of revival encouraged conservative attitudes within the church. Newly active members were usually homecomers in search of the familiar rather than adventurers looking for novelty. They were interested in knowing what the church had to say, not what it hesitated to say. Unlike Canadians of the previous generation, who had often found it difficult to believe what they were taught, they scarcely knew what they were supposed to believe and eagerly sought information and explanation. Above all, they desired the reassurance and direction that are most readily provided by structured systems of belief and practice.

The churches were, on the whole, able to give what was asked with a good conscience. Theologians were already turning from speculations about the goal of the religious quest to explorations of classical Christian doctrine as expounded by Karl Barth or St. Thomas Aquinas. Seminarians shared their interest in affirmative theology, and university students responded most positively to missioners who spelled out the basic elements of Christian belief. Parish clergy gave what time they could spare from their building programs to the encouragement of religious literacy among their people. In contrast with the United States, where the reaction against theological liberalism proved divisive in many denominations, the general mood in Canada was one of sober reappraisal. Wild charges of Communism against respected church leaders that abounded in the United States during the ascendancy of Joseph McCarthy were seldom echoed in Canada.

Nationally, churches maintained and sometimes intensified traditional emphases. Historical continuity through bishops, once the watchword of a party, was now taken seriously by the great majority of Anglican clergy. Graduates of such conservative schools as Westminster Seminary, Philadelphia, accentuated an element of doctrinal rigidity that had been present in the Presbyterian Church since union. The Catholic hierarchy of Quebec reiterated its support of rural colonization, which it promoted as an alternative to contraception and abortion.[2] To the general public, however, the most forceful reminder of the apparent changelessness of the church was the continued and vocal opposition of The United Church of Canada to any extension of facilities for drinking, gambling, indulging a taste for pornography, or going to the races on Sunday. No representative of this church was more widely known than J. R. Mutchmor, secretary of its board of evangelism and social service, who lost no opportunity to warn Canadians of moral dangers. So long as he was at the helm, it seemed, the old verities were safe.

The postwar situation was not conducive to closer relations among the denominations. Suburban expansion offered them many opportunities to erect buildings that could be filled and paid for with unprecedented ease. Their natural tendency was to pre-empt desirable sites and to think of possible cooperation only when it became obvious that they had overextended themselves. Competition for areas where more than one church would clearly be undesirable occasionally led to friction, as between United and Presbyterians in the foothills of western Alberta. There were also more fundamental factors that inhibited ecumenicity. One was the apparently secure position of the church in North America, which made competition seem less risky. Another was the general desire for reassurance and stability, which was more readily satisfied within familiar denominational compartments than in ventures into the unknown. The ecumenical recession was by no means limited to Canada. Reaction against wartime dislocation encouraged Christians everywhere to seek solid footing in familiar traditions, and conservatives readily identified ecumenism with theological vagueness.

Existing interdenominational enterprises languished, and most proposals for new ones were stillborn. The Canadian Council of Churches failed to break much new ground, despite the devoted labours of its general secretary W. J. Gallagher, and churches continued to work separately in such vital areas as Christian education and mass communication.[3] The appointment of university chaplains by individual denominations led to increasing fragmentation of effort on campuses, and an attempt in the late 1950s to unite teachers and students in a broadly based university Christian movement did not succeed. There were some experiments in community churches, especially in isolated company towns, but difficulties with sponsoring denominations soon caused most of them to break up.

Union conversations between United and Anglican churches suffered from the denominational backlash. In 1946 joint committees issued a plan for the provision of a ministry acceptable to both churches through mutual ordination. Its theological assumptions have been widely questioned, but rapid cooling of interest was chiefly responsible for the failure of either church to take it very seriously. Conversations continued throughout the next decade with little visible result beyond increased frustration. They seemed on the point of collapse in 1958 when the general council of the United Church declared, "The time has come when, in our judgment, the Anglican Church of Canada should make plain whether it really wishes to continue these conversations, or whether it now desires to terminate them."[4] Few at that time expected the Anglican reply to open the way to any significant advance towards union.

## THE SECULARIZATION OF CANADIAN LIFE

While the churches were retaining or even solidifying their traditional shapes, Canada was changing at an accelerating pace. The nation became steadily more urban as factories that had sprung up during the war were converted to the production of consumer goods, and as wealth from newly exploited resources of iron, oil, and uranium flowed back to the cities. The most conspicuous product of the new urbanism was not the industrial slum but the more or less affluent suburb. Each suburb consisted of a number of builders' subdivisions where families of young couples and young children shared their social life with similar families of roughly equivalent income. Life in suburbia was geared not to production but to consumption, giving rise to patterns for which popular sociologists coined such phrases as "built-in obsolescence," "conspicuous consumption," and "status seeking." Standards were set, most often, not by what others said but by what others bought.

Despite frequent complaints of suburban conformism, Canadians were becoming increasingly cosmopolitan in their tastes. Wartime refugees, of whom the Dutch royal family were the most eminent, gave Canadians a new sense of belonging to the world. The publishers of Paris, who during the German occupation made Montreal the centre of the French-language book trade, extended this influence to the province of Quebec. Soldiers brought back to Canada memories not merely of Flanders mud and *mademoiselles* from Armentières but of varied cultural patterns in many parts of the world. The Pearson era of diplomacy made Canadians directly aware of international trouble spots. More influential than all of these factors, perhaps, was the affluence that made Europe accessible not only to the well-to-do but to retired school teachers and to students on vacation.

Cosmopolitan tastes were also furthered by immigration, which after falling off sharply during the depression and second world war returned to something like its earlier volume. Many came to Canada in search of better material conditions. Others left Europe as a result of the Soviet occupation of the Baltic states, the Hungarian rising of 1956, and other disturbances, and many of these were doctors, lawyers, artists, or artisans. Accustomed to the amenities of European living, they soon constituted a clientele for distinctive restaurants, boutiques, and cultural centres. Instead of merely posing a problem in assimilation they were quickly able to enrich Canadian life. Their impact was heightened by the coming to maturity of earlier immigrant groups, which were beginning to emerge from their defensive seclusion and to become full participants in the national culture. Many pioneers of the transition were of Jewish origin. A. M. Klein, Irving Layton, and Eli Mandel all showed, in poems differing greatly in style and content, that works could be unmistakably Canadian without disguising in any way their distinctive ethnic origin. Among the élite of arts and letters, at least, the Anglo-Saxon monopoly was finally breached.[5]

Such contributions would have little effect on Canada as a whole, however, if native Canadians had been unwilling to receive them. Many nationalities had brought cultural gifts in earlier immigrations, but Anglo-Saxon self-esteem had confined them to ethnic ghettoes. Even after the second war there was some tendency to lump together all immigrants as displaced persons or "DP"s, but especially in metropolitan areas it soon became natural to tolerate and even to adopt unfamiliar folkways. The gateway to an appreciation of Italian culture was for some Canadians the opera, for others Chianti, for still others pizza. In one way or another, however, they began to shed their provincial prejudices.

Patterns of moral behaviour changed with the times. Among urban sophisticates and even middle-class suburbanites traditional taboos gave way before a style of life that included social drinking as a matter of course, was lenient towards sexual aberrations, and regarded Sunday as a day like any other day. Pressure mounted on "blue laws" for which moral reformers had struggled, although they still had their defenders. In 1950 the Ontario legislature made it possible for communities to allow professional sports on Sunday, but during the next five years more votes were cast in local plebiscites against than for change.[6] The new anti-puritans desired no return to the rough days of the saloon or the speakeasy. They were essentially well instructed consumers, particular about their brands of liquor, and eager to surround themselves with the amenities of gracious living. They condemned earlier standards not as unrealistically high but as restrictive of natural human freedoms. The moral revolution had its casualties, notably alcoholics in mounting numbers, but these were commonly dismissed as evidence of previous failure to instil civilized habits of moderation.

Although these changes were most obvious in the larger cities, they were taking place in every part of Canada. Prairie farmers, relieved by mechanization of the obligation to feed and water horses, began to use Sunday for travel and recreation rather than for worship. Many of them moved into towns where they were little known and where their behaviour attracted little attention. The entry of Newfoundland into confederation in 1949 was accompanied by an old-fashioned religious row, with most members of The United Church of Canada welcoming closer relations with coreligionists on the mainland and most Roman Catholics fearing that the union would jeopardise the autonomy of their educational system. Its effect was to introduce into the province the benefits and the attitudes of the modern welfare state, along with the CBC and a certain amount of industry. Even Indians and Eskimos were not immune to the effects of change. Church residential and industrial schools began to close down after the war, and by the 1950s Indian children were being integrated into public schools.

The province of Quebec had long been sheltered from the full impact of movements originating elsewhere, and since its accession to power in 1936 the Union Nationale administration of Maurice Duplessis had sought to keep it so. Duplessis also encouraged American and English-Canadian industrialists to locate in the province, however, and industrialization made the preservation of rural values steadily more difficult. After 1939 war jobs attracted many country girls to the cities, and few of them returned. In 1943, during an interlude of Liberal rule, education became for the first time compulsory. An explosion in secondary education for children of all classes followed by about 1950.

The effect of these changes was to raise questions about the fabric of Quebec society at a time when the mood of the rest of Canada was unusually complacent. Many English-speaking Canadians were first disabused of their conception of Quebec as a land of picturesque but priest-ridden *habitants* by reading *The Tin Flute*, Gabrielle Roy's realistic portrayal of slum life in Montreal.[7] Literary insiders knew that the poetry of Anne Hébert was more widely read in Europe than in North America.[8] Quebec writers no longer saw life through the eyes of the church. They derived their inspiration, however, not from the nineteenth-century tradition of *rouge* anticlericalism but from later rebels. Perhaps the most important of these was Emile Nelligan, a poet whose writing career had been limited to three years of adolescence near the close of the nineteenth century but who in that time had made Quebec intellectuals aware of such French writers as Verlaine and Baudelaire.

This readiness to accept far-reaching changes in habit and outlook showed that, despite the popularity of religious observance, Canada was not immune to the secularizing trends that in some other countries led to widespread rejection of the church. Even the striking resurgence of religion in North America was not so exceptional as it seemed. The same desire to emphasize symbols of continuity was reflected in India by the multiplication of Hindu shrines, in Africa by the rise of indigenous semi-Christian sects, and in the USSR by the revival of iconography. The unique feature in North America of this return to the sources of national values was its Christian orientation. Even here, however, secularization offered sources of meaning independent of those provided by the church and commonly led to the application of different sets of axioms to religious and secular behaviour.

## A SILENT REVOLUTION IN CHURCH LIFE

Visitors to Canada in the years after the war were sometimes puzzled by the remarkable popularity in a rapidly changing society of churches that seemed to be living on an accumulated capital of good will. Coming from countries where the church had been pushed to the perimeter of society, they saw little evidence that Canadian churchmen were learning from the experience of others and warned that the favourable conditions of the time could not last. More recent developments have shown that their diagnosis was at least partially correct. Behind a façade of changelessness, however, Canadian churches were adapting themselves in ways that attracted little attention at the time but had a significant cumulative effect.

A silent revolution in church life was mainly the work of the lay people who came flocking in after the end of the war. As we have seen, they were eager to take advantage of the services of the church. On the other hand, they were selective in what they took. They crowded church buildings on Sunday morning, but except for conservative evangelicals, stayed home to watch Ed Sullivan in the evening. They brought new life to the Sunday school, but showed little enthusiasm for weekday communions and in most communities dealt a final blow to the languishing Wednesday prayer meeting. Although in some ways they were traditionalists, they cared little about those elements in the various traditions that had contributed most directly to the formation of the Canadian character.

Churchgoers of the new breed retained few emotional attachments to the ethnic memories that some churches had cherished. Sensing that its old-country associations made it few friends in suburbia, the Church of England in Canada became in 1955 the Anglican Church of Canada.[9] The Presbyterians, who in reaction against the outspoken Canadianism of the United Church had made a good deal of their Scottish inheritance, now found it expedient to play it down. The Lutherans began to move cautiously towards independence from American headquarters and towards the amalgamation of groups that differed chiefly in national background.[10] In 1952 several bodies joined to set up the Canadian Lutheran Council. Even among the Orthodox, who have clung persistently to European languages and groupings, some began to dream of a single Canadian church in which, presumably, English would be the language of worship.[11]

The postwar generation had even less interest in the prosecution of old moral and religious crusades than in the preservation of transplanted folkways. Since 1925 the United Church had looked to the program of its board of evangelism and social service, rather than to its basis of union, as a focus of self-definition. After 1945 it became increasingly evident that this program no longer represented the position of most church members, few of whom even remembered their forefathers' dream of a Canada from which the blighting influence of booze and vice should forever have been removed. The ultramontane vision that had shaped the Catholicism of Quebec suffered a similar loss of credibility. Few of the parishioners who paid for modern church buildings in the suburbs of Montreal had any desire to rekindle the fervour of the zouaves of 1868 or to emulate the heroic pioneering of Maria Chapdelaine. Most of them accounted themselves loyal Catholics, but a rapid decline in fertility indicated the diminishing effect of official pronouncements against birth control. Even those who opted for fundamentalism were more often attracted by the movie-style entertainment of Youth for Christ than by any hankering for the austerity of earlier sectarian movements.

With the fading of traditional badges of identity the denominations began to look more and more alike, at least in those aspects of their life that made the greatest demands on the time and energy of the average member. In theology and ritual they differed almost as much as ever. In parish organization they had become virtually indistinguishable. They employed the same firms to manage their financial campaigns, drew the speakers for their men's clubs from the same rosters, and provided the same kinds of busy work for their voluntary helpers. Denominations insisted, as a matter of principle, on the distinctiveness of their formal procedures of church government. Their administrative hierarchies, which became steadily more important as the range of church activities widened, parallelled each other closely. Despite the lull in ecumenical activity, a common pattern of practical churchmanship was emerging.

Postwar emphases of the churches reflected, in considerable measure, the consumer mentality that dominated the period. Newly active members sought a product called religion in buildings that increasingly resembled attractive retail outlets. They went to church not so much to express convictions as to seek answers to questions, solutions to problems, and guidance in decisions. Church authorities responded by adopting methods of evangelism that closely resembled those of the new art of public relations. After the war the United Church sponsored a series of national campaigns—the Crusade for Christ, the National Evangelistic Mission, and the Mission to the Nation—in which active support of the church by its members was stressed more than individual conversion.[12] Visitation evangelism, in which laymen were sent out to invite others to commit their lives to Christ, had such an appeal to a sales-oriented society that in 1958 the Baptist Convention of Ontario and Quebec found it expedient to dispense with the services of a full-time evangelist. Larger denominations appointed information officers and began to take the mass media more seriously. Even the conservatism of the period often represented not so much a mood of assurance as a self-induced desire not to raise awkward questions about the merits of the product advertised.

The erosion of denominational differences resulted from attempts to meet increasingly similar consumer demands. Suburbanites found it natural to choose denominations, as they chose banks or grocery chains, for their convenience of location or range of facilities. The products offered by the various denominations differed, and the clergy who purveyed them were sincerely convinced of the superior quality of their own brand. The customers became increasingly difficult to tell apart, however, and with constant intermarriage they tended to overlap a good deal. The resulting situation was reminiscent of what some economists call "product differentiation," whereby firms "distinguish products not by price but by small differences, sufficient, however, in connection with advertising, to take the product out of direct price competition with otherwise similar competing products."[13] Church members valued the distinctive features of their denominations, but what most of them sought from the church had little to do with their denominational affiliation.

Comparisons with postwar patterns of consumption, although suggestive, should not be pressed too far. Those who turned to the church in the 1940s may initially have thought more of getting than of giving, but they soon showed a great eagerness for active involvement. The most spectacular result was a great expansion of activities for men. Among Protestants, despite temporary enthusiasm roused by the Laymen's Missionary Movement in the 1900s and the foundation of AOTS clubs from 1924, organization into groups for study and action had largely been left to women. In the 1940s and 1950s, however, men flocked to congregational service clubs, joined informal cell groups for Bible study and prayer, and attended inspirational conferences. Well equipped conference and retreat centres and schools for lay leaders sprang up in all parts of the country and among all major denominations. The United Church, which already had a strong tradition of lay activity, appointed a full-time secretary for men's work in 1946 and set up a board of men in 1950.

With more active participation came a widespread demand for greater recognition of the laity in the church. In all parts of the world there was a new insistence that all Christians, whether ordained or not, equally form part of the *laos* or people of God. The most influential publicist of this concept among Canadian Protestants was Elton Trueblood, an American Quaker whose books were widely read after he had delivered a series of addresses to

United Church laymen in 1953. One consequence was that laymen began to take over a number of positions that had hitherto been reserved to the clergy. In some Protestant denominations there was a revival of lay preaching, and graduates of lay training schools were active in Christian education and group leadership. Roman Catholic laymen were encouraged by the encyclical *Evangelii Praecones* in 1951 to serve as missionaries abroad. In French Canada, with the approval of Cardinal Léger and other members of the hierarchy, they moved into important posts in education and social welfare.

The desire for more active lay involvement in the life of the church was sometimes expressed with a militancy that seemed to threaten the traditional prerogatives of the clergy, and in many Protestant circles any suggestion that ordination confers a superior status within the church was immediately challenged. Yet the new attitude had little in common with traditional anticlericalism, which had sought chiefly to limit the influence of the church on secular affairs. Self-conscious laymen of the postwar years were unequivocally churchmen, eager not merely for a greater voice but for greater opportunities to serve. They wanted to fulfil what they liked to call "the ministry of the laity."

## CHANGING SOCIAL CONCERNS

The Protestant churches are generally supposed to have been so concerned with their own expansion and internal organization during the post-war years that they had little time or thought to spare for social and economic issues. A glance through denominational year books gives a different impression. In fact the churches had never spoken at such length on public affairs. Canon W. W. Judd, secretary of the Anglican council for social service, kept his church supplied with a constant flow of information. Mutchmor issued two reports each year, one for his board and one for the church's committee on international affairs, and each was on the scale of a royal commission report. The Presbyterians, who had never been enamoured of detailed blueprints for society, issued in 1955 a statement of biblical principles that should govern relations between church and state.[14]

If there was no real slackening of social concern after the war, however, there was undoubtedly a fading of political controversy. In the United Church the messianic hopes of earlier radicals were replaced by neo-orthodox reliance on interim solutions, while H. H. Walsh noted among Anglicans "an indecent and precipitous flight from Temple" at the end of the war.[15] On the other hand, the economic bourbonism that had been displayed by many business men in church assemblies gave way to the pragmatic conservatism of a more flexible generation of executives. Collective bargaining and a measure of government intervention ceased to be controversial issues, and a pledge by Bishop Alexander Carter of Sault Ste Marie to prefer union labour indicated a similar trend among English-speaking Roman Catholics. By 1958 traditional objections to the association of church and state no longer inhibited the Baptists from locating a residence on the campus of the provincial University of British Columbia. The chief marks of discussion in church courts of such issues as capital punishment came to be a passion for data and a distaste for extreme views.[16] On the other hand, United Church resolutions in 1952 favouring medicare and *de facto* recognition of the People's Republic of China anticipated government action by some years.[17] The tone of Protestant pronouncements over nearly two decades was largely set by Mutchmor and Judd, who as social pragmatists leaned to Keynesian solutions of economic problems.

In Quebec, meanwhile, the church could by no means be accused of apathy towards social and economic issues. Duplessis was well satisfied with the traditional arrangement whereby Catholic syndicates operated practically as company unions. He presented himself as a defender of Catholic values, and the hierarchy seemed to accept him as a protector. Then in December 1948 an illegal strike of five thousand asbestos miners in the Eastern Townships broke what remained of an alliance that was already subject to greater strains than appeared on the surface. The asbestos strike was one of the most remarkable events in the history of Quebec, remarkable not only because it broke a long pattern of industrial peace but because it was called by a Catholic union, defended by Catholic prelates, and supported financially by the episcopal corporations of several Catholic dioceses. According to J. C. Falardeau, it marked the point at which the syndicates decided to speak for themselves and thus broke a tradition of decision by tripartite discussions among leaders of government, church, and industry.[18]

The early retirement through "ill health" of Archbishop Charbonneau of Montreal, who had spoken on behalf of the strikers, gave rise to a general assumption in English Canada that Duplessis could dictate the policy of the church. It seems likely that the Vatican had decided that Charbonneau's usefulness was at an end, but subsequent appointments of progressives to the episcopate belied any move to the right.[19] In any event, tension between the church and the Duplessis regime steadily mounted. In 1949 the hierarchy opposed, with temporary success, some sections of a new repressive labour code. In 1950 it issued an epoch-making pastoral letter, *Le Problème ouvrier en regard de la doctrine sociale de l'Eglise*, which defined labour organization as a matter of obligation and warned governments of the need to secure the confidence of employers and workers alike.[20] Outside the hierarchy there was even more trenchant criticism. The faculty of social science at Laval University under Father Lévesque was a constant thorn in the side of the Duplessis administration, while pamphlets by Abbés Gérard Dion and Louis O'Neill in 1956 and 1960 roused the conscience of the province against electoral abuses that had been tolerated by successive governments.[21] The new orientation of the church was the outcome of a tradition of careful study of papal documents in relation to local conditions that had been established by *l'Ecole Sociale Populaire* in the 1930s. A series of *journées sacerdotales d'études sociales* was initiated in 1940, and a *commission sacerdotale d'études sociales* that grew out of them was primarily responsible for the promulgation of the pastoral letter of 1950.[22]

## PROBLEM-CENTRED CHURCHES

Whether or not they shared the interest of church leaders in public policy, laymen throughout Canada in the postwar years were primarily concerned with the application of the Christian faith to their own lives. A study by the World Council of Churches on "The Christian and His Daily Work" was eagerly taken up by lay organizations, and lay leaders constantly quoted Hans-Ruedi Weber's description of the Christian life as a rhythm of gathering for worship and scattering for witness in the world.[23] Emphasis on involvement in secular activity as the primary role of the laity appealed to many Christians who were disturbed by the apparent irrelevance of much church work, and to many others who had little taste for technical theology but were greatly troubled by the ethical ambiguities of business and labour relations. Conference planners discovered that many laymen who sat silently through theoretical discussions became voluble when presented with specific cases, often drawn from situations on the job, that called for concrete moral decision. Beginning in 1945, the SCM sponsored a series of projects that enabled students to combine summer employment in industry with discussions of the relation of their faith to the conditions of modern industry.[24] A similar tendency in Quebec was represented by the decline and eventual disappearance of *l'Association catholique de la Jeunesse canadienne*, which had devoted itself largely to pious practices, and by the corresponding rise from the early 1930s of more secularly oriented groups of *Action catholique*. Perhaps the most original feature of the bishops' pastoral letter of 1950 was its contention that the industrial environment, so long condemned as a "murderer of souls," could actually be a means of sanctification.[25]

By the 1950s, however, the industrial environment was no longer the most obvious or the most perplexing fact of life to the middle-class people who composed the most articulate segment of the Canadian church. Just when the churches had begun to approach consensus on the problems of labour they were confronted by the even more baffling ones of unaccustomed leisure. Affluence made it possible for some people to take more time off, while automation and compulsory retirement imposed idleness on others. In either case there were difficulties.

The most acute problems afflicted those whom the affluent society left out: welfare recipients, unemployables, dropouts from school. Among the discards of affluence those who most readily caught the imagination of the church were the aged, who suffered economically from the effects of inflation on fixed incomes and socially from the high cost of housing and the consequent inability of families to provide space for them. Many congregations sponsored recreational programs for lonely pensioners. So many more built "homes for senior citizens," sometimes on a very ambitious scale, that Mutchmor could describe them as "the typical charity of the time."[26] The churches seemed to be less aware of other alienated groups and did correspondingly less for them.

The most pressing demands on the church, however, were made not by the deprived but by those who were enjoying unaccustomed prosperity. People who suffered from no obvious disadvantages suddenly seemed to experience great difficulty in achieving personal stability or in establishing satisfactory relations with others. Pastoral counselling first became popular during the period of demobilization when veterans sought help in re-establishing themselves on "civvy street."[27] The demand for it did not cease with their rehabilitation. Whether affluence intensified personal problems or merely provided more leisure for trying to solve them, churches found themselves drawn into the field of mental health. Some over-eager clerics set themselves up as amateur psychiatrists, but the more responsible soon learned the value of cooperating with doctors and social service workers. It was a sign of the times that Leonard F. Hatfield, who joined the Anglican council for social service in 1950 and became its general secretary in 1956, was a specialist in mental hygiene.[28] Such deep involvement in the problems of individuals gave the church a radically new role in Canadian society. A magisterial presence in early days, sometimes a prophetic voice during the depression, it was frequently called upon during the 1940s and 1950s to serve as a therapeutic agency.

The postwar malaise in personal relations was nowhere more evident than within the family circle. Marital problems were responsible for much of the demand for pastoral counselling during the demobilization years, and by the 1950s tensions between parents and adolescent children had become even more worrisome. Throughout both decades the family and its problems were high on the agenda of all denominations. The United Church appointed in 1944 a commission on Christian marriage and the Christian home, which reported to its general council in 1946.[29] In 1953 the Catholic bishops issued a statement on "Marriage and the Family," and in 1958 another on "The Family in Canada." Such statements stressed the role of the family in preserving social stability, and Mutchmor agreed with the bishops in deploring the employment of mothers outside the home. There also emerged a positive mystique of the family as a focus of Christian living, and couples' clubs and special family services became extremely popular. Despite much urging from the clergy, however, few parents discovered in themselves any great aptitude for leading family worship.

Conscious interest in culture, whether broadly or narrowly defined, flourishes most readily among those who have time and money to spare. Canadian churches had seldom felt a need to adopt any particular attitude to it, although under varying circumstances they had both patronized it and sought to curtail its influence. It was a sign of changed times, therefore, that in 1946 the United Church appointed a commission on the subject. The commission's report in 1950 was well received,[30] and as sequels R. C. Chalmers and John A. Irving edited several symposia on the relation of the Christian faith to various aspects of human creativity.[31]

Direct participation in cultural activities was usually the result of individual initiative. Volunteer effort led to the organization in 1954 of the Christian Drama Council of Canada, which later sponsored a performing group known as the Company of Pilgrims. *Les Compagnons de Saint-Laurent*, under the auspices of the Holy Cross Fathers, had been founded somewhat earlier in Montreal. Both groups specialized in contemporary religious drama, looking for inspiration to England and France respectively. During the early 1960s the authorities of Regis College, a Jesuit seminary in Willowdale, Ontario, instituted a series of exhibitions of religious art to which leading Canadian painters and sculptors were invited to contribute. Invitations were seldom declined, and some outstanding works have been shown.

During the same period, however, the church lost its near-monopoly of the sponsorship of serious music. Hitherto most Canadian musicians had depended on employment as church organists, and the generation of Healey Willan had carried on faithfully the traditions of English cathedral music. By the 1940s the concert hall and the CBC offered an alternate economic base, and composers were turning to the modernism of Schoenberg, Stravinsky, and Bartòk. As church members shifted their attention from ethnic and ecclesiastical traditions to contemporary problems, it seemed, the church exchanged its control of the culture of time for a foothold in that of space.

Thus, despite their apparent changelessness, the churches were adapting in their own ways to a changing social climate. In creeds and rituals they recalled their origins, in public statements they echoed nineteenth-century slogans, but in day-to-day programs they responded to the demands of a generation that was more at home with problems than with traditions or crusades. Some of the most significant changes were in areas where there seemed to be no change at all. The attitude of the United Church to alcoholic beverages has already been cited as an example of the apparent conservatism of the era. What the man on the street saw was unbudging opposition, but to a Methodist or Presbyterian of an earlier generation the church might well have seemed to be in full retreat. Mutchmor at his most militant stopped short of demanding a return to prohibition, which had once been the ideal of almost all evangelical Christians. From 1936 the church officially favoured the nationalization of the liquor traffic as a means of removing the incentive of profit, apparently forgetting that governments too are interested in revenue. For individuals the church advocated voluntary total abstinence,[32] thus expressing a distinct preference but allowing moderate drinkers to be members of the church in good standing. Even more indicative of changing attitudes was the popular appeal of Alcoholics Anonymous, which disclaimed moral judgments and concentrated its efforts on the reclamation of those who seriously desired to overcome drinking problems. Although seldom venturing to query their church's official policy on alcohol, United Church laymen showed by their support of AA that in this field too they were more interested in therapy than in moral reform.

## A NEW RELIGIOUS CONFIGURATION

Despite their crowded services and expanded budgets, the churches with which Canadians had long been familiar faced increasing competition during the postwar years. Religious pluralism, although always an important factor in Canadian society, had previously been limited in practice by the small number of readily available choices. In Quebec the Roman Catholic Church was practically identical with society as a whole. In the rest of Canada social and moral norms were set by a small number of major denominations— before 1925 Anglican, Presbyterian, and Methodist, after 1925 United and Anglican. Signs of the emergence of a new configuration began to appear in the early years of the twentieth century, however, and after 1945 its existence could no longer be ignored. The main-line churches now found themselves sharing the ground with churches based on more recently arrived ethnic groups, with newer denominations of conservative evangelicals, and with unbelievers and other-believers who challenged their status as an unofficial establishment.

Lutherans, Orthodox, and Greek Catholics were well enough organized by 1945 that they were able to take advantage of postwar immigration. At Halifax, where most of the immigrants landed, Catholic and Lutheran workers were joined by a United Church theological professor who welcomed arrivals of other denominations in the name of the World Council of Churches.[33] Several churches maintained information centres in the larger cities, but the major Protestant denominations had little success in attracting immigrants into their fellowship. The Dutch Reformed Church commended departing members to the United Church, then to the Presbyterians, but many found their way into the Christian Reformed Church where the theology was more conservative than at home but the language and the social patterns were familiar. Even existing Lutheran congregations, many of which had been founded by fairly recent immigrants, were seldom able to absorb newcomers. Instead Estonians, Latvians, and Germans who arrived after 1945 were gathered into new congregations where services were conducted in their own languages.[34] The experience made Lutherans of earlier vintage more conscious of the extent to which they had already become Canadian and accelerated their progress towards national organization and national autonomy. The Orthodox, by contrast, were confirmed by the arrival of anti-Communist refugees in their preoccupation with European quarrels.[35] It was no longer possible, in any case, to dismiss churches whose background was mainly other than British or French as exotic features on the religious landscape.

Meanwhile a number of rapidly growing Protestant denominations, varying considerably in doctrine and practice but reflecting a common dissatisfaction with conventional expressions of Christianity, began to emerge as an important third force alongside Roman Catholicism and the traditional Protestant denominations. Still growing in prairie townships, they were now extending their appeal to every part of the country and increasingly gathering in middle-class urbanites. British Columbia was a natural point of entry for Californian movements, and Newfoundland brought into confederation in 1949 a considerable number of Salvationists and Pentecostalists. Several of these groups, although comparatively recent in origin, could no longer be classified as sects. By the mid-1940s, for example, the Pentecostalists had set up separate departments for missions and youth.[36] The newer denominations fell roughly into three main categories, although with almost infinite gradations from one to another.

Most readily identifiable by the general public, perhaps, were groups that laid great emphasis on peculiarities of doctrine or practice. The Seventh-Day Adventists, who combined a lively expectation of the second coming with insistence on the perpetual obligation of elements of the Old Testament ceremonial law, were attracting somewhat fewer converts than in earlier days. They were, however, gaining a reputation for running large and efficient hospitals. The Jehovah's Witnesses, identifying themselves as the faithful remnant of a human race that was rapidly approaching the culmination of its history, condemned all other Christian groups as customers of the whore of Babylon. Having apparently learned a measure of subtlety in their door-to-door canvassing from experts in public relations, they were building up a remarkable following among disgruntled church members. The Mormons, who had not previously expanded far beyond several colonies in southern Alberta, began to be visible in all parts of Canada.

Several important and growing denominations stood for elements of Protestant—and almost always Calvinistic—tradition from which, they complained, the conventional churches had moved away. Members of such groups are more aptly designated as dissenters than as sectarians, for their vision was conservative and they declined on principle to seek new types of religious experience or communal expression. The largest segment in this category consisted of Baptists who had broken with their conventions on the issue of fundamentalism. Known at first variously as Regular or Independent Baptists, they would practically all be affiliated by 1965 with the Fellowship of Evangelical Baptist Churches of Canada. For them the 1950s were a period of exceptional growth, especially in French Canada where they recruited a large missionary force. During the same decade the Christian Reformed Church was suddenly in evidence in almost all parts of Canada as the result of an influx of Dutch immigrants. The product of a major nineteenth-century theological controversy in Holland, it operated on a higher level of theological sophistication than any other conservative denomination and became known to the general public chiefly for its objections to compulsory membership in secularly oriented labour unions.

Less specialized in their appeal than any of these groups were denominations that existed not to maintain distinctive principles but simply to preach the gospel more effectively or to provide fuller opportunities for Christian experience. Their line of descent was not from Calvin's theology but from Wesley's sense of mission, and their most serious charge against the conventional churches was not heresy but spiritual deadness. Some groups in this category merely sought a return to earlier emphases on soul-saving and the cultivation of holiness, while others were distinctly charismatic in nature. The best known representative of more conventional evangelism was the Salvation Army, which despite its centralized organization and efficient public relations, made few innovations in its style of preaching. The largest and fastest-growing of the more charismatic type, and indeed of all the newer denominations, was the Pentecostal. Best known for its revival of the practice of speaking in tongues, it remained largely unknown to many Canadians through its avoidance of public controversy but exerted an influence that spread far beyond its membership. Intrinsic to the evangelistic strain was a carelessness about church order that encouraged a proliferation of loose fellowships and independent congregations. Among the larger groups of this type were the Free Methodists, the Christian and Missionary Alliance, the Church of the Nazarene, and in western Canada the Evangelical United Brethren.

Despite their diversities, most of the newer denominations acknowledged enough common assumptions to enable them to communicate with each other either in cooperation or in controversy. Almost without exception they professed to believe every word in the Bible, although some were developing qualms about speaking of "literal" belief in the Bible. The same conservatism usually extended to enforcement of the moral standards that had long been associated with evangelical Protestantism. Most of the newer groups also insisted on confronting every individual directly with the necessity of making a choice about Christ, declining to accept growth into the Christian life as a substitute for conscious conversion or social involvement as a sufficient form of Christian witness. Many interpreted history in terms of a series of divine dispensations that would culminate in the literal reign of Christ with his saints on earth, although on this point there was less agreement. Having so much in common, conservative evangelicals who were not disqualified by extreme peculiarities of doctrine often found it possible to work closely together. Along with the Mennonites, sectarians of older vintage who also began to recognize their kinship, they directed students to the Prairie Bible Institute at Three Hills, encouraged the work of the Inter-Varsity Christian Fellowship, and participated in the programs of Youth for Christ.

The relation of these groups to the popular piety of the postwar years was distinctly ambiguous. The conservatism of the period, its desire for affirmative answers, and its revival of denominational awareness were all congenial to them. Indeed, the ready consumer demand for religion gave them opportunities they were unusually well fitted to seize. Their unqualified belief in the reliability of the Bible enabled them to commend their product with complete sincerity, while their preference for direct methods of evangelism enabled them to take advantage of current techniques of salesmanship without embarrassment. In other respects, however, evangelical denominations represented a protest against the typical mind-set of postwar religion. They offered informal fellowship in place of its institutionalism, the proclamation of absolute truth in place of its preoccupation with human problems, the demand for a total change of orientation in place of its willingness to accept the gradual impregnation of life with spiritual values. In some ways they themselves conformed to the postwar mood more than they would have liked to admit, but they retained enough sense of their distinctness to rule out any early reconciliation with the conventional churches.

At the other end of the religious spectrum, the churches were compelled to recognize the existence of an increasing number of people who denied the assumption of a Christian Canada on which their leadership had been based. Some right to individual dissent had always been recognized, and Jews had been tolerated on the understanding that it was their responsibility to adjust to the circumstances of a Christian country. The progress of pluralism after 1945 can be traced in changing attitudes to the place of religion in the public schools of Ontario. In 1950, with general public approbation, the Hope commission recommended the continuation of courses specifically Christian in content.[37] By 1960 the Ethical Education Association had mobilized considerable opposition, and in 1969 the Mackay commission would recommend the elimination of such courses.[38] In Quebec, meanwhile, the principle of non-confessionalité was gradually extended from cooperatives into the more controversial field of labour. By 1960, with the transformation of *la Confédération des Travailleurs Catholiques* into *la Confédération des Syndicats nationaux*, the long career of Catholic unionism in the province had come to an end.

## ADJUSTMENT TO A CHANGING WORLD

These changes did not stem from any widespread rejection on the more orthodox churches, although Unitarianism gained ground in the larger cities of English Canada, and anticlericalism became more vocal in Montreal. Instead they reflected a tendency among Canadians of both language groups, including many faithful church members, to pay little attention to what the church said outside a narrowing area within which its special competence was admitted. More than half of those interviewed in an American survey in the late 1940s said that their religion had no effect on their behaviour in business or politics,[39] and the proportion might well have been similar in Canada. A finding of the same series of surveys that the prestige of religious leaders rose rapidly in the United States during the 1940s could not be transferred to Canada with equal confidence. As Canadians emerged late from the Victorian era some opinion-makers began to resent the tutelage of the church and to attribute all that was narrow in Canadian life to its repressive influence.

Overt hostility to the church was still uncommon, but conflict occasionally flared up in areas where remnants of ecclesiastical control persisted. Especially vulnerable were church colleges, where the points of view of secular academics and clerical administrators were not always easily reconciled. As dispute between the principal and some faculty members at United College, Winnipeg, in 1958 and the breakdown of negotiations during 1959 and 1960 to bring the arts teaching of Waterloo Lutheran College within the newly founded University of Waterloo, both of which aroused strong emotions among scholars and churchmen, were symptomatic of a tension between church and society that had implications far beyond the realm of education. English-speaking social workers had secured their independence from the church-sponsored Social Service Council of Canada in 1926, for example, and after 1945 a similar self-conscious professionalism developed in Quebec. Some areas slipped out of the hands of the church without much resistance or even awareness. Philanthropy increasingly became the responsibility of the business community,[40] while schools and community centres claimed much of the free time the churches had used for their midweek programs.

Somewhat analogous developments were changing the face of missions overseas and among native Indians and Eskimos. These had been founded for the benefit of people of other races, but it had always been assumed that effective christianization would require a measure of assimilation to Western culture. By the early years of the twentieth century missionary leaders were aware that the younger churches aspired to equal partnership with the churches of the West, and the discrediting of colonialism after 1945 hastened a drastic readjustment of relationships. Roman Catholics were perhaps readier than Protestants to recognize the necessity of incorporating indigenous social customs and art forms into Christian practice, Protestants readier than Roman Catholics to relinquish Western control. Both admitted the necessity of adapting their aid to the actual needs of the churches that received it, and the role of missionaries was increasingly that of training leaders who would eventually replace them. A similar change of attitude affected Indian work. In a joint brief submitted to the federal government in 1938 the churches insisted on "the solemn duty of the Whiteman with his advanced knowledge, to interpret to those less privileged than himself, the Indians included, the higher values of this present world."[41] By 1959 they all acknowledged, and the Roman Catholic brief explicitly asserted, that integration is "a two-way process of cultural interchange."[42]

These changes, although commendable, came at a time when enthusiasm for service abroad was increasingly being channelled into agencies other than those of the conventional churches. The more conservative Protestant groups were aggressive proselytizers, although in some respects they were more hospitable than the historic churches to the retentions of indigenous customs, they inevitably lacked experience in responding to the aspirations towards equality of Christians of other races. In 1966 there were said to be 5,100 Canadian missionaries abroad, of whom 1,700 were Roman Catholic, 700 were associated with churches belonging to the Canadian Council of Churches, and 2,700 represented conservative Protestant groups.[43] Fundamentalist missionaries were also increasingly active on Indian reservations, where formerly only a few denominations had been seriously represented. At the other end of the spectrum were many Canadians, often active church members, who preferred to serve abroad under the auspices of such secular agencies as UNRRA and CUSO. The effects of Canada's new pluralism were thus felt not only at home but abroad.

The years from 1945 to 1960 constituted a period of uneasy transition when the state of the church was not exactly what it seemed to be. In English Canada its morale was higher than it had been for some years, and it could count on generous support from an expanding membership. In French Canada it was increasingly under attack, and anticlericalism was reviving after a long period of eclipse. Yet in 1955 a Gallup poll reported 93 per cent of the population of Quebec in church on an average Sunday, as against 44 per cent in Ontario.[44] Obviously criticism had not yet seriously affected the Catholicism of Quebec, while elsewhere the return to religion had done more to rouse the careless than to reclaim the lost. The most distressing portent for the future, in all parts of Canada, was a growing gap between the official positions of the churches and the actual interests of members. As institutions the church stood for old-world traditions with which few Canadians felt at home, for moral codes to which few of them adhered, or for beliefs that had little to do with the presuppositions by which most of them lived. Despite the optimism of the moment, such an unstable situation could not long endure.

### NOTES TO CHAPTER EIGHT

1. A. C. Forrest, "The Present," in William Kilbourn, ed., *Religion in Canada* (Toronto: McClelland and Stewart, 1968), p. 64.

2. Jean Hulliger, *L'Enseignement Social des Evêques Canadiens de 1891 à 1950*, pp. 90, 97.

3. W. J. Gallagher, "The Canadian Council of Churches," *The Anglican Outlook*, Vol. VII, No. 6 (April 1952), pp. 8-9.

4. Record of Proceedings of the 18th General Council of The United Church of Canada, 1958, p. 221.

5. John Porter minimizes the significance of such an élite, but in this field as in others there are those who count with insiders and those who do not. See *The Vertical Mosaic* (Toronto: University of Toronto Press, 1965), Chapter 16.

6. R. W. Barker, "The United Church and the Social Question," p. 110.

7. Gabrielle Roy, *Bonheur d'occasion* (Montreal: Pascal, 1943); translated into English as *The Tin Flute* (New York: Reynal and Hitchcock, 1947).

8. Her first major work was *Le Torrent* (Montreal: Beauchemin, 1950).

9. The suggestion had been made by Bishop Anson of Qu'Appelle as early as 1887. Robert Machray, *The Life of Robert Machray*, p. 335.

10. Walter Freitag, "Lutheran Tradition in Canada," in J. W. Grant, ed., *The Churches and the Canadian Experience*, p. 100.

11. Milos Mladenovic, "Canadian Orthodoxy and the Union of Churches," in *ibid.*, p. 115.

12. J. R. Mutchmor, *Mutchmor*, pp. 167, 192.

13. David Riesman, Nathan Glazer, and Reuel Denney, *The Lonely Crowd: A Study of the Changing American Character*, abridged edition (New York: Doubleday Anchor Books, n.d.), p. 64.

14. *A Declaration of Faith Concerning Church and Nation* (Toronto: The Board of Evangelism and Social Action of the Presbyterian Church in Canada, 1955).

15. "Farewell—and Hail," editorial in *The Anglican Outlook*, Vol. XV, No. 8 (June-July 1960), p. 6.

16. The Presbyterian Church affirmed in 1954 the right of the state to inflict capital punishment. Acts and Proceedings of the 80th General Assembly, 1954, p. 263. The United Church declared capital punishment to be "contrary to the spirit and teaching of Christ," while acknowledging the need of suitable alternatives. Record of Proceedings of the 17th General Council, 1956, p. 86; 19th, 1960, pp. 59, 137.

17. Record of Proceedings of the 15th General Council of The United Church of Canada, 1952, pp. 58, 138, 183.

18. J. C. Falardeau, "The Changing Social Structures," in J. C. Falardeau, ed., *Essais sur le Québec Contemporain* (Quebec: Laval University Press, 1953), p. 116.

19. Herbert F. Quinn, *The Union Nationale: A Study in Quebec Nationalism* (Toronto: University of Toronto Press, 1963), p. 163.

20. *Le problème ouvrier en regard de la doctrine sociale de l'Eglise*, Lettre pastorale collective le Leurs Excellences Nosseigneurs les Archevêques et Evêques de la province civile de Québec, 181 (Montréal: Les Editions Bellarmin, 1950), p. 64.

21. *L'immoralité politique dans la Province de Québec* (Montreal: Comité de moralité publique de Montréal, 1956); *Le Chrétien et les elections* (Montreal: Editions de l'Homme, 1960).

22. Jacques Cousineau, sj, in Falardeau, *op. cit.*, p. 210.

23. His *Salty Christians* (New York: Seabury, 1963), originally written at the request of the East Asian Christian Conference, circulated for some years in mimeographed form as a handbook for lay leaders throughout the world.

24. The author was a co-director of the second student-in-industry camp, held at Brantford, Ontario, in 1946. Attendance at these camps was for some students a traumatic experience that changed the course of their lives.

25. *Le problème ouvrier*, 37, p. 12.

26. Mutchmor, *op. cit.*, p. 189.

27. Douglas J. Wilson, *The Church Grows in Canada*, p. 150.

28. W. W. Judd, "The Vision and the Dream," *Journal of the Canadian Church Historical Society*, Vol. VII, No. 4, p. 108.

29. Record of Proceedings of the 12th General Council of The United Church of Canada, 1946, p. 105.

30. Record of Proceedings of the 14th General Council of The United Church of Canada, 1950, Appendix. Also published as R. C. Chalmers, ed., *The Heritage of Western Culture* (Toronto: Ryerson, 1952).

31. Within this period were *The Light and the Flame* (Toronto: Ryerson, 1956) and *Challenge and Response* (Toronto: Ryerson, 1959).

32. For the major statement of policy on alcoholic beverages during this period, see Record of Proceedings of the 13th General Council of The United Church of Canada, 1948, p. 205.

33. I. F. Mackinnon, *Canada and the Minority Churches of Eastern Europe, 1945-1950*, p. 6.

34. Carl R. Cronmiller, *A History of the Lutheran Church in Canada*, p. 209.

35. Paul Yuzyk, *The Ukrainians in Manitoba*, p. 38.

36. E. N. O. Culbeck, "A Brief History of the Pentecostal Assemblies of Canada," in *Canada's Centennial*, pp. 26-27.

37. Report of the Royal Commission on Education in Ontario, 1950 (Toronto: King's Printer, n.d.), pp. 126-127.

38. *Religious Information and Moral Development*, The Report of the Committee on Religious Education in the Public Schools of the Province of Ontario, 1969, p. 93.

39. Will Herberg, *Protestant-Catholic-Jew* (Garden City, N.Y.: Doubleday, 1956), p. 64.

40. See Aileen D. Ross, "Organized Philanthropy in an Urban Community," *Canadian Journal of Economics and Political Science*, Vol. XVIII, No. 4 (November 1952), pp. 474-486.

41. Minutes and Evidence of the Joint Indian Affairs Committee, 1947, p. 443 (Appendix DZ).

42. *Ibid.*, 1960, pp. 731, 795, 811-812.

43. K. MacMillan, "The Influence of the Church on the Life of the Canadian Nation," four lectures given to the Northwest Mission Conference held in Salem, Oregon, August 1966, MS.

44. *Montreal Star*, June 29. 1955.

# NINE

# A Decade of Ferment

Few suspected when the 1960s began that the decade would bring notable surprises in Canadian church life. Suburbanites continued to support their congregations, following a pattern set shortly after the second world war, and most of them could point with pride to well equipped church "plants" that were still almost the last word in ecclesiastical design. Since few of these buildings were yet paid for, a large proportion of the time and effort they could spare for church activities was devoted to the raising of money. The wider life of the church was comparatively devoid of excitement. National and regional bodies passed numerous resolutions, but with a sense that they had already achieved consensus on the most important issues and had ample time to dispose of the rest. The easing of the cold war and the end of the McCarthy era in the United States led to a general cooling of passions, except among a few ban-the-bombers who seemed to most of their colleagues to be making more noise than the peril warranted. The Canadian pew was still comfortable, and the chief complaint of preachers was that they heard so few complaints.

## PAST THE PEAK OF THE BOOM

Already, however, there was mounting evidence that the foundations of the church's recently achieved popularity were not so solid as they looked. Alumni of the swollen Sunday schools of the previous decade, although not conspicuously in revolt against the church, showed little enthusiasm for its youth programs. In 1958 the moderator of the United Church had observed among them considerable interest in personal religion but also exposure to "an endless relativity in faith and morals."[1] Their elders were beginning to complain, after years of faithful attendance, that they found it difficult to grasp the significance of rituals and sometimes even the meaning of sermons. Articulate discontent was still largely confined to the younger clergy, who struggled to relate the traditional roles in which they were often

cast to the technical society in which they had to play them. Clearly, however, the religious boom had already passed its peak. Attendances at worship
was levelling off, and financial campaigns were no longer almost automatically successful.

A growing discrepancy between the teaching of the churches and the
values by which Canadians lived was masked for a time by the rather old-
fashioned rhetoric of the Diefenbaker era but became increasingly evident
as that rhetoric lost its credibility. Canadians slowly realized the anomaly
of a situation in which the churches encouraged sobriety and stewardship
while the media pressed them mainly to get and spend money. The rituals
of the Grey Cup and the Calgary Stampede had an obvious relevance to the
new Canada which those of the churches lacked, and the role of the latter
increasingly seemed to be that of easing the consciences of the bourgeois as
they moved out of the old simple ruralism into a frankly commercial and
industrial age.

Despite the general calm on the religious scene there were tell-tale indications that the churches recognized that the bulk of their members had
moved away from traditional patterns. In 1960 the general council of the
United Church, while continuing to urge total abstinence from alcoholic
beverages as "the wisest and safest course," admitted that some responsible
members conscientiously practised moderation instead.[2] In a sense this had
always been the church's position, but the balanced presentation of arguments on both sides represented a significant break with the past. Later in the
same month Arthur Packman became the United Church's first "padre of
the pubs,"[3] and a report that he had sipped a glass of shandy with his
parishioners created surprisingly little consternation. In Quebec the death
of Duplessis in 1959 and the accession to power of the Liberals under Jean
Lesage in 1960 presaged a series of changes that would make the Catholic
Church something other than the inescapable presence it had been hitherto,
and far-seeing leaders of the church already recognized that its traditional
attitude of paternalism was no longer appropriate. Anglicans were slower
to sense the passing of Victorian Canada but had a sudden awakening in
1963 when overseas delegates to a worldwide Anglican Congress at Toronto
served notice that the patterns of western Christendom were irretrievably
broken.[4] From that time their church seemed more willing to reconsider
traditional positions. In 1965, for example, it moved to relax a rule that had
forbidden its clergy to remarry divorced persons under any circumstances.[5]

## A PROGRAM OF MODERNIZATION

The changes of which the public became dimly aware at the beginning
of the decade seemed few in number and modest in scale. In fact they were
the first tokens of a major process of internal reconstruction that was

engaging the attention of a large number of concerned churchmen. Even in the apparently complacent 1950s the churches had begun to move towards a number of far-reaching reforms in procedure and approach. Most of these came about because clergy and officials observed that current programs were not achieving their intended results, not because the rank and file of church members were expressing dissatisfaction or demanding change. They were inaugurated as a series of independent projects, but together they constituted a carefully planned if not always well integrated program of modernization. All denominations took part in it, although with its centralized polity and its tradition of untraditionalism the United Church was able to move farther and faster than most others. No comparable overhaul of church procedures had taken place since the introduction of new methods of Christian education and missionary support during the last decades of the nineteenth century.

Since church leaders were most conscious of inadequacy in communicating their message, they concentrated at first on improvements in the expression and transmission of the Christian faith. The Anglicans issued a revised *Book of Common Prayer* in 1959. It had long been in preparation, and still reflected the conservatism of the postwar years. The Presbyterians approved in 1964, after considerable debate, a *Book of Common Order* that departed more radically from customary practice. A United Church committee on worship was already at work during the 1950s, although the first of its new *Service Books* would appear only in 1969 when the liturgical climate had changed considerably again. The United Church and the Presbyterians began work on new hymn books. Preachers experimented with dialogue sermons and congregational "buzz groups." Most major denominations issued or imported from the United States new curricula of Christian education. Church broadcasters, who lacked the resources for large-scale television production, began to cooperate closely with the CBC and with private producers. In all these areas there was a subtle change of emphasis about 1960 from the refurbishing of the church's image to the search for a better understanding of the church's message. The era of the ecclesiastical booster was coming to an end.

The new curriculum of the United Church, which began to appear in 1962, was in many respects a classic example of Protestant modernization. The decision to prepare it had been taken by the general council as early as 1952. In 1956 the editors asked for clarification of the theological assumptions on which their work should be based, and with substantial help from the theological colleges a set of presuppositions was approved in 1958.[6] The church's publishing house sought in the actual drafting of the curriculum to make the greatest possible use of available pedagogical skills, and materials were used experimentally in selected congregations before being issued to the public. In view of widespread religious illiteracy, and of a growing gap

in understanding between ministry and laity, the church decided to introduce the program by providing material for study by adults.

The new curriculum came into use more rapidly than even its promoters
had dared to hope. Six hundred thousand copies of the adult study book
were sold during the first summer,[7] and sales of curricular materials during
the first year exceeded the total enrollment in United Church Sunday
schools. Behind the curriculum, which was conceived during the ascendancy
of neo-orthodox theology, lay the essentially conservative intention of increasing the scriptural content of Sunday school teaching. In order to help
adults to study Scripture intelligently, however, the drafters confronted
them directly with difficult problems of biblical authorship and authority
that most ministers had long evaded. Some teachers resigned in protest
against the "modernism" of the curriculum, a few members turned to more
conservative denominations, and many congregations reported an enthusiastic response on the part of their people.

As they reviewed their programs the churches found it necessary to take
a harder look than before at the constituencies for which these programs
were intended. Baptists, who had customarily thought of their congregations as gathered out of society, began to conduct careful surveys of the
communities in which they worked. In 1962 the Anglicans set up a Unit of
Research and Field Study in order to gather more reliable information about
their people; its first major project was a survey of the attitudes of the
clergy.[8] The United Church, which had inherited from its components a
disproportionate number of small rural congregations, was forced to take
the automobile age more seriously after 1958 when a decline in farm income
speeded up the depopulation of the countryside. Church courts used their
authority to combine pastoral charges, and in some localities historic but
dilapidated meeting houses gave way to well-equipped consolidated churches.
Inner-city congregations, which usually consisted mainly of loyal families
who had long since moved their homes to the suburbs, began to give more
attention to those who now lived near their churches. In many cases, however, ministers had to contend with congregational resistance to types of
service that showed little promise of attracting either new members or increased financial support.

Voluntary congregational organizations for particular age and sex groups,
most of which had been founded to meet the needs of an earlier era, came
in for thorough re-examination. Youth programs were modified to take
account of the growing sophistication and self-confidence of teen-agers, and
after one or two false starts became distinctly less paternalistic. Leaders of
women's organizations were also beginning to query the assumptions on
which their patterns of operation had been based. In most Protestant communions these organizations were of two types, one designed to meet specific local needs, the other to support missionary work at home and abroad.

Although both types were represented in almost every congregation, neither was formally related to the other or to official church structures. In 1962, however, the Woman's Association and the Woman's Missionary Society of the United Church joined to form United Church Women, at the same time amalgamating their operations with those of the church as a whole. Anglican Church Women followed in 1966, incorporating the missionary-oriented Women's Auxiliary and any other groups that wished to belong. The formation of mixed groups of men and women seemed to be the logical next step, but segregation by sex is deeply ingrained in Canadian social custom.

As piecemeal reconstruction proceeded, the need for coordination became apparent. Long-range planning committees became a regular feature of the larger denominations. On the advice of technical experts the United Church grouped its boards into divisions, while the Anglicans contrived to do away with their departmental structure altogether. The resurge of regionalism in Canada was reflected in attempts to decentralize the process of decision-making. The United Church set up a conference office in British Columbia, and later others elsewhere, while Anglicans faced with declining revenues were under pressure to make cuts in national rather than in diocesan appropriations. Simultaneously there were strenuous efforts to inject new life into regional legislative bodies.

The weakness of most experiments in restructuring ecclesiastical bureaucracies was that those who proposed them thought mainly in terms of doing more effectively what the church was already doing rather than of examining critically the role of the church in an increasingly secularized Canada. Attention was focused on the latter problem largely by the discontent of ministers who were no longer certain of the relevance of their traditional functions but apprehensive at the prospect of becoming "mere cogs in a lifeless machine—running forever at high speed to distribute and use the endless outpourings of a central headquarters."[9] A search for new avenues of service led to the foundation of the Canadian Council for Supervised Pastoral Education in 1965 and the Canadian Urban Training Project in 1966. In 1964 the United Church appointed a commission on "Ministry in the Twentieth Century," and in 1966 the Anglicans held a consultation on the theme "Ministry to a Changing World." The problem of finding effective ways of using the talents available to them seemed likely to trouble the churches for some time.

## VATICAN II AND CATHOLIC *AGGIORNAMENTO*

Roman Catholics were the last to undertake major reforms, but they soon outstripped all others. The impulse came mainly from the Second Vatican Council, which was convened in 1962 at the call of Pope John XXIII and held its final sessions in 1965 during the pontificate of Paul VI. Although the council neither took place in Canada nor concerned itself with specifically Canadian problems, it must be accounted one of the most important events in Canadian religious history. The Canadian bishops, unlike their counterparts in most other countries, had met annually for consultation since 1943 in what came to be called the Canadian Catholic Conference. Thus accustomed to teamwork, they were able to press their ideas systematically through successive stages of debate, as Bishops Charbonneau of Hull, Doyle of Nelson, and De Roo of Victoria did with notable effectiveness in the definition of the lay apostolate. Cardinal Léger of Montreal, although not especially a committee man, was one of the leading charismatic speakers on the progressive side. Canadians also accepted the decrees and general spirit of the council with an alacrity that was by no means universal in the United States. Even before the final session, the shape of the church in Canada was changing with a speed that startled Catholics and Protestants alike.

One result of Vatican II was to initiate a program of modernization similar to that which was already going on in most Protestant churches. *Aggiornamento* or "updating" was the term used by Pope John XXIII, and its progress was all the more dramatic because so much of it needed to be done. Celebration of mass in the vernacular was the aspect of modernization that was most immediately visible to the general public. Equally significant were other reforms of worship—greater participation by the people in hymns and responses, the downgrading of pious devotional practices that distracted individuals from common worship, and the adoption by priests of the basilican posture in which they faced the rest of the congregation across the altar. Church architecture, less dependent than in Protestant churches on the whims of local committees, was speedily adapted to the new liturgical practices. Christian education, which had been almost unaffected by modern pedagogical methods, began to take on a new look. Previous catechisms had been in a stilted question-and-answer form suitable for memorization. They were gradually replaced during the 1960s by a new series of textbooks in French and English that undertook to deal with questions actually asked by modern children. Clerical training had long been based on manuals of scholastic logic that provided priests with a highly systematized version of Catholic doctrine. It now began to emphasize theological dialogue and to encourage awareness of secular academic disciplines as well as of other religions.[10] One centre of the new-style theological education was the faculty of theology of the University of Montreal, which was formed in July 1967, by the union of several small seminaries. Its four hundred students, with their teachers of various orders, would henceforth be exposed to the stimulating and disturbing influences of a large university campus.[11]

"Collegiality" was one of the key words of the Vatican Council. Strictly speaking, it referred to the association of bishops, acting collectively as a "college" with the pope, in the government of the church. In practice, its popularity encouraged a great deal of consultation at all levels. The Canadian Catholic Conference, with a growing secretariat that included both priests and laymen, was able to make decisions that would previously have had to be referred to Rome. Bishops began to consult priests, and sometimes the laity, before making clerical appointments. Parish councils gave the laity a larger voice in local programs. Paternalism in missions overseas and among native peoples was given a further blow. The growing acceptance of collegiality ensured that historians of Catholic thought would no longer be able to limit themselves to papal encyclicals and episcopal *mandements* but would have to take into account the opinions of theologians both clerical and lay.

Associated with these changes was a general openness and readiness to innovate that confounded those who had known the older "fortress Catholicism." The most popular targets of abuse at the Vatican Council were "triumphalism" and "juridical" modes of thought. Triumphalism was precisely the desire of the church to dominate society that had inspired the circles of Bourget and Laflèche. Juridical behaviour meant a dependence on regulations that had been typical of the church in Canada as elsewhere. With their eclipse there was a general thaw in the Catholic attitude to society. Episcopal pronouncements began to lose their tone of finality. An Anglican student who spent a weekend at the Jesuits' Regis College was heard to exclaim in dismay, "But they have no rules!" "The Theology of the Renewal of the Church" was the theme of a centennial congress at St. Michael's College, Toronto, in 1967, and those invited included leading thinkers of many countries and several faiths.[12]

## THE EXTENSION OF DIALOGUE

As the churches turned their attention from expansion to reappraisal, their enthusiasm for ecumenicity began to revive. The preparation of new liturgies and curricula revealed unexpected areas of agreement, as well as a virtual identity in contemporary trends. Surveys of the constituency indicated that many Canadians chose their denominations almost at random and that comparatively few took their peculiar principles seriously. Attempts to rationalize church structures highlighted the irrationality of overlapping effort. An easing of international tensions contributed to good feeling, and the progress of secularization moderated fears that if the churches were to get together they would reclaim their earlier domination of society. In Canada, interest was further stimulated by the sessions of the fourth Faith and Order conference at Montreal in 1963. Responsive to the new climate, the venerable Canadian School of Missions changed its name and emphasis to become the Ecumenical Institute of Canada.

The most exciting ecumenical development of the decade was the dramatic entry of the Roman Catholic Church into conversation with other communions after four centuries of controversy or silence. Insistence on submission to Rome as a condition of union had seemed to make Catholic participation in the ecumenical movement *a priori* impossible, and several popes had plainly said so. Such influential theologians as Yves Congar had long been urging a more open attitude, however, and at the Vatican Council their view prevailed. The council served the cause of ecumenism in many ways. It promulgated decrees on Ecumenism and on Other Religions that were couched in terms friendly to non-Catholics. It issued a decree on Religious Freedom that declared in unambiguous terms that "a wrong is done when government imposes upon its people, by force or fear or other means, the profession or repudiation of any religion, or when it hinders men from joining or leaving a religious body."[13] It invited Protestant and Orthodox observers, and paid serious attention to their comments. It took a step beyond well meant references to "separated brethren" by designating Protestant communions as "ecclesial communities,"[14] and on a less formal occasion Pope Paul even used the word "churches." Most helpful of all, perhaps, was the concern of the council to state positions in terms that would leave openings for ecumenical discussion. Protestants were grateful for what the council said about Scripture and about the laity, and even more grateful for some things it left unsaid about the Virgin Mary. Vatican II made such a difference, indeed, that it rendered obsolete all previous accounts of the ecumenical movement.

Whatever hesitations there might be in some other countries, most Canadians were ready to make up old religious quarrels. The first public sign of reconciliation was an address by Cardinal Léger to the Faith and Order conference in 1963. Joint worship services began in 1965, and people soon ceased to remark on them. Groups for the discussion of outstanding issues met in some of the larger cities, but lost their glamour as informal contacts became more frequent. Soon one took for granted the presence of Catholic scholars in theological societies, of priests in ministerial associations, and of seminarians in the activities of the Ecumenical Institute. Roman Catholics established in 1966 a national office for ecumenical affairs under the bilingual direction of Fathers John Keating and Irenée Beaubien. Protestants, a little surprised to find the ecumenical initiative for once in other hands, tended to accept more invitations to dialogue than they issued. A sharp exchange in 1962 on the Ontario school issue showed that renewed friendship did not solve all problems, but such differences of opinion would increasingly be resolved by direct encounter and not made occasions for appeals to popular prejudice. Perhaps the most startling evidence of this trend was the institution in 1967 of joint counselling by Catholic priests and Protestant ministers of couples contemplating mixed marriages.[15]

Montreal, the centre of French-Canadian nationalism, was also the scene of some of the most significant pioneering in interdenominational understanding. In 1958, four years before the first session of the Vatican Council, Irenée Beaubien set up an ecumenical centre there at the behest of Cardinal Léger. Soon Protestant and Catholic clergy were meeting monthly "for prayer, discussion and friendship in the mode of the 'spiritual ecumenism' fostered in France by the Abbé Couturier."[16] The dialogue was gradually widened to include not only scholars but youth groups, seminary students, men's and women's organizations, and sometimes entire congregations. A striking feature of ecumenical activity in Quebec has been the contribution of the tiny minority of French-Canadian Protestants. Long regarded by their compatriots as traitors both to language and to religion, they were now able to serve as catalysts to bring together those who were separated by both barriers.

## A RENEWED DRIVE TOWARDS CHURCH UNION

The new ecumenical climate brought fresh encouragement to those who for many years had been trying to negotiate formal unions of churches. Those that actually took place in Canada during the 1960s were, in a sense, overflows from the United States. Mergers in 1960 and 1962 brought together most American Lutherans into two large churches, the American Lutheran Church and the Lutheran Church of America, each with Canadian units. In 1967 the Canada district of the American Lutheran Church became the Evangelical Lutheran Church of Canada, and in the same year this body collaborated with the Lutheran Church of America to form the Lutheran Council in Canada. Canadian Lutherans were well on the way towards autonomy and unity, although several difficult steps remained to be taken.

Another American union that would affect Canadians was proposed between the Methodists and the Evangelical United Brethren Church. The two Canadian conferences of the latter church were thus faced with a choice between becoming part of a vast American organization or attempting to maintain a precarious independence. The Western Canada conference, which was extremely conservative in theology and evangelistic approach, arranged to remain separate while receiving aid from the American Methodists. The more liberal Canada conference in the east, which had begun to discuss union with the Canadian Wesleyans before confederation, would become part of The United Church of Canada shortly after its centennial.

Conversations between the Anglican and United churches, after almost breaking down in 1958, were resumed in 1960 with new committees. Both churches felt a renewed sense of urgency, and a study guide entitled *Growth in Understanding* was widely circulated. The Anglicans had hitherto shown considerable reluctance, but the Lambeth Conference of 1958 was enthusiastic for union, and in 1962 Bishop Stephen F. Bayne challenged the general synod to contemplate the disappearance of the Anglican communion into a reunited church.[17] Rigid attitudes on both sides were undercut by Roman Catholic willingness to reopen old questions, although there were occasional suggestions from members of the Anglican and United Churches alike that they might have felt more at ease negotiating with Rome than with their actual partners. Expectations of early action were aroused by the appearance in late 1964 of a plan of union sponsored by the London conference of the United Church and the Anglican diocese of Huron.[18]

On June 1, 1965, after years of frustration and deadlock, the official committees were at last able to issue a statement of principles on which an organic union of the two churches might be based.[19] Committee members, who ranged from Anglo-Catholic to former Congregationalist, spoke of a "breakthrough" into unanimity which they regarded as almost miraculous. The secret, as they explained it, was recognition that a fruitful union would bring into being "not a merger of two existing ecclesiastical bodies, but rather a new embodiment of the One Church of God."[20]

The initial public response was favourable, and with scarcely a dissenting voice the Anglican general synod of 1965 accepted the *Principles* as a basis on which the details of union might be worked out.[21] Then much of the impetus was dissipated by delays inherent in ecclesiastical government. The next general council of the United Church did not meet until September 1966, and by then ministers and members had found time to catalogue their doubts. The general council approved the *Principles* in language that was intended to be as positive as the Anglican resolution of the previous year, but only after a vigorous debate during which amendments had been offered in bewildering variety.[22] Some Anglicans wondered whether the United Church was really serious, others whether they themselves had examined the document critically enough. Once the necessary assurances had been given and accepted, there was further delay while new commissions were appointed to work out the details of union and inevitably to offer fresh suggestions of their own. By 1967 the process of refinement was under way, however, and in 1969 the Christian Church (Disciples of Christ) would join the conversations.

Meanwhile, churches were quietly beginning to do together many things they had previously done separately. In a number of new suburbs and industrial towns several denominations combined to erect buildings for common use. St. Michael's College of the Basilian order became part of the Toronto Graduate School of Theological Studies, the Presbyterian College in Montreal moved closer to affiliation with the faculty of divinity of McGill University, and by 1967 a proposal for concentrating theological education in four ecumenical centres was being seriously discussed. Roman Catholic and Protestant seminarians organized a national conference of theological students, under the aegis of the Ecumenical Institute, that attempted to be not only interdenominational but bilingual. In Newfoundland, where education had always followed strictly denominational lines, the Anglicans, the United Church, and the Salvation Army agreed to consolidate their educational facilities and organization. A broadly representative committee on the Church in Industrial Society laid plans for a congress in 1968. Some co-operative projects were by-products of union descussions: Anglican and United churches projected a joint hymn book, Covenant College and the Anglican Women's Training College moved towards amalgamation, and in the Kootenays of British Columbia the two communions began to set up ecumenical parishes. In other cases, such as the preparation of materials for Canada's centennial, participants included not only a wide spectrum of Christian communions but Jews, Muslims, and Buddhists.

Less visible to the general public than organized cooperation was an emerging pattern of informal consultation across denominational lines. Experts in Christian education or in family life discovered that they shared more concerns with their opposite numbers in other churches than with colleagues who specialized in different areas. The approach of the major churches to the mass media became practically a single operation, to the astonishment of more denominationally bound Americans. Workers in the inner city were brought together by common problems and by common complaints of indifference at headquarters. Theological teachers began to work out joint curricula. By 1964 the Canadian Council of Churches was compelled to undertake a serious reappraisal of its constitution. Whereas it had formerly been hampered by the unwillingness of churches to cooperate at all, it was now often by-passed by the telephones on secretaries' desks. As its function as a coordinator of denominational activities became less important, it moved towards a greater stress on study, research, and the encouragement of serious dialogue across denominational lines. The stream of ecumenism carved out new channels for itself that occasionally left old ones high and dry.

Whereas the key word of early Canadian projects of union had been "consolidation," and that of the early stages of the ecumenical movement "agreement," pride of place in the 1960s belonged to "dialogue." Dialogue, as understood in ecumenical circles, means a conversation that presupposes not agreement on belief but willingness to take seriously the convictions and concerns of others. Its aim is not the attainment of a predetermined program but the achievement of openness to the other and to the future. The concept, which emerged in the early twentieth century from discussions among Protestant and Orthodox churchmen, was adopted enthusiastically by the fathers of the Second Vatican Council and affected all cooperative ventures and union negotiations of the 1960s. It could also be applied more broadly to conversations between Christians and Jews, members of other religious communities, or adherents of such secular ideologies as Communism. In 1962 the Anglican diocese of Toronto commissioned the Rev. Roland de Corneille to a special ministry of reconciliation between Christians and Jews. The Catholic Sisters of Sion, who had been founded to seek the conversion of Jews to Christianity, began to concentrate their efforts on improved understanding on both sides and had remarkable success in winning the confidence of the Jewish community.

## REBELLION AND EXPERIMENT

As if the astonishing developments of the early 1960s were not enough for church members to absorb, towards the middle of the decade the pace of change suddenly speeded up. The initiative in innovation, which up to this point had remained firmly in the hands of church leaders, passed to impatient and often younger critics. What had begun as an orderly process of reform began to look more like a revolution. Calm reappraisal by those in authority proved, for by no means the first time in either ecclesiastical or secular history, to be a prelude to the violent expression of discontent by those who were prepared to challenge authority.

The initial stimulus to criticism of the church came from church officials themselves, who were anxious to jolt people out of their complacency and to put steam behind their programs of modernization. Anglicans planning their Lenten study for 1965 decided not to issue the usual devotional booklet but to ask journalist Pierre Berton to give an outsider's view of the church. The result was *The Comfortable Pew*, which was destined to become one of Canada's all-time best sellers.[23] Not to be outdone, the United Church replied with a hastily compiled symposium entitled *Why the Sea Is Boiling Hot*.[24] *Brief to the Bishops* in the same year was a more spontaneous offering of advice by the Catholic laity to leaders then attending the Vatican Council, and the book was coldly received by the hierarchy.[25] In this case too the advice had been solicited, however, and the Catholic Information Centre of Toronto held copyright to the volume. For a time, headquarters secretaries on tour could almost be counted on to point out the shortcomings of the church and to dissect its structures. Outsiders marvelled at the readiness with which churchmen absorbed and even asked for punishment.

The attack on complacency in the pew succeeded beyond the wildest dreams of those who had launched it. Young people, many of whom were sensitive to the apparent aimlessness of bourgeois society and aroused to indignation by the civil rights struggle in the United States, had no difficulty in believing that the church was irrelevant and inept. What leaders now told them only confirmed what they had already suspected. Even many older people confessed, when their opinions were sought, that they found little meaning in many aspects of the church's worship and program. It soon became apparent that few people were prepared to defend the existing state of the church, although prescriptions for its future varied tremendously.

Every aspect of church life was suddenly subject to review, revaluation and sometimes protest. Questioning began with the institutions of the church: the local parish (especially in suburbia), church headquarters (most of which were vulnerably located in Toronto), theological colleges (often identified as the source of the church's backwardness), Catholic schools, eventually the very existence of institutions. It extended to the bases of authority in the church: age, ministerial status, hierarchical rank, membership in ecclesiastical "establishments." It did not spare the teaching of the church: the theological language in which it was expressed, the vestiges of pre-scientific thinking it preserved, its alliance with outdated forms, ultimately even the concept of God it presupposed. Missionary work overseas was decried as a relic of western arrogance. Increasingly, too, the church was charged with complicity in injustice as represented by the Vietnam war, the oppression of Indian and black minorities, and the continuance of economic colonialism.

Criticism of the church in Quebec constituted a distinct chapter in the story of dissent, and clergy, religious and laity vied to outdo each other in irreverence towards a hitherto sacrosanct institution. Frère Untel—Brother Anonymous to English readers—became a national figure overnight by poking fun at the religious orders who imposed their monastic inhibitions on the schoolchildren of the province.[26] Although promptly whisked off to France for further study, he returned as Brother Pierre-Jerôme Desbien to take a serious part in the reform of Quebec education. *Maintenant*, a Dominican magazine that had long taken a radical line, survived the brief removal of its editor, Father H. M. Bradet, and became more influential than ever. Jean LeMoyne, a journalist who was also a philosopher, portrayed the church as an over-protective parent who would not let Quebec society and culture grow up. His articles were later published as a book in French and English.[27] Students in the conservative classical colleges were reputed to be the most trenchant critics of the church, but they were closely rivalled by nuns.

On the more positive side, a wave of experimentation demonstrated that alternate methods and ideas were available to the church if it wished to adopt them. The chaotic state of Catholic liturgy in the wake of the Vatican Council made worship a particularly inviting field for innovation. Masses were invaded by electric guitars, singing nuns contributed to a new repertoire of folk hymns, and serious liturgists explored the use of new idioms of music and language. Protestants took up the Catholic practice of addressing God as "you" and found that as a result they had to revamp their whole vocabulary of worship. A "psychedelic" service in Vancouver under the joint auspices of an Anglican parish and a United Church congregation momentarily caught the attention of the nation, while elsewhere local churches laboriously worked out their own patterns of worship. Service projects were no longer limited to prim homes for unmarried mothers but extended to drop-in centres for hippies in which solid citizens found it difficult to distinguish clergy from flower children. Experiments in new styles of Christian living caught on more slowly than in the United States, but few Canadians were unaware of efforts to define a "new morality." Meanwhile a new theological system appeared every few months, only to be superseded by another that was even more radical in its denials of received truth. Most of these were imported from Britain or the United States, but the presence of such influential and sometimes controversial figures as Leslie Dewart, Gregory Baum, and Bernard Lonergan made Toronto one of the main centres of theological innovation among English-speaking Roman Catholics.

Neither rebels nor experimenters were greatly impressed by the programs of modernization into which the churches had put so much effort a few years earlier. They regarded the new curricula as already antiquated, and many of them wrote off proposed new official liturgies and hymn books in advance. Although suspicious of the clergy, they showed little interest in official lay movements that had been in the vanguard of change during the 1950s. In the Roman Catholic Church, where the reforms had been most far-reaching, the dissatisfaction seemed to be most acute. The initiators of change in the church might have reflected on the fates of Mirabeau and Kerensky.

The same scepticism was extended to the church's official participation in ecumenical activities. Enthusiasts for change were undoubtedly ecumenists of a kind. They had no interest in denominationalism and avoided denominational labels on their enterprises whenever they could. On the other hand, many of them dismissed closer relations among church bodies, and especially formal unions, as so many efforts to keep dying institutions alive. It was a misfortune for the framers of the *Principles of Union* that their work appeared during the same publishing season as *The Comfortable Pew* and *Why the Sea Is Boiling Hot*. They had performed well the tasks assigned them and even broken new ground in seeking to orient their work towards the future. Within a few months, however, their language seemed rather stodgy and the questions to which they had given most of their attention had lost much of their currency.

## NEW LINES OF CLEAVAGE

As the ferment continued to work, dialogue was often replaced by confrontation. Resolutions were debated with a vehemence that had been absent since depression years, although the grounds of objection were not always those expected by their sponsors. Ecumenical discussions frequently bogged down, as experts who were familiar with the complexities of one set of problems were suddenly called upon to deal with another. Among all the churches there appeared a new line of fissure that bore little relation to traditional denominational and party differences, a good deal more to those of age and ecclesiastical status. Demands quickly followed for the more effective representation of groups that felt themselves to be deprived of power in the church—the laity generally, but especially women, youth, and ethnic minorities. Even those who showed no great desire for radical change seemed reluctant to trust decisions to boards or committees on which their peers were not strongly represented. Hierarchical and conciliar churches alike were pressed to institute participatory democracy.

To many on either side the cleavage was one that could be described in simple terms. In 1964, when the Rev. Russell Horsburgh was charged with contributing to juvenile delinquency in the course of an experimental program for teen-agers, dissatisfied radicals could readily attribute the failure of the United Church to underwrite his eventually successful defence to its involvement in existing social structures. In 1967, when an Anglican priest named Ernest Harrison wrote a book with the provocative title *A Church Without God*, he was informed that his views were unsound and that a licence to officiate within the diocese in which he lived could therefore not be granted. Often, however, differing points of view met obliquely rather than head on. Many who had been accustomed to regard themselves as progressives were as baffled as acknowledged conservatives by the new vocabulary. Two sets of presuppositions were in conflict, with the result that each side constantly complained of being misunderstood.

Older and newer styles of churchmanship were basically the products of incompatible attitudes to time. Orthodox Christianity defined itself chiefly in relation to the past. Its adherents based their faith on a revelation that had been given and recorded at particular points in time, and they looked for its preservation to confessions of faith, ordained ministries, and other forms of authoritative witness. The social gospel, on the other hand, had been oriented to the future and found its most natural expressions either in vague hopes for the conversion of society or in detailed blueprints for an ideal order. Rebels of the 1960s, in line with Northrop Frye's description of the contemporary vision of life as "a discontinuous sequence of immediate experience,"[28] sought meaning chiefly in the present. Truth is discerned, they claimed, not by viewing current events from the perspective of either history or eschatology but by becoming involved in specific encounters on such issues as the war in Vietnam or the grievances of Canadian Indians. Their complaint against orthodoxy was not so much that it was incredible in detail as that its concern for absolutes was really a device by which establishments sought to retain power. They were more sympathetic to the social gospel but did not share its fondness for planning, which they regarded as merely another means of control.

Two main streams of influence affected theology in the 1960s. One, which might be called existential, dominated the thought of many Protestants. It made much of Dietrich Bonhoeffer's vision of a "religionless" Christianity in which man, freed by the gospel from the tyranny of idols of his own fashioning, would devote himself without embarrassment to the attainment of his own creaturely and therefore secular ends. Bonhoeffer's vision, which in some aspects recalled Nietzsche's assertion that man "come of age" had outgrown his need of supernatural aid, gave rise in turn to Harvey Cox's celebration of the secular city on the one hand and to various "death of God" theologies on the other. Another line of thought, which affected the pronouncements of the Vatican Council and profoundly influenced most progressive Catholics, was impatient of all distinctions between the sacred and the profane. It leaned heavily on A. N. Whitehead's "process" philosophy, Paul Tillich's definition of God as "the ground of all being," and the evolutionary theology of Teilhard de Chardin. The former position virtually eliminated the concept of the sacred, the latter that of the secular, but John Robinson attempted to combine the two in his *Honest to God* and his avid readers apparently sensed no incongruity. Whatever their divergences, both approaches at least made possible a view of the world as open to human initiative and innovation rather than as programmed in advance to a precise goal.

Church authorities listened to the new voices and sought to respond to them. The Roman Catholic Church swept away regulations that had bound monks to irrelevant austerities, nuns to outmoded dress, and all the faithful to meatless Fridays. J. Raymond Hord, a United Church minister who had shown few signs of nonconformity as a pastor, delighted many young people as secretary of the board of evangelism and social service by promoting support for civil rights and opposing American intervention in Vietnam. The Anglicans called in an expert on social work to review their policy on Indian missions, which many critics had accused of paternalism.[29] Typical of new pastoral approaches was a Catholic program for young adults called "Youth Corps," which in contrast with the social and athletic orientation of the Catholic Youth League was dedicated to service and geared to the age of ecumenicity and electronics.[30]

Some changes had the appearance of having been made under pressure. Some gestures, such as the appointment of youth observers to committes or conferences, were often dismissed as "tokenism." Sometimes authorities over-reacted in a manner that suggested condescension or a fear of losing prospective members. Sometimes they seemed to step on the accelerator and the brake at once, as when Hord arranged for emergency aid to American draft-resisters in Canada and the executive of the general council promptly dissociated itself from his action.[31] It could certainly not be said, however, that the churches were ignoring calls for a new approach. Even the secular press was amazed by the unconventionality of Anglican and United submissions to Parliament that called for the recognition of "family breakdown" as a ground for divorce and for the broadening of grounds for legal abortion.

## VARIED RESPONSES TO CHANGE

It would be easy to give the impression that during the 1960s beleaguered ecclesiastical establishments were bombarded from all sides by insatiable demands for change, but the impression would be false. Responses to change among church members varied with age and temperament, with social and ethnic background, with denominational affiliation, and not least with closeness to centres of ecclesiastical power. Almost all segments of the church were affected by the ferment of the times, but in varying ways and to varying degrees. Change was greeted in some quarters with enthusiastic approval, in others with hostility and even shock, and in still others with scepticism or an almost complete lack of interest.

The initiative for the overhaul of church structures that began about 1960 came almost entirely from the more highly educated and more socially mobile segments of the middle class. The officials who planned the first phase of modernization had in mind chiefly the needs of young sophisticates who responded most readily to provocative and professionally packaged programs. Most of those who pressed for more radical changes were products of the same social milieu, which they reflected even in opposition. Much less enthusiasm for experiment was evident among farmers, blue-collar workers, and well established business men. The confusion and discontent of the church in the 1960s had their source, it would seem, in the suburban neighbourhoods on which its prosperity during the 1950s had been based.

In local congregations, where the church impinged most directly on the lives of its members, awareness of innovation varied greatly from denomination to denomination. Roman Catholics could not escape change. They participated each Sunday in a simplified and readily intelligible mass, absorbed the new ecumenical atmosphere, and gradually became accustomed to their new freedom to talk back. Most of them retained enough of their earlier habits of disciplined obedience to take seriously the advice of their leaders to think for themselves, although it was not yet clear how much of this discipline their thinking would leave intact. In Quebec, where the social structure had depended for stability on the absolutes of the Catholic faith, the novel spectacle of officially sponsored self-criticism induced what one pair of clerical dropouts described as a kind of *traumatisme national*.[32]

In most Protestant communions the effects of upheaval were somewhat less pervasive. Ministers wondered about their vocations, theological students participated in campus protests, and young people's groups showed a distinct preference for experimental programs. Older members of the laity were at least made aware of the unsettlement of the time as they listened to sermons, read their church papers, or picked up their children's Sunday school lessons. In some advanced congregations they made room for youth representatives on sessions or parish committees. Many of them were sympathetic to experiment, for they too were confused by the old language and bored by the old hymns. As yet, however, they had been spared the profound shocks to which Catholics had been subjected. Most of them were happy enough to turn over a service or two each year to young people with guitars so long as they could depend on the familiar pattern Sunday by Sunday.

Conservative evangelicals were in some ways affected least of all, less even than they had been by the affluence of the 1950s. Attacks on constituted authority and deviations from conventional morality were to them symptoms of a society in full flight from the obedience it owed to God, while the advent of new theologies and the inauguration of dialogue with Rome were further proofs of the long-suspected apostasy of the conventional Protestant churches. If the conservative denominations changed their posture at all, it was in the direction of seeking not merely to rescue individuals from the damning effects of worldliness but to provide an alternate set of values for the nation. They began to show interest for the first time in serious projects of general education, especially at the secondary and university levels. The Christian Reformed were most active in this respect, sponsoring not only specifically Christian schools and labour unions but an ambitious centre for intellectual synthesis at Toronto known as the Institute for Christian Studies. As an alternative to the official ecumenical movement a number of conservative groups organized the Evangelical Fellowship of Canada,[33] and within the older denominations conservative evangelicals became more vocal and more cohesive. What these movements offered was essentially a return to patterns of the eighteenth and nineteenth centuries that most Canadians had long since discarded, but to many in the 1960s it began to seem a credible option.

Colette Moreux, a French-Canadian sociologist, portrayed another response to change within the church in a study of the semi-urban parish of "St. Pierre" rather portentously entitled *Fin d'Une Religion?*[34] Religion as practised by the women of St. Pierre in the 1960s was conventional and other-directed, drained of fervour, and even of belief. Parishioners attended mass regularly, said their prayers, and crowded the schoolhouse when a priest lectured on marital relations, but avoided retreats and pilgrimages and took little part in official parish organizations. The interviewer drew only laughter when she asked whether religious observance was prompted by fear of the local priests, and a response only slightly more positive when she suggested either the fear or love of God as a motive. People went to church because it was the thing to do, without reluctance and without enthusiasm. Most of them were neither troubled nor excited by the movement of renewal inaugurated at the Second Vatican Council. So far as they were concerned, it was just one more program from headquarters. Similar blends of complacency and scepticism probably existed in many English-speaking communities both Protestant and Roman Catholic.

Whether the predominant response to the ferment of the 1960s would be radical renewal, conservative revolt, or stubborn conventionality remained uncertain in 1967. Some people complained that all familiar landmarks had been removed, others that nothing significant had yet changed. It is always thus in periods of transition. Among Canadian Christians generally, however, there was no sign of any widespread desire to turn the clock back. The leaven of change continued to work, while those who had been affected by it waited impatiently for the loaf to rise.

## THE DISESTABLISHMENT OF RELIGION

In English-speaking areas of Canada the unofficial establishment of Christianity had virtually come to an end by 1960, although it would take time for many people to adjust mentally to a situation in which churches were no longer moral policemen but pressure groups or even interest groups. Where further retreat was forced upon the church in these areas during the decade it was usually for financial rather than ideological reasons. Roman Catholics, who had moved seriously into the field of higher education outside Quebec only after the second world war, were the first to admit that the price tag was too high. Both money and disagreements over policy were factors in persuading Maritime Baptists to relinquish control of Acadia University in 1966. Surviving church colleges depended increasingly on government support, and the institution of the Ontario Tax Foundation Plan in 1964 brought long-delayed relief to the hard-pressed Catholic schools of Ontario. The contribution of the churches to social welfare, although still considerable, could no longer be compared in scale with that of governments or of specialized secular agencies.

In Quebec, where despite secularizing trends the Catholic Church had maintained unimpaired its position in society, the accession in 1960 of the Lesage administration inaugurated a new era in the relations of church and state. One of the first acts of the new government was to institute a study of education, which it entrusted to a commission chaired by A.-M. Parent, vice rector of Laval University. In 1963 and 1964 the commission submitted reports that proposed sweeping changes in educational procedure and in teacher training. Its most daring proposal was for the establishment of a ministry of education, which the church had always opposed as an invasion of its prerogatives. The hierarchy was able to bring about some modification in Bill 60, which incorporated many of the commission's suggestions, but an amended bill was passed unanimously by the legislature early in 1964. Another signal of change was the taxing of religious communities that engaged in business. Rural Quebec was not ready for secularization at such a pace, and the Union Nationale swept back to power in 1966. A process had begun, however, that would not readily be reversed. The influence of the church was a steadily diminishing factor in Quebec politics, and priests were rapidly being displaced from positions of power in normal schools, labour unions, and cooperatives.

That the end of the Duplessis regime should mean a change in the position of the church was not particularly surprising. The Liberals had always been somewhat suspect among the clergy, and the intellectuals who inspired many of the changes represented a spirit of lay independence that had been growing for some years. Much more surprising was the widespread support for innovation that appeared within the church itself. A domestic prelate gave his name to the controversial report on education. Cardinal Roy of Quebec expressed satisfaction with the legislation that followed and has been credited with a major role in shaping it.[35] Charles de Koningk, the most influential lay theologian of the province, actively campaigned for legislation that would permit civil marriage and nonconfessional French-language schools. By 1966 the Canadian hierarchy was prepared to admit, in flat contradiction of earlier ultramontane claims, that on such matters as birth control Christian legislators should make decisions in terms of their own understanding of the common good rather than of Catholic doctrine.[36]

Before 1960 religion had been regarded as one of the most divisive elements in Canadian life. In 1930 Dr. J. U. Tanner, the United Church missionary superintendent for Quebec, had written of relations between French and English:

> Prejudices and antipathies on both sides are giving way to better understanding and mutual respect. The religious barrier remains. It is the only barrier that stands in the way of intermarriage and the fusion of the two races of the Province into a united Christian citizenship.[37]

By the 1960s ethnic "prejudices and antipathies" were stronger than ever, and even French-Canadian Protestants were urging that French should be recognized as the official language of Quebec.[38] Religion, by contrast, had ceased to be a serious factor in national disunity. French-Canadian nationalism in Quebec, although supported by many Catholics, was no longer in any sense a religious crusade. The churches, if one may judge by the submissions of the three largest of them to the Laurendeau-Dunton commission, were solidly on the side of bilingualism and biculturalism.[39]

## LOSS AND GAIN

Churches that had looked forward during the 1950s to a period of quiet consolidation were shaken to their foundations during the "seething sixties." Questioning and criticism weakened the convictions of many Christians and led others to reject their faith altogether. Membership failed to keep pace with growth in population, attendance at church and Sunday school declined, and money was steadily more difficult to raise. Recruiting for church work fell off sharply, except among conservative evangelicals, while ministers, priests, and religious deserted their posts in alarming numbers. Those who remained in the church were constantly reminded of their failings by critics both within and without. The religious boom was definitely over.

To many Canadians, however, membership in the church brought a sense of exhilaration that had long been lacking. Young people, and many older people as well, found that in new forms of worship and more intimate types of personal encounter the gospel spoke to them in unexpected ways. The search for new styles of Christian living in a secular age, although sometimes bewildering, was an antidote to the dullness that had long infected much church life. In the Roman Catholic Church, where the frustrations were sometimes greatest, the excitement also reached its highest pitch. There seemed to be almost no ventures that could not be tried—despite Paul VI— and there were many that had not yet been tried. No one could fail to observe "a widespread desire among the laity to feel on their own faces the winds of new theological thought"[40] that were changing the church. Whatever their discouragements, Christians could not complain of a lack of interest in religion. University courses in religious studies multiplied, and students flocked to them. Plays on religious themes abounded, as often in secular theatres as in church chancels. The hippies who congregated along Yorkville Avenue in Toronto and Fourth Avenue in Vancouver were obsessed with religion. The gods invoked by the new religious enthusiasts were not always the Christian God of Canadian tradition, but at least some of the relevant questions were being asked.

The position of the church in Canadian society had unquestionably changed and in some ways diminished. The church was no longer the keeper of the nation's conscience, and few Canadians seemed to regret its dethrone-ment. On the other hand, it had become one of the places where the action was—especially if you were a Roman Catholic. There was gain as well as loss in the exchange. The church's former role as mentor and guide to the nation had inspired it to raise up statesmen and prophets, but it had also laden it with a heavy weight of institutional responsibility. Having shed most of its political power it could, if it would, concentrate on its primary task of offering good news to people.

## NOTES TO CHAPTER NINE

1. J. S. Thomson, "The State of the Church Now—a Moderatorial Report," *The United Church Observer*, October 15, 1958.

2. Proceedings of the 19th General Council of The United Church of Canada, 1960, p. 283.

3. E. L. Homewood, "The Padre of the Pubs," *The United Church Observer*, February 1, 1961.

4. See Report of Proceedings, Anglican Congress, 1963, Toronto, Canada, August 13-23, 1963 (Toronto: Anglican Book Centre, 1963).

5. Journal of Proceedings of the 22nd Session of the General Synod of The Anglican Church of Canada, 1965, pp. 114-117. In accordance with regular procedure, the change took effect only after confirmation at the 23rd Session in 1967. Journal, 1967, pp. 25-28.

6. Prospectus of the New Curriculum of The United Church of Canada (Toronto: Board of Christian Education and Board of Publication, 1961), pp. 17-28.

7. D. M. Mathers, *The Word and the Way* (Toronto: United Church Publishing House, 1962).

8. The results were published in W. S. F. Pickering and J. L. Blanchard, *Taken for Granted: A Survey of the Parish Clergy of the Anglican Church of Canada* (Toronto: The General Synod, 1967).

9. An Anglican minister, quoted in *ibid.*, p. 102.

10. See Elliott B. Allen, csb, "The Roman Catholic Seminary: Changing Perspectives in Theological Education," *Canadian Journal of Theology*, Vol. XIV, No. 3 (July 1968), pp. 159-168.

11. Gilles Langevin, sj, "L'Evolution récente et l'état actuel de l'enseignement de la théologie au Canada français: Dossier," *Canadian Journal of Theology*, Vol. XIV, No. 3 (July 1968), pp. 169-179.

12. For addresses and summaries of the discussions, see L. K. Shook, csb, ed., *Renewal of Religious Thought*, Proceedings of the Congress on the Theology of the Renewal of the Church, Centenary of Canada, 1867-1967, 2 vols. (Montreal: Palm, 1968).

13. Declaration of Religious Freedom, 6, in Walter M. Abbott, sj, ed., *The Documents of Vatican II* (New York: Angelus Books, 1966), p. 685.

14. Decree on Ecumenism, 19, in *ibid.*, p. 361.

15. Edward L. Bader, "New Approaches to Interfaith Marriage: A Report," *The Ecumenist*, Vol. 6, No. 5 (July-August 1968), pp. 172-174.

16. George Johnston, "The Future of Ecumenism in Canada," in Philip LeBlanc and Arnold Edinborough, eds., *One Church, Two Nations?* (Toronto: Longmans, 1968).

17. From a sermon preached at the opening service of the synod at Kingston on August 22, 1962. Included in Stephen F. Bayne, jr., *An Anglican Turning Point* (Austin, Texas: The Church Historical Society, 1964), pp. 271-272.

18. *A Suggested Plan for the Reunion of the United Church of Canada and the Anglican Church of Canada as submitted to the two Communions by a joint committee appointed by the London Conference of the United Church and the Anglican Diocese of Huron.* No publishing details are given.

19. *Principles of Union Between The Anglican Church of Canada and The United Church of Canada: The Report of the Committee on Christian Unity and the Church Universal of The Anglican Church of Canada and the Committee on Unity of The United Church of Canada* (Toronto, 1965).

20. *Ibid.*, III, 1(a), p. 12.

21. Journal of Proceedings of the 22nd Session of the General Synod of The Anglican Church of Canada, 1965, p. 23.

22. Record of Proceedings of the 22nd General Council of The United Church of Canada, 1966, pp. 52, 54.

23. Pierre Berton, *The Comfortable Pew* (Toronto: McClelland and Stewart, 1965).

24. *Why the Sea Is Boiling Hot: A Symposium on The Church and The World* (Toronto: Board of Evangelism and Social Service of The United Church of Canada, 1965).

25. Paul T. Harris, ed., *Brief to the Bishops: Canadian Catholic Laymen Speak Their Minds* (Toronto: Longmans, 1965). See also Paul T. Harris, "The 'Aggiornamento' (Up-

dating) and the Catholic Church in Canada," in *Canada and Its Future*, 42nd Annual Report of the Board of Evangelism and Social Service of The United Church of Canada, p. 26.

26. *Les Insolences de Frère Untel* (Montréal: Les Editions de l'Homme, 1960); translated into English as *The Impertinences of Brother Anonymous* (Montreal: Harvest House, 1962).

27. Jean LeMoyne, *Convergences* (Montreal: HMH Ltee, 1961); translated into English by Philip Stratford as *Convergence: Essays from Quebec* (Toronto: Ryerson, 1966).

28. Northrop Frye, "The University and Personal Life," *University of Toronto Graduate*, Vol. II, No. 3 (June 1969), p. 43.

29. The results of this study are incorporated in Charles Hendry, *Beyond Traplines* (Toronto: Ryerson, 1969).

30. See *Resource Book* of Youth Corps (Ottawa: The Catholic Centre, 1968), Series 1.

31. The United Church of Canada Year Book, 1968, Vol. II, p. 5.

32. Charles Lambert and Roméo Bouchard, *Deux Prêtres en Colère* (Montréal: Editions du Jour, 1968), p. 8.

33. Opposition to the ecumenical movement was officially affirmed by the Pentecostal Assemblies of Canada in 1964, the Fellowship Baptists in 1965, and the Christian Reformed Church in 1967.

34. Colette Moreux, *Fin d'une Religion? Monographie d'une paroisse canadienne-française* (Montréal: Les Presses de l'Université de Montréal, 1969).

35. L. Dion, as quoted in *Le Devoir*, January 18, 1966.

36. Brief to the House of Commons Standing Committee on Health and Welfare, October 11, 1966.

37. The United Church of Canada Year Book, 1930, p. 177.

38. *Breaking the Barriers*, Report of the Board of Evangelism and Social Service of The United Church of Canada, 1964, p. 216.

39. For the Roman Catholic position, see Jean Hulliger, *L'Enseignement Social des Evêques Canadiens de 1891 à 1950*, p. 165. The Anglican brief is printed in full in the *Bulletin* of the Council for Social Service of the Anglican Church of Canada, No. 191 (June 1965). An MS. of the United Church brief, submitted over the signature of Eugene A. Forsey, is at United Church House.

40. Janet Somerville, "Women and Christian Responsibility," in Harris, ed., *op. cit.*, p. 147.

# TEN

# The Church in Canada, 1867-1967

By 1867 Canadians were already familiar with the principal components that would give their church history its distinctive colour and texture; familiar although varied heirlooms of religious practice that could practically be classed as settlers' effects, successive waves of revival that overflowed a religiously undefended frontier, romantic movements reasserting the primacy of Christ over Caesar that were transplanted to the new world by the zeal of their adherents, and the need of adapting all of these influences to the conditions of a country that was not quite like any other. As they interacted with each other these movements expressed themselves in two complementary thrusts—one of recall to a past that was in danger of being left behind, the other of adventure into a future that was yet to be shaped. The history of the church over the next century would consist in large measure of their logical working out under changing circumstances.

## TENSION BETWEEN PAST AND FUTURE

This tension between past and future has been by no means peculiar to the Canadian churches. It reflects a tendency, evident in every culture, for some to be more hospitable to change than others. It has always been characteristic of Christians, who sustain themselves at once on the memory of their Lord's incarnation and on the anticipation of his final triumph. It has usually been most acute in immigrant societies, where choices constantly have to be made between the preservation of ancestral patterns and the formulation of new ones. In the United States, which has been in many ways the typical immigrant society of modern times, it has been a major theme both in literature and in popular mythology. Henry James believed that only by drawing upon the European past could a transplanted culture avoid rawness and sterility, Henry Ford dismissed history as "bunk," and Americans have never quite made up their minds between the two.

In Canada the circumstances of national existence have caused the contrasting pulls of past and future to be felt with unusual intensity. On the one hand, the people of a loyalist, counterrevolutionary nation have naturally demonstrated an attachment to tradition that would seem to most Americans undesirable and to most Europeans unnecessary. On the other hand, the formation of social values has required an unusual amount of conscious effort in a country where these were provided neither by an inherited pattern of establishment, as in Europe, nor by a powerful secular vision of national destiny, as in the United States.[1] Circumstances also allowed both sets of attitudes an exceptionally long and uninterrupted run in Canada. The impact of revolutionary attacks that discredited tradition in Europe was considerably delayed by the Atlantic barrier, while Canada retained the stimulus of a western frontier for some decades after the United States had been effectively settled. From one point of view, the contrary pulls of memory and anticipation have been part of a perpetual Canadian tug of war between overseas and North American influences. Tradition has almost always had Europe as its point of reference, while innovators even when most self-consciously Canadian have usually looked to the United States for their models.

The persistence of traditional patterns in Canada has been made visible in church buildings whose design often recalled the countryside of England or the Ukraine but seldom recorded an impulse born on Canadian soil. It has expressed itself in public rituals that have almost invariably echoed the language of the Book of Common Prayer, in vestiges of a connection between church and state that has never been renounced with thoroughgoing conviction, and in a retentiveness of ancestral affiliations that has made a change of religious denomination seem to many Canadians a more serious step than a change of citizenship. The traditional element has held its place mainly by inheritance from generation to generation in a land that has known no sudden breaks with the past, but it has been renewed from time to time by borrowings from older lands and constantly strengthened by a simple determination that it should not be lost. Its adherents have ranged from well established élites who have thought of themselves as its natural custodians to insecure immigrant groups who have found in it their readiest defence against absorption. Although the preservation of the European religious heritage has often seemed incidental to the perpetuation of ethnic and class identities, its implications for Canadian church life have far transcended the frequently mixed motives that have secured it. Canadians became inescapably aware, as many Americans did not, of being immersed in a continuing stream of Christian history within which the Atlantic crossing constituted a minor incident rather than a revolutionary break.

A strong urge to adapt ecclesiastical practice and to extend the influence of the church into new areas has been an equally significant factor in shaping the mentality of Canadian Christians. It has been conspicuously present in numerous missionary projects at home and abroad, in busy programs of education, group fellowship and social action, in ambitious campaigns against real and alleged evils, and in a remarkable sense of identification with national aspirations whether Canadian or French-Canadian. This activist temper was nourished by early missionaries and revivalists, stimulated by the challenge of a religiously divided society to voluntary effort, maintained by the intensely expansionist spirit of nineteenth-century Christianity, and constantly reinforced by the spread of American movements across the border. Although the programs to which it has given rise have been bewildering in their variety, their ultimate purpose has been to stake a total claim for Christ on the future. Their existence has constantly reminded Canadians that the continuity of the church has not only a past but a future dimension.

Once one has called attention to the polarization of Canadian church life between the traditional and the contemporary, the urge to classify denominations as belonging to one or the other becomes almost irresistible. The Churches of England and Scotland, and above all the Church of Rome, suggest themselves as consistent upholders of continuity. The free churches, notably the Methodists, the Canada Presbyterians, and later The United Church of Canada, come to mind as aggregations of forward-looking activists. This categorization is valid up to a point, but it fails to describe adequately a tension that has constantly operated within as well as among denominations. The Anglican bishop John Strachan, despite his last-ditch stand on behalf of a doomed establishment, had a remarkable capacity for putting a lost past out of his mind and building for an uncertain future. The Methodist John Carroll, on the other hand, spent his later days collecting anecdotes of circuit-riding days in order to give his denomination a history and even a mythology.[2] The contrasting pulls of past and future have been felt, indeed, not only by every denomination but by almost every church member. Each seems to correspond to a facet of the Canadian character.

The quiet preservers of ancestral patterns tend to be overshadowed in the historical record by the busy promoters of campaigns and causes. In part this has come about because historians are better equipped to deal with change than with its absence, and because innovations and controversies are more newsworthy than the inner life of prayer, the routines of pastoral work, or the attempts of Christians to live out their faith day by day. Yet there can be no doubt that in some respects the more contemporary-minded denominations have shown greater vigour than the more traditional ones. They have raised more money, involved more people in a greater variety of projects, and sent more workers into various fields of endeavour. Spokesmen for the more activist communions have habitually claimed a lien on the future, while the clergy of once-established churches have complained ever since pioneer times that more aggressive competitors were making inroads into their flocks.

Although the traditional element in Christianity has always seemed to be giving way before the contemporary, there is little reason to think that over the years the balance between the two has shifted very much. The Anglican Church, which has been as conscious of continuity as any communion, has maintained from census to census its ratio of adherents in relation to other major Protestant denominations and sometimes improved it. Over the decades, too, its role as a custodian of ethnic and ecclesiastical memory has been taken up by Lutherans and Orthodox, as well as by such conservative Protestant groups as Mennonites and Hutterites. The church life of Canada, like the nation itself, has always seemed to remain poised on the brink of complete Americanization without actually going over it. In part the balance has been maintained by successive waves of European immigration. Mainly, one suspects, it persists because Canadians have never been willing to make a final choice between the old world and the new.

Tension between the past and the future, which among English-speaking Canadians expressed itself at least to some extent in denominational rivalries, worked itself out in French Canada within a single communion that was closely knit by ethnic loyalties and even family ties. It accordingly generated more bitterness than elsewhere and more urgently demanded resolution. It came to the surface most conspicuously in nineteenth-century conflicts between ultamontanes and liberals, although in terms for which English Canada provides no precise parallels. In some respects, the ultramontanes strikingly resembled those elements of Protestantism that particularly emphasized the contemporary thrust of Christianity. Like the Protestant evangelicals of their day they were aggressive, missionary-minded, and devoted to programs of action. Since the aim of their *programme* was to maintain the integrity of tradition, however, they encouraged French Canadians to look to the past for solutions to their problems and sought to protect them from the infiltration of new ideas.

The triumph of ultramontanism, which thus combined respect for tradition with an activist and missionary temper, relieved for a time the tension of past and future that had troubled Quebec throughout most of the nineteenth century. By the early years of this century the church in Quebec seemed to have achieved unanimity on a wide range of issues. The same priests who extolled the rustic virtues of earlier days busied themselves with the promotion of agricultural societies, cooperatives, and labour unions. Nowhere else in Canada were the clergy so dedicated to ancestral values, and nowhere else did they devote so much effort to the social and economic betterment of their people. This combination of traditional loyalties with aggressive programs of improvement could not—or at any rate did not—last indefinitely. Ultimately the forces of modernization would break loose again from what they had come to regard as an unnatural alliance. It was not by accident, however, that ultramontanism provided the matrix from which such forces would emerge.

Having rejected revolution, Canadians discovered that the past had nevertheless an inexorable tendency to recede into memory. Having committed themselves to nationhood, they found that their new identity was extremely fragile even in the most favourable times. Thus, driven by necessity to devote an unusual amount of conscious thought both to the preservation of the past and to the shaping of the future, they have shown the effects of this double obsession in their churches as in other aspects of their national life. The activist and missionary strain, both evangelical and ultramontane, was chiefly instrumental in determining their norms of moral behaviour and their understanding of the role of the church in society. Fidelity to the past, both ethnic and theological, was evident in their diverse forms of worship and styles of spiritual formation.

## THE MOTIF OF CHURCH UNION

In sharp contrast to the polarization between the traditional and the contemporary that has shaped so much of Canadian church history has been a persistent trend towards the union of churches. During the nineteenth and twentieth centuries the desire for Christian unity has been a worldwide phenomenon, and especially in English-speaking countries few denominations have not at one time or another discussed plans of formal union. Subgroups have merged into strong denominations, and such consolidations have regularly been followed by proposals for broader union. In almost every case, however, unions between comparable groups have been achieved in Canada earlier than in any other Western nation, and the union that brought The United Church of Canada into being almost fifty years ago has not yet been duplicated in Britain, the United States or any other British dominion. This apparently inexorable trend has clearly been a major motif of Canadian church history, although its effects thus far have largely been limited to the middle range of the ecclesiastical spectrum.

The peculiar fascination of church union for Canadians reflected the unusual circumstances of the country in which they lived. The churches of Canada had to contend with almost unparalleled difficulties of communication. They had to span immense distances, maintain their cohesion across formidable internal barriers of geography and language, weld together provincial units that had grown up in isolation, and in many areas minister to populations that would always remain too scattered to pay their own way. As if these obstacles were not enough, the nation that looked to the churches for moral and spiritual guidance suffered from a permanent crisis of identity as it responded to the conflicting metropolitan attractions of Britain and the United States. There was also a desire, seldom mentioned in official documents but always tacitly recognized, for a solid Protestantism to balance the weight of a monolithic Roman Catholic Church. Such considerations did not give rise to proposals for union, but they provided an undergirding of practical utility that ensured them a serious hearing. There existed in Canada, at least from the time of confederation, a vacuum that only a united church could fill. Canadian realities also determined some of the specifications that such a church would have to meet. It would have to be large and comprehensive enough to cope with the size and diversity of the country. It would have to involve itself deeply in national life in order to help in the shaping of a Canadian identity. It would have to combine the traditional and the contemporary if it were to match the universality of its opposite number in Quebec.

The idea of a national church appealed to both traditional and crusading elements within the Canadian churches, especially since both were prepared to accept a large measure of responsibility for the well-being of society. The two elements differed considerably in motivation, however, and their vision of union differed accordingly. Traditionalists thought mainly of what a united church would stand for. It would serve as a reminder of the continuity of Christian history, declaring the allegiance of the citizens of a new land to the faith of their fathers and maintaining unimpaired a pattern that had already existed over many centuries. Activists were more interested in what a united church would be able to do. They looked to it for a combination of resources that would make possible a more thorough occupation of the land and a deeper penetration by Christian leaders than any single denomination could achieve. In general the former was the vision of Anglicans, the latter of free churchmen, but the distinction was never clear-cut. George M. Grant, a Presbyterian although significantly of Kirk background, dreamed of a united church that would be the result of God's gift of "all the good and beauty that he has ever evolved in history."[3] Herbert Symonds, an Anglican, insisted that "for the realization of the ideal of Christ, 'the Kingdom of Heaven', there must be a visible unity of the Church."[4]

The activist element predominated in the union that took place in 1925, as it had to a considerable extent in earlier ones. Union was urged more often as a step towards the effective christianization of the nation than as a testimony to the primacy of the Christian tradition in Canadian life. This bias was probably inevitable. Among the four denominations that seriously considered union, the three that ultimately consummated it were deeply committed to prohibition and other restrictive measures with which most Anglicans had little sympathy. The same three denominations faced a crisis in church extension in the west which Canadian Anglicans were largely spared through dependence on British aid. It was natural that communions with common problems and common goals should proceed with a type of union that was congenial to them, leaving the reconciliation of divergent traditions to a time of greater leisure. Their preoccupation with the future may well have been a major factor in the refusal to enter the United Church of many Presbyterians who were out of sympathy with parts of their program or feared the loss of theological, social, or ethnic elements in their inheritance. They never entirely forgot, however, that the concept of church union had a traditional as well as a contemporary dimension. Anglican initiatives towards union in 1886 and 1921, and again in 1943, served as reminders of this aspect of the movement. It was significant, too, that on June 10, 1925, when representatives of the uniting churches joined in the official act of unification, they did so by solemnly offering to the new body the various traditions they represented.[5]

## THE PRESUPPOSITION OF CHRISTENDOM

That it was possible even to discuss the comprehension of traditional and reforming elements into a single church indicates that, at least within a wide range of the denominational spectrum, the contrast between them was less stark than a superficial view might suggest. What they most notably had in common, beyond the Christian faith itself, was a conviction that in the main the institutions and values of Western society rested on a Christian foundation. They believed in the existence of an entity that over the centuries had come to be known as "Christendom" and assumed that Canada was destined to become a part of it.

In Europe the belief that church and society (or church and nation) constitute two sides of one coin had normally led to the official establishment of a particular form of Christianity by the state. Colonial legislators had determined by the time of confederation that no church or churches should receive such official recognition in Canada. The purpose of this arrangement, however, was not to deny the nation's allegiance to the Christian God but merely to allow equal opportunities to all denominations. The status of Canada as a Christian nation was never in question, and in practice the churches were regarded more as public than as private institutions. This belief in the existence of Christendom and in Canada's place within it was a common presupposition that made possible mutual understanding and occasionally even collaboration among Christians of various denominations.

Both traditionalists and activists owed their particular emphases to impulses that had been generated within Christendom. The former represented the recoil of Christendom against forces that sought to destroy its classic shape, the latter its expansive energy which in the nineteenth century was in process of transforming the world. Neither pattern was to any significant degree a spontaneous response to the Canadian environment, and even those who were most active in introducing changes into church life viewed the future less as a realm of unrevealed possibility than as a plastic mass to be shaped in terms of a prearranged program. Thus the conflict between past and future, while always a major factor in Canadian church history, was never total. Both parties were committed to the basic values of Christendom, and in this perspective their disagreements were over comparatively marginal issues.

A corollary to this constant reference to an existing Christendom was the virtual lack of any suggestion that the task of the churches in Canada might be to institute a new Christian society that would be an alternative to older ones and perhaps even render them obsolete. The recurrent theme of a new Christendom led in the United States to almost endless experimentation. In Canada, by comparison, church life was strikingly devoid of the bizarre or even the novel. Canadian ecclesiastical struggles were usually local reflections of controversies originating elsewhere. Suspected heretics were popularizers of European critical ideas rather than innovators in their own right. Even church union, which Canadians could claim with the greatest plausibility as their own specialty, was typically conceived not as the construction of a new ecclesiastical model but as a projection of existing ones. This deference to precedent, notable even among some radical exponents of the social gospel,[6] may account for what William Kilbourn has called the lack of a "messiah complex" he saw at the heart of American history.[7] The church history of Canada was always intended to be a part of a larger whole, and any attempt to portray it as a new beginning is defeated from the start.

Advocates of stability and of change had in common a desire to incorporate Canada more fully into the existing framework of Christendom. Whether they emphasized continuity with the past or impact upon the future, the churches that most readily prospered in Canada were those that identified themselves closely with community activities and national aspirations. They did so, as S. D. Clark constantly reminds us, at the cost of losing to sectarian movements many of those who sought to make their way from the fringes of society towards its centre.[8] As he readily concedes, however, these movements never succeeded in putting their stamp on the national character to the same extent as their American counterparts.[9] The country did not prove very hospitable, as a Baptist ruefully noted, to denominations that conceived of the church as a "gathered community" or drew a sharp line between the concerns of church and state.[10] Canada required the active participation of its churches if it were to be viable as a nation, and equally the churches required a strong Canada if they were not to lose their most promising young people to the United States.

Canada had not always been a part of Christendom but represented a new province added to it or in process of being added to it. Since this extension of the frontiers of Christendom called for much heroic effort, often against overwhelming odds, Canadian church history has often taken the form of epic narrative. Traditionalists concentrated on the beginnings of Christian work, when the difficulties were more conspicuous than the opportunities. They found their inspiration in accounts of Jesuits who won martyrs' crowns in Huronia or of high-born Oblates who immured themselves in draughty northern cabins. Those whose vision was shaped by future possibilities inclined to a more optimistic view, finding typical protagonists in the go-getting Presbyterian superintendent James Robertson or in Bishop Bompas who chose the more remote portion whenever his diocese was divided. Dom Paul Benoit inscribed on the title page of his *Vie de Taché* the motto *gesta Dei per Francos*, "the mighty acts of God through the Franks," thus claiming for Roman Catholic efforts in Canada the same heroic stature as the medieval adventures of Charlemagne and the crusaders. Edmund H. Oliver made "the winning of the frontier" the theme of the first serious ecumenical study of the history of the church in Canada.[11] The winning, in every case, was on behalf of a Christendom already existing and already known.

The movements that gave shape to Canadian church history sprang from the womb of Christendom and assumed its continued vitality. Traditionalists wished to transfer the patterns of Christendom to the new world and to conserve its values against the disintegrating influences of the frontier. Reformers endeavoured to adapt these patterns and perfect these values. Romantic movements of the nineteenth century, represented notably by ultramontanes, Anglo-Catholics and Scottish evangelicals, called attention to forgotten or neglected element in the heritage of Christendom and found unusual opportunities to cultivate them among the relatively unformed communities of the new world. Churchmen of all parties assumed that it was their responsibility to impart a Christian content to Canadian nation-hood and to ensure that this content would be passed on both to future generations and to newcomers to the country. Movements towards church union can only be fully understood when set within the same frame of reference. On the one hand, union would demonstrate the Christian con-sensus on which the nation rested. On the other, it would be a significant step towards making the nation more perfectly Christian.

## THE PASSING OF CHRISTIAN CANADA

So long as Christendom existed, and so long as Canada was demonstrably part of it, Canadian church history flowed with a certain inevitability. Churchmen played their contrasting but complementary roles as conservers or reformers, and gradually came to see the unity of the church as "in-dispensable in order to enable it to provide society with a unified program and outlook for its integration."[12] But the assumption that Christian faith provides the recognized values of Western society had been increasingly questioned in Europe since the "enlightenment" of the eighteenth century, and indeed ever since the end of the Middle Ages. The decline of the concept was masked during the nineteenth century by the resurgence of faith that accompanied the romantic movement, a resurgence that largely coincided with the years in which Canada's major denominations came to self-awareness. It was brought into full view by the moral and physical trauma of the First World War, however, and the Russian Revolution became its most graphic symbol. After the Second World War and the Chinese Revolution no one believed in Christendom any longer, or at any rate no one outside North America.

Canadians were shielded from the full impact of the assault on Christendom by their lingering ruralism and isolationism, and they did not immediately recognize the signs that warned of its decline. Some symptoms could have been observed in the 1920s, but they were obscured by the vehemence of counterattack from the religious right. They persisted through the 1930s, only to be hidden from sight by the euphoria of the postwar return to the church. Throughout this period, however, industrialization and the provision of urban amenities were producing a new breed of Canadian whose outlook owed more to salesmanship and the mass media than to Bible-reading and the mass. Realization that Christendom was dead, even in Canada, dawned with surprising suddenness in the 1960s—at some time during 1965, for many people.

Official attempts to modernize the church and unofficial protests against ecclesiastical establishments did not come about merely because in a few readily identifiable areas the church had failed to keep up with changes in society. They reflected the disappearance of Christendom as a universally intelligible frame of reference. The old vocabulary became obsolete not because it contained an excessive number of archaisms but because for many Canadians the world in which it had been understood no longer existed. The same problem affected the church's forms of worship, organizational structures, and styles of presence in society. And since the entity that had been known as Christendom was substantially identical with Western civilization, the upheavals that affected the church were also taking place in every other segment of social and political life. The discontent of the 1960s, which expressed itself on the surface as rebellion against existing institutions, may have had as its more fundamental cause the need to fill a vacuum whose existence had suddenly become apparent.

The end of Christendom does not imply the end of Christianity or necessarily even any diminution of the influence of the church on its members or on society. The church grew and permeated Graeco-Roman society for centuries in the face of official hostility and mob hatred, and there are many who regard its adoption by the emperor Constantine as its greatest misfortune. A period of exile to the periphery of power might well release Christian energies that have been smothered for centuries. Obviously, however, the drastic change in the situation of the Canadian church that took place during the present century could not leave unaltered structures and patterns that had been evolved to meet the circumstances of an earlier era. In particular, it was bound to modify some of the aspects of church life that had seemed most typically Canadian.

Those who campaigned energetically to complete the christianization of Canada were the first to feel the effects of secularization, seeing their long-cherished goals begin to recede just when they seemed close to realization. The signs were already visible in the 1920s with the disarray of the liberal social gospel, the defeat of prohibition in one province after another, and the failure of the church union movement to retain its momentum after 1925. They became even plainer when the United Church, despite the vigorous leadership of its board of evangelism and social service, declined to become the crusading moral force in had been intended to be. Social criticism continued to be heard within the church, but it steadily derived less of its inspiration from the perfectionism of Wesley, the bourgeois humanitarianism of Chalmers, and the updated medievalism of Maurice, more from the class awareness of Marx and the neo-orthodox realism of Reinhold Niebuhr. United Church recognition of moderate drinking in 1960, however grudging, represented a significant step in the winding up of the old campaign to establish a certain kind of Christian Canada.

Retentiveness of tradition was not so quickly affected, partly because it depended less on the ability to achieve immediate goals and partly because immigration constantly reinforced the ethnic loyalties that helped to undergird it. Indeed, the debacle of the social gospel in the 1920s was followed by a resurgence of traditionalism within the more Protestant churches. This trend manifested itself most visibly in such superficial changes as the gowning of choirs and the remodelling of sanctuaries to include divided chancels, but it indicated a desire to recover from the past a sense of direction that the future no longer seemed to give. Respect for tradition was to have its knocks in turn after the second world war. Having triumphantly survived earlier pressures towards assimilation, it was unable to escape the effects of urbanization and of the increasing mobility of Canadians. The picturesque and nostalgic aspects of religion lost much of their attraction as consumers became accustomed to planned obsolescence, and demands for relevance to the contemporary scene became steadily more insistent.

In Quebec, where the maintenance of the pattern of Christendom had been not merely implicitly assumed by all segments of society but actively fostered by a network of active organizations, the process of disintegration was delayed even more than in the rest of Canada. As late as 1960, despite the growth of a restive intelligentsia, church and society were blended more intimately than they had ever been in most other provinces. Even in Quebec, however, industrialization was preparing the way for change, and when French Canadians realized that their survival as a people no longer depended on the support of the church the old bonds snapped with a suddenness that startled the entire nation.

## OLD EMPHASES IN NEW FORMS

Like an earthquake that disarranges the topography of a region and blocks the outlets of its streams, the dramatic secularization of Canadian society interrupted the flow of Canadian church history and deflected some of its main thrusts from what had seemed to be their predetermined targets. One's first impression is inevitably that the forces that motivated the churches in the past have largely ceased to operate. The old-world traditions, the spiritual and moral causes, even the desire for a national church, seem to have little relevance for Canadians in the age of the computer and the space laboratory. After the earthquake, however, the streams make new channels for themselves. After the demise of Christendom, likewise, the primal tendencies that have shaped Canadian church life have begun to assert themselves in new guises.

The most obvious line of continuity links the old moral crusades with current movements of protest. Both have drawn on large reserves of moral indignation, whether against individuals or against entrenched systems from popery to the "military-industrial complex." Both have been sustained in hope by apocalyptic visions of a perfect future that has many features in common whether it is described as the coming of the kingdom of God or as the dawning of the age of Aquarius. Both have been able to keep themselves going only by maintaining a large head of emotional steam, and the techniques could as reasonably be called psychedelic in the one case as the other. There has even been a remarkable similarity in method between former raids on saloons and current demonstrations against the purveyors of napalm. Contemporary social protest is, however, recognizably a product of the post-Christendom era. It is conceived as a secular movement with secular aims, although theological students and nuns are prominent among its sponsors. Even in its in-church manifestations it seeks not the enforcement of a predetermined moral standard but the release of latent human powers. Christian faith serves it as an irritant to social action rather than as a source of social values.

The links between old and new crusades were even more direct in Quebec than in English Canada. There the first stirrings of rebellion against the alliance of the church with foreign capitalists were inspired by nationalist interpretations of the great social encyclicals. The blend of ultramontane moralism and economic nationalism that emerged from them lay behind every significant movement of reform during the 1930s and thereafter. The Liberal program of the 1960s was a secularized version of it, and its support by a large segment of the clergy can be explained by the fact that they had been its original instigators. In the meantime, however, what had been planned as the renovation of a Christian society became the transition to a secular one.

What place there would be for the traditions of the churches in a secular age had not become so clear by 1967. The whole career of Christendom was under a cloud, and references to the past were most often unfavourable. One had only to observe the labels on church buildings, however, to realize that theological and especially ethnic memories were far from dead. One possibility was that those concerned with preserving the values of the past would retreat into readily available ghettos and forfeit any possibility of affecting the course of the future. Already, however, one aspect of Canadian traditionalism had demonstrated its compatibility with significant change. Having always thought of their own history as continuous with that of the universal church, Canadians were sometimes more open to the influence of such international events as the Vatican Council and the Anglican Congress than were the more self-sufficient Americans. Traditionalism, if freed from lingering remnants of the colonial mentality, could help to protect the Canadian churches from a temptation to take refuge in the provincialism of "fortress America."

The movement towards church union, which after 1925 appeared to have been relegated to the category of a pious hope, seemed to gather momentum as the nation became more secular. Conversations between the Anglican and United churches began during the crisis of war and issued in a concrete proposal for organic union shortly after the postwar religious tide had begun to recede. On the surface the new project of union appeared to be merely a logical sequel to earlier ones. The church it proposed would be a splendid substitute for the establishment that Strachan had struggled to preserve, and equally a long step towards the completion of the work of the founders of the United Church. It would be national in a sense that neither existing communion could claim to be, able to deploy its resources effectively in every part of the country, and comprehensive both of British tradition and Canadian national feeling. Its pronouncements would presumably have behind them the support of a preponderance of English-speaking Canada. Surprisingly, however, relatively little was heard about such considerations, and nothing at all about a solid front against a monolithic Roman Catholicism that patently no longer existed. Much more emphasis was placed on "the belief that God has created One Church"[13] and on the frivolity of denominationalism in an increasingly unchurched nation. The chief impulse to union came, not as before from those who were deeply immersed in local problems but from those who were most aware of international developments.

Like earlier Canadian movements towards union, the current proposal was the local expression of a world-wide interest. Conversations elsewhere had gone through most of the same stages as in Canada. They began when Europe and America were still assumed to be Christian and unity was valued chiefly for its practical advantages on frontiers of the faith at home or abroad. With the collapse of Christian Europe after the First World War there was a natural desire to explore together the common sources of a shared faith. The motivation was undoubtedly partly defensive, but an important result was that Christians of various traditions came to know and understand each other better and to find bases for common action. After the second war, Christians gradually realized that they would have to take part with others in solving the problems of a plural world and that for this purpose they would need not only to recover the fulness of their common heritage but to discover appropriate styles of contemporary presence. This concern dominated the Second Vatican Council. One of its first expressions in a formal proposal for union was the Canadian anticipation of "a new, visible expression in structure, in worship, in life and witness, for that oneness of the Church which already exists."[14] By 1967 counterparts to the Anglican, United, and Christian churches in most other countries were engaged in similar negotiations, often on terms that bore a striking resemblance to the *Principles of Union*. Conversations in all parts of the world were based on a common recognition that existing denominations were products of Christendom, admissible luxuries perhaps in a society that took basic Christian assumptions for granted but serious impediments to effective witness in a world where Christianity had become one of many options.

It soon became clear that the promoters of union would have no easy task, for the familiar problem of reconciling the traditions and programs of three churches was complicated by that of reconciling traditionalists and experimentalists within all denominations. There were many Canadians whose confidence in Christendom had not yet been shaken by world events and who therefore saw no need for a radical rethinking of ecclesiastical positions. There were many others who would not easily be persuaded that the generation chiefly responsible for union discussions could be trusted to advance beyond earlier and more institutional concepts. The planners of union would have to learn to think no longer of a magisterial national church but of a unified Christian presence in a secular and pluralistic Canada.

A radically different reaction to the secular age was represented by the rapidly expanding group of conservative Protestant denominations. Most of these had originated as protests against the formality of the more traditional churches and against the political orientation of the social gospel.

On the other hand, they had important affinities with both. They were strongly traditional (they would have preferred to say "scriptural") in their condemnation of modernism and in their appeal to the nation to come "back to God." They resembled liberal Protestants in their background of evangelical revival, their emphasis on a common set of moral taboos, and their readiness to adopt new methods.

Sectarian movements have customarily arisen in opposition to the "worldliness" of churches that have accepted social obligations, seeing in these the source of compromises that inevitably dilute the purity of the church. With some justice, therefore, they have always been regarded as enemies of Christendom. Their origin and outlook in Canada have been similar. Drawing their adherents chiefly from those who had been excluded from participation in the existing order, they viewed with considerable scepticism the efforts of the churches to sanctify national life. As the secularization of society has proceeded, however, a strange reversal of roles has been taking place. Conservative evangelicals now seem to constitute the only important segment of the church that seriously believes in the continued existence of Christendom. Their allegiance, indeed, is not to the European version but to the rurally based Protestant piety of North American bible belts. They see this Protestant America as battered and beleaguered by materialism at home and Communism abroad. It remains for them the authentic America, not only a defensible bastion of the faith but a feasible base for the evangelization of the world. Because of their confidence they display remarkable *élan* and missionary zeal. They see no occasion for accommodation with the world, no advantage in church union, and only peril in associating with those who advocate either. It may be a significant sign of the times that in 1967, when the larger churches decided to emphasize contemporary problems in their special centennial events, it was a Pentecostal spokesman who recalled the famous story of Sir Leonard Tilley's choice of the word "dominion" as a recognition of God's claim upon Canada.[15] Perhaps the radical fringes of the major churches had become the most fertile breeding ground of genuine sectarianism with its hostility to earthly principalities and powers.

## CHANGES OVER A CENTURY

In 1967 the configuration of the church in Canada differed in a number of respects from what it had been a century earlier. Among the major communions a series of unions had brought about a remarkable measure of consolidation. Five groups of Presbyterians and six of Methodists had been reduced to two major denominations, and by 1967 the Lutherans were well on the way towards a similar achievement. The most remarkable of these unions was that which in 1925 brought together Methodists, Congregationalists, and most Presbyterians to form The United Church of Canada. In later years this church would absorb a number of congregations that in 1867 had called themselves simply "Christians" as well as a small group of United Brethren, and in 1967 what had been the Evangelical Association was about to enter it.

Despite this trend to consolidation the total number of separate church bodies had steadily increased over the century. The Quakers and Universalists had almost vanished, and any remaining Second Adventists had long since found homes in newer denominations of similar emphasis. On the other hand, many new groupings had made their appearance. Immigration had added Doukhobors, Hutterites, and Christian Reformed, along with Orthodox of various jurisdictions, and transformed Lutherans, Mennonites, and Mormons from communities of merely local significance into important churches. Two important groups, the Fellowship Baptists and the Ukrainian Orthodox, were products of dissatisfaction within existing denominations. Others appeared during the century as new foundations, although the Christian and Missionary Alliance was the only sizeable group that could claim a distinctively Canadian origin. Some, such as the Free Methodists, the Salvation Army, the Seventh-Day Adventists, and Christian Science, were by 1967 already long-familiar and past their peak of growth. The Pentecostalists and Jehovah's Witnesses were more recent and still expanding rapidly. The supporters of many other groups that were too small to be included in census tables constituted in sum a substantial body of people.

Confederation had inevitably initiated a process by which colonial segments of European communions evolved into national churches or at least set up organs for action on a national scale. Unions contributed considerably to this process. Other milestones were the formation of the general synod of the Church of England in Canada in 1893, the Baptist Federation of Canada in 1944, and the Canadian Catholic Conference in 1948. Long before 1967 most denominations had set up national headquarters, with staffs that tended to grow steadily. Despite one hundred years of nationhood, however, regionalism and local independence had held this trend towards centralization within fairly narrow bounds. The Baptist Federation never became as influential as regional conventions, residual power in the Anglican Church remained with the dioceses, and national councils in the Roman Catholic Church still exercised less authority than either the pope or the individual bishops. Moreover, denominations of more recent foundation tended to be rather loosely structured. The name of the Pentecostal Assemblies of Canada correctly suggested a federation of autonomous congregations, and the ethnic sections of the same denomination were able to exercise a fair measure of initiative. Even in denominations with active and well equipped headquarters the flavour of church life varied considerably from region to region, and in 1967 such differences were becoming more rather than less pronounced.

One of the most striking examples of the force of regionalism was the limited success of eastern-based national churches in retaining the confidence of western Canada. Their beginnings in this region had been auspicious. Energetic bishops and superintendents had taken advantage of opportunities offered by an influx of settlers from eastern Canada to erect church buildings, organize congregations, and introduce a variety of familiar programs. For a time it had seemed that, apart from Quebec, the Canadian ecclesiastical pattern might be almost homogeneous from sea to sea. Then, as settlers from continental Europe began to move into a land that was still almost empty, some of their denominations briefly rivalled the old Canadian churches in census returns. In 1881 there were almost as many Mennonites as Methodists in Manitoba, and in 1901 the Doukhobors tallied almost half as many adherents as the largest denomination in the district of Assiniboia. Churches already on the ground sought to provide spiritual homes to the newcomers, but in the end they had to share the ground with the newcomers' churches. By the 1920s they were having difficulty even in holding their own members as newer groups from the United States spread through the rural areas and into the cities. In 1967 a western town of ten thousand people might require as many as thirty congregations to satisfy its varied theological, emotional, and linguistic tastes. Even within the more conventional churches, it was often noted, members tended to be more volatile than in eastern Canada.

Despite these changes, Canadians as a whole had shown remarkable denominational stability during their first century of nationhood. There had been some unions and some disruptions. Even in eastern Canada there had been changes in relative strength, some large enough to be significant. Roman Catholics, who had been a third of the population of New Brunswick in 1871, constituted a majority in 1961. In Ontario they had advanced from 17 per cent to 30 per cent, while Methodists, Presbyterians, and Congregationalists had declined from a combined total of 51 per cent to 33 per cent for United Church and Presbyterian adherents. Such fluctuations were the results not of major religious upheavals or of widespread shifts of allegiance but of movements of population and differing rates of natural increase. For the most part they were more obvious to statistical analysts than to local observers. Six denominations with deep roots in Canadian history—Anglicans, Baptists, Catholics of various rites, Lutherans, Presbyterians, and United—accounted in 1961 for 91.4 per cent of the Canadian population, and for 85.6 per cent even in the four western provinces. The religious affiliations of Canadians had been fixed, by and large, several decades before confederation.

The place of the church as a whole in Canadian society had changed much more dramatically, especially during the second half-century of nationhood. Total rejection of the church was still rare, if one is to attach any significance to the fact that the number of those who professed no religion to census enumerators remained negligible. It was evident, however, that many people had quietly dismissed the church as a serious factor in their lives. Even more noticeable was the extent to which the nation had come to carry on its business as if the church were not there. Major newspapers no longer represented denominational interests, even informally. Voters had ceased to be influenced by ecclesiastical issues except as inherited party loyalties reflected forgotten church struggles of the past. The clergy had been replaced as all-round pundits and after-dinner speakers by university professors and public relations consultants, and as confessors by psychiatrists and social workers. The nation could no longer claim, like the editor of the *Christian Guardian* in 1868, to have "the best kept Sabbath in the world."[16]

In 1967 the church was still seeking to determine its appropriate response to the increasingly secular society in which it was set. Some of its members carried on as if there had been no change in circumstances, perhaps hoping that the twentieth century would go away. Some seemed prepared to jettison almost any element of Christian belief or practice that was likely to prove offensive to the secular mind. Most persevered with a mixture of bewilderment and hope, no longer presuming to offer cut-and-dried answers to the problems of society but welcoming signs of renewal that came as they sought to be faithful to the will of God as they understood it. One prediction that could be made with confidence was that, although apparently destined to be servants of the nation's conscience rather than its masters, churches that had always accepted responsibility for the shaping of the Canadian character would not relinquish it now.

## THE CHURCH IN CANADA, 1967

The place of the church in the Canada of 1967 was graphically symbolized by the manner of its presence at Canada's centennial fair. When Expo '67 was being planned, a group of French-speaking priests and ministers in Montreal determined that the church should be worthily and imaginatively represented.[17] The Christian Pavilion that resulted was an ecumenical venture, sponsored by Roman Catholic, Protestant, and Orthodox churches, and planned by members of several linguistic and cultural groups. In this respect it marked an advance over the slightly earlier New York fair, where Catholics had had a separate building. The contents of the pavilion marked an even greater departure from previous practice. There was no explicit preaching. Instead the visitor was catapulted into a series of audio-visual experiences that graphically reminded him of human suffering and human indifference, finally emerging into a meditation room where quiet music, pastoral murals, and Scripture texts suggested but never argued the possibility of redemption.

The general theme of the fair was "Man and His World," a tribute to human achievement that reflected the secular spirit of Canada and especially that of French Canada one hundred years after confederation. The planners of the Christian Pavilion accepted this environment, designing their building to harmonize with its general pattern and offering its contents as a corrective rather than as an alternative to the human vision of Expo. Many church members were puzzled and annoyed by the failure of the exhibits to make the Christian message more obvious and compelling. To citizens of the secular city, especially the young, the pavilion was a surprising and gratifying discovery. It was also significant, however, that in the end there were two Christian pavilions at Expo '67. Conservative evangelicals would have nothing to do with the ecumenical project but sponsored an exhibit of their own entitled "Sermons in Science." Here the message was clear, positive, and unambiguously religious.

Canadians of 1967, like visitors to Expo, were offered a choice of Christian responses to the growing secularization of society. One was experimental and ecumenical, the other traditional and exclusive. Did either point the way to the future of the church in Canada? It seemed unlikely that the golden age of belief recalled by "Sermons in Science" would return, although for many it would continue to be a source of reassurance and a standard of judgment. It seemed equally unlikely that the frank experimentalism of the Christian Pavilion would become the permanent posture of the church, for men and institutions can bear to live out of suitcases for a relatively short time. Some day the church might reach a new point of equilibrium, but exploration was its mood in 1967.

## NOTES TO CHAPTER TEN

1. Some implications of the lack of an implicit national consensus are discussed in Allan Smith, "Metaphor and Nationality," *Canadian Historical Review*, Vol. LI, No. 3 (September 1970), pp. 247-275.

2. John Carroll, *Case and His Cotemporaries, or The Canadian Itinerants' Memorial: Constituting a Biographical History of Methodism in Canada, from Its Introduction into the Province, till the Death of the Rev. Wm. Case in 1855*, 5 vols. (Toronto: Samuel Rose, 1867-77); also *Past and Present, or a description of persons and events connected with Canadian Methodism for the last forty years by a Spectator of the Scene* (Toronto: Alfred Dredge, 1860).

3. W. L. Grant and Frederick Hamilton, *Principal Grant*, p. 155.

4. Herbert Symonds, *Lectures on Christian Unity* (Toronto: William Briggs, 1899), p. 75.

5. Act of Inauguration of The United Church of Canada. A copy is in the Archives of Victoria University and The United Church of Canada.

6. See Salem G. Bland, *The New Christianity; or, The Religion of the Age* (Toronto:

McClelland, c. 1920). The author argued that the church of the future would be in some respects closer to Roman Catholicism than to Protestantism.

7. William Kilbourn, "Epilogue," in William Kilbourn, ed., *Religion in Canada* (Toronto: McClelland and Stewart, 1968), p. 123.

8. S. D. Clark, *The Developing Canadian Community* (Toronto: University of Toronto Press, 1962), p. 119.

9. *Ibid.*, p. 127.

10. Stuart Ivison, "Is There a Canadian Baptist Tradition?" in J. W. Grant, ed., The *Churches and the Canadian Experience*, p. 67.

11. E. H. Oliver, *The Winning of the Frontier* (Toronto: United Church Publishing House, 1930).

12. Jose Miguez Bonino, "Christian Unity in Search of Locality," *Journal of Ecumenical Studies*, Vol. 6, No. 2 (spring 1969), p. 189.

13. *Principles of Union*, III, 1(a), p. 12.

14. *Loc. cit.*

15. T. Johnstone, "Our Spiritual Heritage," in *Canada's Centennial*, p. 11.

16. *Christian Guardian*, January 1, 1868, p. 2.

17. Claude de Mestral, "When Should the Church Speak?" in Philip LeBlanc and Arnold Edinborough, *One Church, Two Nations?* p. 163.

# Bibliographical Note

The last hundred years of Canadian church life are only now beginning to be submitted to serious historical study. Churchmen seeking to stake claims on the past have been drawn to the era of beginnings, dismissing the later process of maturation as somehow less "historic." Secular historians have done justice to the influence of the church in colonial days, but most of them have included the church in a general neglect of social and cultural developments since confederation. Books and articles on various aspects of the life of the church abound, but most of them reflect official interests and many important subjects have not yet been investigated. The works mentioned here, although admittedly unequal in quality, are offered as among the best available in their respective fields. It is hoped that they will be of assistance to readers who wish to learn more about the church history of Canada than can be included in these volumes.

## GENERAL WORKS

The only comprehensive history of the church in Canada is still, fifteen years after its publication, H. H. Walsh, *The Christian Church in Canada* (Toronto: Ryerson, 1956). Douglas J. Wilson, *The Church Grows in Canada* (Toronto: Canadian Council of Churches, 1966), adequately serves its purpose as a study book for lay groups and contains more detailed information about smaller Protestant bodies than any other general work. E. H. Oliver, *The Winning of the Frontier* (Toronto: United Church Publishing House, 1930), is of interest today chiefly as the first serious attempt by a Canadian to submit the church history of the nation to historical analysis. In J. W. Grant, ed., *The Churches and the Canadian Experience* (Toronto: Ryerson, 1963), representatives of various denominations trace the interaction of their traditions with Canadian circumstances. Primary and secondary documents relating to Canadian church life are reproduced in J. S. Moir, ed., *The Cross in Canada* (Toronto: Ryerson, 1966). Briefer accounts include A. R. M. Lower,

"Religion and Religious Institutions," in George W. Brown, ed., *Canada* (Toronto: University of Toronto Press, 1950); John S. Moir, "Religion," in J. M. S. Careless and R. Craig Brown, eds., *The Canadians, 1867-1967* (Toronto: Macmillan and Maclean-Hunter, 1967); and H. H. Walsh, "Church History," in the *Encyclopedia Canadiana*. Articles on the church history of various regions in Adam Shortt and Arthur G. Doughty, eds., *Canada and Its Provinces* (Toronto: Glasgow, Brook and Co., 1914), are still worth consulting.

The church scarcely appears after confederation in most general histories of Canada by English-speaking writers, exceptions being A. R. M. Lower, *Colony to Nation: a History of Canada*, 4th rev. ed. (Don Mills: Longmans, 1969), and, to a lesser extent, Donald G. Creighton, *Dominion of the North*, rev. ed. (Toronto: Macmillan, 1957). Some material can be found in J. H. Stewart Reid, Kenneth McNaught, and Harry S. Crowe, *A Source Book of Canadian History* (Toronto: Longmans, Green, 1960). Neglect of the church by secular historians emphatically does not extend to French Canada. Robert Rumilly's massive *Histoire de la Province de Québec*, 37 vols. in 31 (Montreal: several publishers, 1940-1968), although virtually undocumented, contains a great deal of information on ecclesiastical matters. So does his *Histoire des Acadiens* (Montreal: the author, 1955). Much of this material is available in English in Mason Wade, *The French Canadians, 1760-1967*, rev. ed., Vol. II (Toronto: Macmillan, 1968).

## DENOMINATIONAL HISTORIES

The most ambitious denominational history is Philip Carrington, *The Anglican Church in Canada* (Toronto: Collins, 1963). Regional studies of Anglicanism in greater depth are T. C. B. Boon, *The Anglican Church from the Bay to the Rockies* (Toronto: Ryerson, 1962), and F. A. Peake, *The Anglican Church in British Columbia* (Vancouver: Mitchell, 1959). The history of the Presbyterian Church before union is well treated in J. T. McNeill, *The Presbyterian Church in Canada, 1875-1925* (Toronto: Presbyterian Church in Canada, 1925). A more recent survey of Presbyterianism, scholarly although brief, is N. G. Smith, A. L. Farris, and H. K. Markell, *A Short History of the Presbyterian Church in Canada* (Toronto: Presbyterian, 1965). Carl R. Cronmiller, *A History of the Lutheran Church in Canada* (Evangelical Lutheran Synod of Canada, 1961), is a careful narrative account.

Comprehensive histories of other major denominations, when they exist, are too old and usually too sketchy to provide anything like adequate coverage of the period. There has been no general history of Canadian Baptists since E. R. Fitch, *The Baptists of Canada: a History of Their Progress and Achievements* (Toronto: Standard, 1911). The Maritime section of the story has been treated adequately in George E. Levy, *The Baptists of the Maritime Provinces* (Saint John: Barnes and Hopkins, 1946). The Baptist Convention of

Ontario and Quebec marked its jubilee with a symposium, *Our Baptist Fellowship, 1889-1939* (Toronto: the Convention, 1939), but only a part of this slim volume is devoted to history. Baptist growth in western Canada is described in C. C. McLaurin, *Pioneering in Western Canada: a Story of the Baptists* (Calgary: the author, 1939). For the Fellowship of Evangelical Baptists the best source is C. A. Tipp, *Ten Years of Fellowship: a Historical Review and 1963 Year Book* (Toronto: Trans-Canada Fellowship of Evangelical Baptist Churches, 1963).

There is no good national history of Methodism in Canada. The least unsatisfactory may be Alexander Sutherland, *Methodism in Canada: Its Work and Its Story* (Toronto: Methodist Mission Rooms, 1904), which mingles sober narrative with descriptions of miracles of grace in a manner that itself tells something of the ethos of an older Methodism. A good regional study with national overtones is J. H. Riddell, *Methodism in the Middle West* (Toronto: Ryerson, 1946). No history of the United Church of Canada has yet been written. From time to time the church has commissioned interim reports of progress, the most recent being W. F. Munro, *These Forty Years* (Toronto: United Church Publishing House, 1965). Otherwise the most accessible account is by Arthur G. Reynolds in the 1967 volume of the *Encyclopaedia Britannica.*

The most serious gap of all is the lack of a comprehensive history of Roman Catholicism in Canada. For Ontario one can turn to W. P. Bull, *From Macdonnell to McGuigan* (Toronto: Perkins Bull Foundation, 1939), for the west and north to A. G. Morice, *History of the Catholic Church in Western Canada,* 2 vols. (Toronto: Musson, 1910). No formal history of the church in Quebec exists, although Rumilly's volumes help to make up for the omission.

Two smaller groups have been the subjects of excellent studies: Victor Peters, *All Things Common: the Hutterian Way of Life* (Minneapolis: University of Minnesota Press, 1965), and George Woodcock and Ivan Avakumovic, *The Doukhobors* (Toronto: Oxford University Press, 1968). Two brief but useful sources for Mennonite history are J. W. Fretz, *The Mennonites in Ontario* (Waterloo: Mennonite Historical Society of Ontario, 1967), and Frank H. Epp, *Mennonite Exodus* (Altona, Man.: D. W. Friesen for the Canadian Mennonite Relief and Immigration Council, 1962); the latter is particularly helpful in distinguishing various strands of Mennonite immigration. Accounts of other small denominations vary enormously in quality and scale. The following are the best and sometimes the only ones available: A. G. Dorland. *The Quakers in Canada: A History,* 2nd ed. (Toronto: Ryerson, 1968); Reuben Butchart, *The Disciples of Christ in Canada since 1830* (Toronto: All Canada Committee, 1939); on Pentecostalism, Gloria Culbeck, *What God Hath Wrought* (Toronto: Pentecostal Assemblies of Canada, 1958); and on the Salvation Army, Arnold Brown, *What God Hath Wrought,*

2 vols. (Toronto: Salvation Army, 1952). The *Encyclopedia Canadiana* contains useful articles on practically all denominations of any size.

## MISSIONARY LITERATURE

Missionary projects at home and abroad have inspired a voluminous literature, most of it the work of participants and promoters rather than of professional historians. In a class by itself among general surveys is Lionel Groulx, *Le Canada Français Missionnaire* (Montreal and Paris: Fides, 1962). Anglican missions are the theme of W. E. Taylor, *Our Church at Work: Canada and Overseas*, 2nd ed. (Toronto: MSCC, n.d.), which is useful although distinctly out of date. The best single source for the home missions of the United Church and its antecedents is E. H. Oliver, *His Dominion of Canada* (Toronto: Women's Missionary Society of the United Church of Canada, 1932). On the Methodist side this may be supplemented by Annie D. Stephenson, *One Hundred Years of Canadian Methodist Missions, 1824-1924*, Vol. I only (Toronto: Missionary Society of the Methodist Church, 1925), on the Presbyterian by a perusal of James Robertson's reports in Appendix 1 to the Acts and Proceedings of each general assembly. Regional studies of the church in western Canada by Morice, Riddell, Boon, and Peake, to which reference has already been made, are also rich in missionary material. For overseas work it is usually necessary to have recourse to accounts of particular fields. These are far too numerous to mention individually, although some of them are very good.

Work among Indians and Eskimos has given rise to an extensive literature of its own. Almost the whole of Morice's *History of the Catholic Church in Western Canada* is devoted to Indian work, and the same is true of much of Mrs. Stephenson's *One Hundred Years of Methodist Missions*. Much useful information on early Anglican missions is contained in S. Gould, *Inasmuch: Sketches of the Beginnings of the Church of England in Canada in Relation to the Indian and Eskimo Races* (Toronto: MSCC, 1917). Otherwise one must look to biographies of outstanding individual missionaries, of which only a small selection can be mentioned: on Bishop Bompas, H. A. Cody, *An Apostle of the North* (New York: Dutton, 1908); on Lacombe, Katherine Hughes, *Father Lacombe, the Black-Robe Voyageur* (Toronto: Briggs, 1911); on George McDougall, J. E. Nix, *Mission among the Buffalo* (Turonto: Ryerson, 1960); on Isaac Stringer, F. A. Peake, *The Bishop Who Ate His Boots* (Toronto: Anglican Church of Canada, 1966). A fascinating although sometimes tantalizingly incomplete account of missionary work among the Eskimos is Bishop A. L. Fleming's autobiography, *Archibald the Arctic* (Toronto: Saunders, 1965). The current trend is towards a more critical appraisal of the church's approach to the native peoples, but this approach has not as yet inspired any serious historical studies.

## THE CHURCH IN CANADIAN LIFE

Interest in the social and economic concerns of the churches is increasing. Invaluable for the development of official Roman Catholic policy is Jean Hulliger, *L'Enseignement Social des Evêques Canadiens de 1891 à 1950* (Montreal: Fides, 1958). How policies were applied in practice during a period of unusual economic growth is the theme of W. F. Ryan, sj, *The Clergy and Economic Growth in Quebec (1896-1914)* (Quebec: Laval University Press, 1966). The closest Protestant counterpart to Hulliger's book, also strongly slanted towards the recording of official policies, is Stewart Crysdale, *The Industrial Struggle and Protestant Ethics in Canada* (Toronto: Ryerson, 1961). Richard Allen, *The Social Passion: Religion and Social Reform in Canada 1914-28* (Toronto: University of Toronto Press, 1971), is an excellent and long-needed study of the later years of the social gospel. It is likely to remain for some time the standard work on the subject, although studies of individual denominations by younger scholars raise questions about some of its conclusions. One perceptive treatment (incidentally by an American) is W. H. Magney, "The Methodist Church and the National Gospel, 1884-1914," *Bulletin*, No. 20 (1968). Most others are still in the form of unpublished theses or essays. Insights into the institutional development of agencies for social action and into the minds of the men who guided them may be garnered from J. R. Mutchmor, *Mutchmor* (Toronto: Ryerson, 1965), and W. W. Judd, "The Vision and the Dream," *Journal of the Canadian Church History Society*, Vol. VII, No. 4 (December 1965), pp. 76-118.

Changing attitudes to immigrants may be traced through a series of books, largely by Protestant authors. The pioneer studies were those of J. S. Woodsworth, *Strangers Within Our Gates, or Coming Canadians* (Toronto: Missionary Society of the Methodist Church, 1909) and *My Neighbor: A Study of City Conditions, a Plea for Social Service* (same publisher, 1911). A trend towards greater acceptance of immigrant ways is evident in W. T. Gunn, *His Dominion* (Toronto: Canadian Council of the Missionary Education Movement, 1917), and W. G. Smith, *Building the Nation: the Church's Relation to the Immigrant* (same publisher, 1922). The earlier assimilationist policy is abandoned completely in I. F. Mackinnon, *Canada and the Minority Churches of Eastern Europe, 1946-50* (Halifax: The Book Room, 1959).

Two excellent studies of the place of religion in state-supported schools, based on traditional Protestant and Roman Catholic assumptions respectively, are C. B. Sissons, *Church and State in Canadian Education* (Toronto: Ryerson, 1959), and Franklin A. Walker, *Catholic Schools and Politics in Ontario* (Toronto: Nelson, 1964). For the rest of Canada the latter may be supplemented by D. O'Brien, "Education in Canada: the Varying Position of Catholic Schools," *Tablet*, No. 218 (June 1964), pp. 632-634. A much-needed account of the relation of the church to higher education has been provided by D. C.

Masters, *Protestant Church Colleges in Canada: a History* (Toronto: University of Toronto Press, 1966).

The *Theological Bulletin* of McMaster Divinity College devoted an entire issue (No. 3, January 1968) to the theme, "Christianity and the Development of Canadian Culture." A corresponding study in the French-Canadian setting is Marcel Rioux, ed., *L'Eglise et le Québec* (Montreal: Les Editions du Jour, 1961). References to the church are also frequent in Julian Park, ed., *The Culture of Contemporary Canada* (Toronto: Ryerson, 1957), in Marcel Rioux and Yves Martin, eds., *French-Canadian Society*, Vol. I (Toronto: McClelland and Stewart, Carleton Library No. 18, 1964), and in John A. Porter, *The Vertical Mosaic: an Analysis of Social Class and Power in Canada* (Toronto: University of Toronto Press, 1965). On the whole, indeed, sociologists and students of culture take the place of the church in the post-confederation era more seriously than do secular historians.

MOVEMENTS AND CONTROVERSIES

Spokesmen for the churches have generally been concerned to accentuate the positive, calling attention to the heroic deeds of pioneer missionaries and playing down divisions within their own ranks. Controversy has been plentiful, but systematic analysis of controversy has been scarce. Even the primary polarity of Canadian religion, that between Protestants and Roman Catholics, has been studied at length only in relation to such specific issues as education. Useful in this connection, however, is Roy C. Dalton, *The Jesuit Estates Question, 1760-1888* (Toronto: University of Toronto Press, 1968).

The most compendious source for ultramontanism in Quebec is Rumilly's *Histoire de la Province de Québec*, which is heavily weighted on the ultramontane side. Useful as an antidote is an illuminating article by Philippe Sylvain, "Quelques aspects de l'antagonisme libéral-ultramontain au Canada français," in *Recherches sociographiques*, Vol. VIII, No. 3 (septembre-décembre 1967), pp. 275-298. For a brief guide to the literature on the subject see Pierre Savard, "Note sur l'étude de l'ultramontanisme au Canada français," *Sessions d'étude de la Société Canadienne d'Histoire de l'Eglise Catholique*, 1966, pp. 13-16.

The complicated story of the prohibition movement is traced in great detail in Ruth E. Spence, *Prohibition in Canada* (Toronto: Dominion Alliance, 1919). An excellent brief study of the critical period of controversy over Lord's day legislation is A. M. C. Waterman, "The Lord's Day in a Secular Society: a Historical Comment on the Canadian Lord's Day Act of 1906," *Canadian Journal of Theology*, Vol. XI, No. 2 (April 1965), pp. 108-123. S. D. Clark, *Church and Sect in Canada* (Toronto: University of Toronto Press, 1948), is a comprehensive sociological account of sectarian movements and of the conflict of sectarian and ecclesiastical tendencies within major denominations. W. E. Mann, in *Sect, Cult and Church in Alberta* (Toronto: University of Toronto Press, 1955), applies the same type of analysis to a single province.

Canada's numerous unions of churches have attracted unequal attention from students. The story of Methodist union has been well told in J. Warren Caldwell, "The Unification of Methodism in Canada, 1865-1884," *Bulletin*, No. 19 (1967), pp. 3-61. For Presbyterian union, where there is no published account, one must seek out J. A. Johnston, "Factors in the Formation of the Presbyterian Church in Canada, 1875," Ph.D. thesis, McGill University, 1955. The only comprehensive study of the 1925 union is C. E. Silcox, *Church Union in Canada* (New York: Institute of Social and Religious Research, 1933). A briefer account that touches on various unions and proposals for union is J. W. Grant, *The Canadian Experience of Church Union* (London: Lutterworth, 1967).

Much information about contemporary developments in various branches of the church can be gleaned from *Canada and Its Future* (Toronto: United Church Publishing House, 1967), the 42nd Annual Report of the Board of Evangelism and Social Service. A popular account that catches the mood of the 1960s very well is A. C. Forrest's chapter, "The Present," in William Kilbourn, ed., *Religion in Canada: The Spiritual Development of a Nation* (Toronto: McClelland and Stewart, 1968). A symposium edited by J. C. Falardeau, *Essais sur le Québec Contemporain* (Quebec: Les Presses Universitaires Laval, 1953), although no longer as contemporary as its title suggests, provides valuable insights into the background of recent changes within the church in Quebec.

## NOTES FOR THE RESEARCH STUDENT

Up to this point this note has been intended chiefly for the interested reader who would like more detailed information on various matters than a book of this size can supply. Anyone who wishes to make a serious study of some aspect of Canadian church history will find that published books and major articles can do little more than whet his appetite. He will quickly need to go beyond them to biographies of individuals, to periodicals, and to primary sources. Professor Moir has indicated in "A Select Bibliography" to Volume Two of this series the chief sources of material and of scholarly guidance for the student, and no attempt will be made to duplicate here all the information given there. It may be helpful, however, to call attention to some of the most important resources available for the post-confederation period.

Among periodicals the *Canadian Historical Review* and the journals of the various provincial historical societies are all important for the period after 1867. The files of the *Canadian Journal of Religious Thought* and of the

*Canadian Journal of Theology* contain many articles on historical subjects, and the newly founded *Studies in Religion / Sciences Religieuses* should continue to do so. Several scholarly journals specialize in denominational history: the *Journal of the Canadian Church Historical Society* for Anglicanism; the *Bulletin* of the Committee on Archives of the United Church of Canada; and the bilingual *Report / Rapport* of the Canadian Catholic Historical Association, recently retitled *Study Sessions / Sessions d'étude*. Beyond these the student should be aware of many popular religious journals in which the history of the church has been recorded as it has been made. In particular, practically every missionary society and missionary order has regularly kept its constituency informed of its work, and these seldom-consulted periodicals contain an enormous amount of information. For missions in the north and northwest the Hudson's Bay Company's *Beaver* is also an invaluable source.

Almost all denominations publish year books, as well as proceedings of national and regional legislative bodies. For the Roman Catholic Church a similar function is served by *Le Canada Ecclésiastique*, an annual review published by Beauchemin of Montreal. Reports of church boards of missions and of social service, as well as of men's and women's organizations, may be equally important. So may those of the Canadian Council of Churches, the Student Christian Movement of Canada, and such quasi-religious organizations as temperance federations. For the student seeking new areas of historical investigation the field is even broader, extending to sermons and catechisms, to liturgical manuals and hymn books, to Sunday school lessons and seminary calendars.

Most of these latter materials, along with manuscript collections relating to important figures and movements, will be found most readily and sometimes only in archival repositories. The archives of the United Church of Canada and its antecedents are largely concentrated in Toronto, although there are small regional collections in all but the central conferences. Those of the "convention" Baptists are divided between Acadia University in Wolfville, for the Atlantic provinces, and McMaster University in Hamilton for the rest of Canada. Anglican and Roman Catholic records are for the most part dispersed in diocesan collections. The Archives of the General Synod of the Anglican Church of Canada house materials of national concern, however, and the Archives de la Province de Québec are a rich source for the study of both Roman Catholic and Anglican history in the region. The Public Archives of Canada are chiefly important for the never-to-be-forgotten religious dimension of Canadian politics.

# Index